US–UK Counter-Terrorism after 9/11

D0705986

This book provides a qualitative analysis of post-9/11 counter-terrorism strategy undertaken by the United Kingdom and United States of America.

Since 9/11, both the UK and the US have significantly revamped their counter-terrorism approaches. The approaches apply, to varying degrees, three key policy instruments – intelligence, law enforcement and military force. However, the success or failure of these counter-terrorism strategies has never been satisfactorily validated. Analysts and policymakers alike have assumed their success due to the inability of terrorists to conduct 7/7 and 9/11, respectively, scale attacks upon each state. This assumption has existed despite the fact that it fundamentally underestimates the impact of transnational terrorism.

This volume provides an in-depth qualitative assessment of the three primary policy instruments implemented to counter the transnational threat of terrorism during the period 2001–2011; an approach somewhat neglected by the current body of literature which utilises primarily a quantitative methodology. Drawing upon previously unpublished data collected from interviews with policymakers, specialists and academics, this book fills this lacuna by ascertaining and analysing both UK and US counter-terrorism strategies and based upon this examination providing policy recommendations for both states.

This book will be of interest to students of terrorism and counter-terrorism studies, security studies and IR in general.

Edgar B. Tembo is a Lecturer at Sheffield Hallam University, UK.

Contemporary Terrorism Studies

Understanding Terrorist Innovation
Technology, tactics and global trends
Adam Dolnik

The Strategy of Terrorism
How it works, why it fails
Peter Neumann and M.L.R. Smith

Female Terrorism and Militancy
Agency, utility, and organization
Edited by Cindy D. Ness

Women and Terrorism
Female activity in domestic and international terror groups
Margaret Gonzalez-Perez

The Psychology of Strategic Terrorism
Public and government responses to attack
Ben Sheppard

The De-Radicalization of Jihadists
Transforming armed Islamist movements
Omar Ashour

Targeting Terrorist Financing
International cooperation and new regimes
Arabinda Acharya

Managing Terrorism and Insurgency
Regeneration, recruitment and attrition
Cameron I. Crouch

Religion and Political Violence
Sacred protest in the modern world
Jennifer L. Jefferis

US–UK Counter-Terrorism after 9/11

A qualitative approach

Edgar B. Tembo

Routledge
Taylor & Francis Group

LONDON AND NEW YORK

First published 2014
by Routledge
2 Park Square, Milton Park, Abingdon, Oxfordshire OX14 4RN

and by Routledge
711 Third Avenue, New York, NY 10017

First issued in paperback 2015

Routledge is an imprint of the Taylor & Francis Group, an informa business

British Library Cataloguing in Publication Data
A catalogue record for this book is available from the British Library

Library of Congress Cataloging-in-Publication Data
Tembo, Edgar B.
  US–UK counter-terrorism after 9/11 : a qualitative approach / Edgar B.
  Tembo.
    pages cm. – (Contemporary terrorism studies)
  Includes bibliographical references and index.
  1. Terrorism–United States–Prevention. 2. Terrorism–Great Britain–
  Prevention. 3. War on Terrorism, 2001–2009. 4. September 11 Terrorist
  Attacks, 2001–Influence. I. Title.
  HV6432.T424 2013
  363.325'170941–dc23
                                                              2013027603

ISBN 13: 978-1-138-94022-2 (pbk)
ISBN 13: 978-0-415-64378-8 (hbk)

Typeset in Times
by Wearset Ltd, Boldon, Tyne and Wear

Contents

Illustrations

Figures

Table

Boxes

Acknowledgements

It is of course apt that I should thank the University of Sheffield, particularly the Department of Politics and the Graduate Research Centre, for providing the guidance, time, space, and – through a University Scholarship funding – to undertake the research that informs this work. I would also like to thank the editorial team at Routledge, particularly Annabelle Harris and my anonymous reviewers, for their informed and timely comments on early drafts. It goes without saying that any errors are completely my own.

Critical to the viability of the work were my interviewees, some of whom, for obvious reasons, are not identified here. Interviewees came from both the United Kingdom and the United States, working at all levels of government, law enforcement, intelligence and military force. Without them, their time and their trust, this work simply would not have been possible. I am eternally grateful.

The commissioning of a research-based, single-authored monograph is not only time consuming but emotionally draining. It is my friends and family that have supported me and for whom the greatest amount of thanks is reserved. Many perhaps do not realise how valuable their presence – be it via email, on the phone or in person – has been. Of particular note are those who acted as informal proof-readers and critics at various stages of my research. Nicholas Hyman, Andrea Sterling and of course Mum. From the bottom of my heart I thank you.

Last but not least, and to whom this book is dedicated, I would like to thank all those who I have had the pleasure of teaching at the University of Sheffield (2007–2011), University of Nottingham (2011–2012) and Sheffield Hallam University (2012–2013). There is no greater joy then being party to the learning process of young, fertile minds. It is, however, a two-way street. Many of you have, without knowing it, helped me finesse many of the arguments and rationales that appear in this work.

Thank you.

For my students past and present let this serve as an example of what can be achieved when you put your mind to it.

Edgar B. Tembo
September 2013
Sheffield, United Kingdom

1   Introduction

It has been over ten years since planes were flown into symbols of economic and military might of both the United States and the world. Still, even with a change of President, the 2011 death of Osama bin Laden, an increase in economic woes and competing priorities, the United States continues to engage in counter-terrorism initiatives both at home and abroad. The success of the Global War on Terror cannot simply be measured by the internment or killing of insurgents and/or terrorists. The fear that comes with the acknowledgement that, as an Irish Republican Army member put it in the 1980s, '[w]e only have to be lucky once, you have to be lucky always', is part and parcel of the rationale and associated *modus operandi* of terrorist violence.

This book draws upon original and previously unpublished interview material conducted by the author. Most of these interviews were conducted in 2009 and included, among others, counter-terrorism professionals with specialist expertise in the implementation of intelligence, law enforcement and military force. The aim of these interviews was to ascertain the changes and effectiveness of policy instruments after the 11 September 2001 terrorist attacks upon the United States (9/11). In one interview, conducted in the United States, with an individual who was at that time working on an oversight committee for the Department of Homeland Security, a statement was made that in many ways led to further research and, indeed, to this book. When asked whether the Department of Homeland Security had been effective at countering the threat of transnational terrorism, the interviewee said: 'Well, I think it's been effective in that there hasn't been a major terrorist attack on United States soil since 9/11.'[1] Not least due to issues relating to causality, this struck me as an interesting rationale that deserved further consideration. How can the failure of a terrorist to succeed in an attack denote the success of a state in countering the threat? One does not have to equal the other. Indeed, the failure of a terrorist to succeed may well be due to their own incompetence and have nothing to do with the state's tactics of interdiction. Beyond this, the research became drawn to issues related to the perceived effectiveness of post-9/11 counter-terrorism strategy, particularly with reference to the primary policy instruments in this area: intelligence, law enforcement and military force.

A number of failings in analysis from this era were quickly identified. For example, analysis that discussed the effectiveness of strategy tended to focus on quantitative metrics. While this is perfectly understandable (would 9/11 have been as significant if only 100 people had died?), it does not facilitate an understanding of the full picture. Broadly speaking, in order to realise their aims, those who use terrorist violence aim to not only kill as many as possible (although this has not always been the case) but also to cause fear or, more accurately, terror. Indeed, the Department of Defense stated, quite rightly, that "terror is a natural phenomenon; terrorism is the conscious exploitation of it".[2] Tragic as it may be, the number of people killed in any one particular terrorist attack is not directly comparable to the fear that is induced. Indeed, the effectiveness of a counter-terrorism strategy should not be measured purely on quantitative methodologies nor, perhaps more so, on utilising exclusively qualitative metrics. If the aim of a terrorist is to gain a qualitative result (be it short or long term), an assessment of its effectiveness should incorporate a qualitative metric.

Counter-terrorism: a qualitative problem

Terrorist violence, by its very design, is intended to strike fear in a manner that resonates beyond the immediate. It is, however, incumbent upon the state to design policies to counter terrorist violence which are not driven by fear. The metric of success of these policies is not simply reducing the amount of violence that is prevented, but rather, and simultaneously, ensuring the continuation of 'normal' life. States must therefore develop strategies that strike a balance between effectiveness and acceptability. States, as ultimate securers of individual security, must constantly ask themselves whether the qualitative benefits of a particular strategy outweigh the costs. In doing this they have to strike a balance between the acceptability of a counter-terrorism strategy to the general populace and its effectiveness at stemming the perceived threat while still adhering to such democratic norms as freedom of speech and *habeas corpus*.

Makinda states that counter-terrorism policies have varied 'from the most liberal to the most authoritarian and, even within democracies frequently span both extremes of the ideological spectrum'.[3] Liberal democracies are disadvantaged in the struggle against terrorism, as 'rule by the majority while respecting the right[s] of the minority' has invariably meant the application of 'measured, rule based force [... placing the state] at a tactical disadvantage in the conflict with an anonymous opponent showing no restraint'.[4] Undeniably, 'by tolerating the intolerant, democracies allow terrorists to plan and prepare their strikes'.[5] In contrast and 'by definition totalitarian regimes suppress all effective opposition within their boundaries and are entirely unimpeded by any judicial or humanitarian constraints'.[6] The preservation of values such as equality, freedom of speech, justice and tolerance are not values to which totalitarian-authoritarian regimes necessarily subscribe. As such, these regimes are able to employ harsh, unyielding forms of oppression and retribution, and to selectively apply counter-terrorist-related activity to their own, often politically motivated, ends. Liberal-democratic states (broadly defined) therefore have, when it comes to counter-terrorism, asked themselves, 'do we want to sacrifice some democratic substance in order to be effective against terrorism or do we have to tolerate a certain level of terrorism for the sake of maintaining the civil liberties and political rights which we cherish?'[7] States must therefore find an adequate balance so as not to infringe upon civil liberties in the pursuit of security.

In the aftermath of 9/11 both the United States and the United Kingdom sought to revamp their counter-terrorism strategies. At the centre of these strategies, but to varying degrees of implementation, were three distinct policy instruments: intelligence, law enforcement and military force. Did the United States and the United Kingdom strike an adequate balance between the effectiveness of their counter-terrorism strategies and their acceptability? Qualitatively speaking, how effective were these strategies in not only preventing terrorist violence but also the possible contagion of fear surrounding these acts? In essence, this book investigates and analyses the qualitative effectiveness surrounding the use of intelligence, law enforcement and military force in the decade following 9/11, at the level of practitioners drawing upon both interviews and primary documents.

All too frequently, scholarly evaluations of the effectiveness of counter-terrorism initiatives have been based either on quantitative methodologies or value-free statements. There are good reasons for this. Indeed, the road to an objective qualitative appraisal of a policy is fraught with difficulty as, essentially, any qualitative analysis has a higher degree of subjectivity than rudimentary quantitative analysis. This, however, does not mean it should not be attempted. The study of terrorism lends itself readily to qualitative analysis due to the fact that the long-term objectives of terrorists themselves are rarely wholly quantitative but are in fact mostly frequently qualitative. Logically, it is argued here, it makes sense to consider the implementation of counter-terrorism strategy, certainly over the long term but also in the short term, in ways that are more attuned to qualitative rather than quantitative metrics of success or failure. Beatrice de Graaf adopts an approach that is based on in-depth case study analysis of counter-terrorism professionals. She analyses the relationship between counter-terrorism measures and radicalisation processes across multiple states during the 1970s.[8]

This book is structured in such a way as to provide a unique holistic understanding of both United Kingdom and United States post-9/11 strategies to counter the threat of transnational terrorist violence espoused by al Qaeda. The United Kingdom and United States faced a broadly similar threat of transnational terrorism insofar as the overarching organisation, al Qaeda, had affirmed its desire to target both states. That said both states have divergent social, cultural, political and economic foundations. Moreover, a deeper analysis of the threat, as undertaken in Chapter 2, highlights differing conceptualisations of the danger posited by al Qaeda. For the United Kingdom, the threat was considered to be one that originates, both domestically and internationally, whereas for the United States it is seen as one that originates, wholly, internationally. The divergent social, cultural, political and economic foundations of each state, combined with the differing conceptualisations of the threat posed by al Qaeda, should serve as a warning regarding the usefulness of comparing each state's counter-terrorism strategies. This book assesses the implementation of each policy instrument largely from the perspective of counter-terrorism practitioners.

The United Kingdom first published its counter-terrorism strategy, CONTEST, in July 2006, one year after 7/7.[9] The strategy itself had actually been in existence, but classified as secret, since 2003. A revised edition was published in March 2009 and another in July 2011 under a new coalition government.[10] In CONTEST-2009 it was stated that the British government believed that, to date, it had achieved its aim of reducing the risk to the United Kingdom and protected its interests overseas from the threat of terrorism.[11] This assertion was based on the fact that no terrorist attack on a scale of 7/7 had been successfully undertaken in the United Kingdom since the 2006 publication. As is argued throughout this book, such a quantitative methodology fails to take account of the qualitative aim and objectives, such as the spread of fear and reduction in confidence of the state to provide security, that terrorists aim to achieve.

In the same year that CONTEST-2006 was published, the United States under the Bush administration released its own counter-terrorism strategy, the *National Strategy for Combating Terrorism*.[12] To date, this strategy has not been revised. The January 2009 inauguration of United States President Barack Obama, however, represented a sea change in United States counter-terrorism thinking. With more of an emphasis on diplomacy and development assistance, the Obama administration also set about putting in motion the closure of Guantánamo Bay Detention Centre and ending enhanced interrogation methods – a probable euphemism for torture – through the signing of United States Presidential Executive Orders and the establishment of the Office for the Closure of Guantánamo.[13] These changes in the United States counter-terrorism approach indicated that the new administration did not believe that the National Strategy for Combatting Terrorism could achieve the overarching aim of success in the global War on Terror.[14]

Counter-terrorism assessments: Cold War evaluations

Contemporary terrorism represents a unique threat to both the United Kingdom and United States, due to the fusion of religious rhetoric and political aims that has also led to an increase in apocalyptic aspirations to acquire weapons of mass destruction in order to facilitate the realisation of the terrorist movement's aim. In order to best counter the threat it is critical that an explanation of core characteristics, the nature of the response so far and the costs and benefits of that response are known. The realist perspective of international relations theory lends itself to this particular approach. This is because realism serves as a means of explaining events that have occurred and, based on this, predicting how things may transpire. In line with realist thought and in order to explain why international events have occurred, it is necessary to identify the context in which policies were adopted by looking at the threat, the strategies and their purpose. Thus, this book centres on three main areas: the nature of the threat that is posed by transnational terrorism; the response that has been undertaken by states to counter this particular threat; and the effectiveness of that response.[15]

One way of understanding the threat of contemporary transnational terrorism is to distinguish it from traditional forms of terrorist violence. Indeed, analysing the characteristics that make up transnational terrorism aid further in the understanding of the context in which the counter-terrorism strategies, used by both the United Kingdom and United States, were created. As such, this book discusses the aims, objectives and key policy instruments that have been used to counter the threat of transnational terrorism. The book identifies the actual, as opposed to the planned, role of the three policy instruments under analysis: intelligence, law enforcement and military force. Understanding the costs and benefits for each state is of critical importance. This is because understanding, in this area, resolves any disconnect between what was planned for each of the policy instruments, i.e. what their intended role was and what their actual role turned out to be.

Systematic research that undertakes an analysis of multiple policy instruments using a qualitative methodology is scarce in the area of counter-terrorism. Cold War counter-terrorism literature was driven by the geopolitical, theoretical interpretations of the day and as such formed the backdrop for the emergence of critical ways of thinking about terrorism and security more broadly. The principal concern for theorists and practitioners, supported by realist theoretical conceptualisations of state interactions, centred upon security threats posed by other states. The state was the primary actor in the international arena and non-state actors were subservient to the moves that states made. Consequentially, the analysis and study of security was irrevocably linked to that of state security. The effect on the academic pursuit of terrorist-related research was profound. Scholars rarely examined the characteristics of countering non-state-sponsored terrorism, let alone transnational terrorism, but instead examined security threats from other states under the disciplinary rubric of *Strategic Studies*.

The literature that characterises the *Strategic Studies* discourse tends to fall into one of three categories. First, counter-terrorism literature is in edited books as single chapters, which detract from the consistency of single-author conception needed for a detailed analysis – journal articles, due to their length, fall into this category.[16] Second, they form the concluding chapters of books on other areas of the terrorism debate – particularly so on issues of definition and motivation also detracting from the method and associated benefits, such as consistency of analysis in counter-terrorism studies.[17]

The third category, namely studies conducted by current or former counter-terrorism *professionals*, was typically authored by intelligence, law enforcement and, more frequently than not, military officials. One source that falls into this latter category is Frank Kitson's *Low Intensity Operations – Subversion, Insurgency, Peace-keeping*. Kitson, a British Army officer who had a keen interest in insurgency and low-intensity conflict, investigates the development, response and cessation of insurgencies.[18] His work not only focuses on the United Kingdom's experience in dealing with terrorist violence overseas, such as Malaya (modern-day Malaysia and Singapore), but also on domestic problems related to Northern Ireland.[19] Kitson acknowledges three actors which impact upon the outcome of an insurgency that uses terrorist violence: the perpetrators of violence (typically nationalists or anti-colonialists), the civilian bureaucracy that oversees the armed forces' response and the military.[20] Kitson argues that if a government's strategy is to be successful, 'it must base its campaign on a determination to destroy the subversive movement utterly, and it must make this fact plain to its people'.[21] On the other hand, the late Professor Paul Wilkinson of St Andrew's University and former officer in the Royal Air Force argues that while a government should declare its 'intention to maintain its authority and to implement its policies', it should shy away from announcing any intention of annihilating the terrorist opposition.[22] This point is indicative of the importance, when considering military responses to counter-terrorism, of recognising the need for governments to appreciate the balance between the acceptability of the chosen strategy and its effectiveness. Recognising the significance of the relationship between the government and the military is also of critical importance. Kitson goes on to state that:

> The process of tying civil and military measures together into a single effective policy is clearly a complicated one. No matter how well aware of the problem the authorities are, they will only be able to solve it if they can devise machinery at every level which can assess all the factors whether they be operational or administrative, short term or long term, make a plan, and put it into effect.[23]

In countering sub-state threats, Wilkinson suggests the adoption of strategically applicable rules based on historical experience. Indicative of a historical methodology, akin to the realist theoretical approach popular at the time, one such rule is that the state 'must not be seen to give in to terrorist blackmail or intimidation'.[24] Doing so, he argues, would not only demoralise the resolve of the security services, but also and more importantly that of the general population. Furthermore, unimpeded concessions may encourage further terrorist actions. Governments should publicly reiterate that they can protect civilians from terrorist attack. If not, a risk exists of the emergence of ad-hoc vigilantism and a *street violence* type of retributive crime wave, similar to the backlash seen against those stereotyped as being a terrorist because of their Arab appearance, in the United States shortly after 9/11. Accordingly, states should 'avoid alienating the support of the mass of the population'.[25] This is not to suggest that they should alienate minority communities through draconian legislation or ostensibly racial profiling, but rather to underscore the importance of proportionality in their response.

Doing so, in a liberal democracy, may serve only to heighten perceived injustice and hypocrisy on the part of the state. Certainly, 'it is the terrorist's intention to provoke a campaign of governmental repression which will turn the people against' them.[26] This suggests that government should govern in a manner that is acceptable to the domestic population they represent. Not doing so risks a reduction in government support among the population at large. This may mean that if a government wishes to continue governing, while faced with a distinct lack of confidence by the electorate, it will need to bring in ever more stringent measures to mitigate the risk of rebellion. Starting with draconian emergency legislation and culminating in martial law, theoretically, through the suspension of civil rights and *habeas corpus*, the emergence of an authoritative totalitarianism may occur in place of the previous ideals consistent with liberal democracies.

Wilkinson affirms that '[t]he cardinal aim of [a] strategy [should be] to isolate the terrorist[s] from their host population'.[27] Thus, the strategic tactician's role should be the adoption of an appropriate balance between the acceptability of the techniques or initiatives used and the effectiveness of their implementation. For example, using draconian legislation may be effective in the short term but would be considered, over a longer period, unacceptable by the general population. It is recognised that governments need to use proportionate force 'to deter terrorist aggression while avoiding any damage or injury to the innocent whose moral support and cooperation they require'.[28] Too much oppression will lead civilians to rebel and sympathisers of terrorist causes to become practitioners of terrorist violence. Thus terrorist recruiters will be able to point not only to the failure of the state to provide adequate protection but also justification in their cause through the use of draconian measures. Too little force and the demands of the terrorists may increase along with the frequency of the attacks.

Wilkinson's final and perhaps most challenging ground rule refers to the task of defeating violent elements within groups, while simultaneously engaging 'with the political wing of the terrorist movement to win the allegiance of the people'.[29] It is not unusual for organisations that employ terrorist violence to have some kind of link to a more mainstream political group. Examples include the Provisional Irish Republican Army and Sinn Fein and Euskadi Ta Askatasuna (also known as ETA) and Batasuna. This engagement, more often than not, will take the form of negotiation and will prove controversial among the population. However, *engagement* or *negotiation* need not be synonymous with *concession*. If deals are to be made, the benefits to the state must be clear.[30] It is also important to note that in such negotiations one key condition often set by the targeted state is that the political branch renounce terrorist violence.

Another *specialist* Cold War publication on counter-terrorism was by G. Davidson Smith, a counter-terrorism expert and former member of the Canadian Security Intelligence Service. Smith suggests that there should be a debate within the field regarding the use of emergency powers and the employment of the military in countering terrorism within liberal democracies. For him, the strength and robustness of institutional mechanisms are critical to a counter-terrorism strategy's success. Smith's work takes as its case study the Canadian response to domestic terrorism pre-1990. Of particular interest to the author was the response to threats from the 1950s through to the 1990s, specifically in relation to the Front de Libération du Québec – a largely domestic terrorist organisation. Smith continually draws on the experiences of the United Kingdom and United States to support his arguments. As the purpose of his study is the investigation of 'government *policies* associated with response to terrorism', it is unsurprising that he spends considerable time defining the core characteristics of *policy*.[31]

Smith divides policies into two categories: macro and micro. A '[m]acro policy is one which has a wide application and a general dimension'.[32] Such policies are broad and have a sweeping effect upon terrorist activities. Examples may include the introduction of new legislation, improved security or any other general measure which is applied in an ad-hoc fashion. In other words, a macro strategy is one which is not adopted for a specific threat. In contrast, a micro policy has 'a more narrow involvement, such as hostage negotiations and surveillance techniques'.[33] At first glance, the difference between macro and micro policies appears to be similar to that between strategic and tactical approaches. This, however, is not so, as a micro strategy may be identified as one developed to deal with a specific threat, such as '[t]he Canadian Government's decision to allocate responsibility to the Royal Canadian Mounted Police for the development of a national hostage rescue team'.[34] The Royal Canadian Mounted Police being designated the responsible agency for a national rescue team was a micro policy decision that emanated 'from the macro policy of use of security forces in response to terrorism'.[35]

Smith's approach to the study of counter-terrorism is both clear and concise. He discusses the decision-making processes and use of crisis management systems, resources and capabilities of the Canadian counter-terrorism response. Smith also enters the debate regarding the role of the military in counter-terrorism.[36] He notes that historically, successive Canadian governments have accepted the 'need to maintain constitutional principles throughout any crisis situation, that is, barring a major catastrophe'.[37] This is not to say that the military option has never been used, just that it was traditionally seen as subordinate to that of the elected government. An example of when the military was used was during the 1970 October crisis. During this crisis, in which the War Powers Act was invoked, military assistance was requested from 'the Federal Government [... in the form of A]id to the Civil Power', thus keeping the civilian infrastructure as the lead force.[38] Smith does not explain why, when military force was called upon to counter a specific terrorist threat, civilian agencies were seen as the decision-making authorities. Is this because liberal democratic governments were worried that the military might not relinquish power and perhaps feared a coup? Alternatively, governments may have been concerned that the military would use force that was considered disproportionate within the confines of the home state but proportionate when tackling large anti-colonial insurgencies overseas? Does it not seem illogical, if the military have the expertise, capabilities and the experience, to use the civilian infrastructure rather than the military one?

Smith does note that the idealist notion of the rule of law, which is bound up with the mind-set of liberal democratic states, may suggest an inherent reluctance, within such states, to lead counter-terrorist operations using military force.[39] There seems to be a perception that using the military in some way impedes the role, or notion, of democracy. This perception is prevalent throughout the literature, as well as in the post-9/11 United Kingdom and United States counter-terrorism strategies. Smith's work highlights the mechanisms by which strategy can and has been formulated. It constructs a logical, coherent argument, beginning with an outline of the threat, before deconstructing and scrutinising the mechanisms in place to counter that threat. Although useful by, for example, offering significant insight into areas such as the use of the military in times of national emergency, Smith does not explore in any great depth actual polices that have, or should be, adopted.[40]

Kitson, Wilkinson and Smith may all be seen as Cold War counter-terrorism specialists. Their work, while insightful, also highlights shortcomings in the discourse of this period that continued into the post-Cold War era. All of the publications discussed thus far were published throughout this period and have a narrow focus on the topic of counter-terrorism. Kitson's work centres purely on the use of the military, whereas Wilkinson's counter-terrorism analysis comes on the back of a much broader study of *Political Terrorism*.[41] Therefore, his work on counter-terrorism is limited due to a focus on other issues in the terrorism discourse. Smith's work in contrast provides, perhaps, the clearest appreciation for counter-terrorism in one geographic region.[42] However, it fails to consider other terrorism issues, such as transnational terrorist organisations and the effects these may have had on Canada's security. Moreover, Smith's study is focused primarily on the decision-making mechanisms of the Canadian state with particular reference to emergency legislation, as opposed to broader policies, such as police intervention and dealing with underlying and historical causes.

Counter-terrorism assessments: contemporary evaluations

Towards the end of the Cold War, realism was challenged by a number of contending theories emerging from within the discipline of international relations. Chief among the criticisms laid at the door of realism was its insistence that states should form the referent object of analysis. The term *security* was no longer irrevocably linked to that of states. The term, as a result and highlighted by *Security Studies* theorists, became an increasingly contested concept. Dalby's observation that 'Cold War security policy, premised on the necessity of ensuring military preparedness, maintaining secrecy, and working out strategies for using nuclear weapons in international conflict' appears to be an accurate description of the narrow focus that the term – security – had during the period.[43] Security was, to *Security Studies* theorists, believed to be 'more than the contest for political supremacy in the process of superpower rivalry'.[44]

Walt, writing shortly after the collapse of the Soviet Union, argued that 'military power is not the only source of national security, and military threats are not the only dangers that states face'.[45] The rapid decline in the relevance of superpower relations had a profound effect on the study of security. The notion of security being intrinsically linked to that of the relations between states was undermined by the development of interests in other areas that could be considered matters of national security. Such areas included environmental degradation and water scarcity. The subdiscipline of *Security Studies* began to fill the void created by orthodoxy focus on areas pertaining almost exclusively to national, or state, security. The lack of analysis of individual human security provided fertile breeding ground for the development of new theories of international relations and, by extension, security.

Walt notes that the Cold War conceptualisation of security was argued to be obsolete and not in line with the changing times of the world.[46] Dalby concludes that security is not just about military matters. Rather, security includes those threats which affect the stability of the community.[47] Security is 'about the protection of a political community [...] with community understood as a population with attributes in common'.[48] Such an understanding left ample room for manoeuvre in terms of what was meant by a political community, which may, for example, be defined as a state, a region or a non-state actor such as the European Union. Buzan suggests that the analysis of the concept of security needs to consider three aspects: first, the political context in which the concept of security is used; second, its scope of operation, which includes military, economic, societal and environmental dimensions; finally, an analysis of security should consider 'the logical contradictions and ambiguities that are inherent in any attempt to apply the concept to international relations'.[49]

Paul Rogers, writing in 2008, stated that the

> broad trend that constitutes the security paradigm that is now evolving [...] is quite different from the Cold War era. At the heart of this paradigm are three factors or 'drivers', the widening wealth–poverty divide, environmental constraints on development, and the vulnerability of elite societies to paramilitary action.[50]

Similarly to contemporary terrorist threats, these security factors are not constrained by the traditional territorial borders of a state. In the context of globalisation, the proliferation of technologies, trade and economies are considered to be critical security issues that can arise in one area of the world and have the power to affect another, not necessarily in weeks or months but possibly instantaneously.

Within this new concept of security, literature on counter-terrorism emerged. However, similar problems to Cold War literature are seen in post-Cold War studies on terrorism. Publications were in multi-authored books, or in journals, continuing the failure of the field to recognise the need for consistent analytical study. A key development that emerged in the post-Cold War literature was that the study of counter-terrorism was not undertaken purely by specialists. The topic of counter-terrorism was seen as an area to which criminologists, sociologists and political theorists, to name but a few, could and did contribute.[51]

Gus Martin's work is illustrative of this and is representative of the literature when arguing that the fundamental consideration to any contemporary counter-terrorism approach is that of practicality. Will the strategy be successful? Will the terrorists be deterred? Is it acceptable within the current legal framework of the state? Given the subject and format of the study, it seems unusual to pay so little attention to the topic of counter-terrorism. Although the author is willing to discuss the challenges of terrorism in detail, he does not discuss how these challenges could be met. This *afterthought* approach, in the analysis of counter-terrorism, is symptomatic of books on terrorism.

Another example of this approach is Kenneth Christie's work. Christie discusses the costs of the Global War on Terror in relation to human rights. Costs are related specifically to human rights and are seen in the manner in which quasi-liberal democratic states utilise the military to suppress domestic threats of terrorism.[52] Christie's work does not look at any counter-terrorism policy instruments beyond those of the military for which, he states, success is evidenced by an increase in the amount of investment by those involved in military business. This success, however, has come at the expense of human rights.[53]

Michael Ignatieff also looks at the ethical dimension of terrorism. Rather than focusing on human rights, as Christie does, he centres his discussion on the broader political ethics of the Global War on Terror.[54] He argues that terrorism poses a unique threat to liberal democracies and asks what states, with this ideological perspective, should do when faced with such a threat.[55] Among his suggestions, he argues that '[a]ssassination can be a justified lesser evil, but only against bona fide terrorist target'.[56] He does not offer detailed analysis as to the success or failure of the implementation of this or other policies, preferring, instead, to offer suggestions and ideas.[57] This idea of *justifiable* assassination also features in other studies such as Tamar Meisels' work.[58]

Like Ignatieff, Meisels discusses the political and also moral difficulties of terrorism. In looking at problems of countering terrorism Meisels disagrees with Ignatieff, arguing that targeted assassination is inherently problematic. Targeted assassination may aid terrorist recruiters by provoking those who sympathise with terrorist causes to becoming practitioners of terrorist violence.[59] Both Ignatieff and Meisels are representative of literature from this period that looks at terrorism, offers suggestions on what is right or wrong, but seldom focuses on broader counter-terrorism strategies. Rather, for such works, the focus is on other areas of the terrorism discourse.[60] Martin does make some interesting contributions to the counter-terrorism discourse, particularly with regard to the conceptualisation and indeed categorisation of counter-terrorism policies. He states that counter-terrorism policies are 'traditionally regarded as a choice between so called hard-line and soft-line responses'.[61] Hard-line responses, he states, are military and paramilitary operations, whereas soft-line approaches 'incorporate diplomacy, compromise, and social reforms as possible options'.[62] The latter is problematic, since it may lead to the legitimisation of grievances and consequently implies understanding of terrorist causes and their *modus operandi*.

A key consideration for policymakers should be the practicality of the options available. Practicality, Martin suggests, involves addressing questions such as 'will the option work? Will the terrorists' behaviour change? Can the terrorist environment be co-opted or suppressed?'[63] This view is useful insofar as it acknowledges the gap that needs to be reconciled between theory and practice.

The developments of theoretical concepts, or constructs, should always precede the development and subsequent employment of practical steps. The development of a theoretical concept and all that it entails, such as analysis and consideration of alternatives, may help justify the development and employment of a practice. Neglecting this step may lead to the development of a *trial by error* methodology which can be detrimental to the state, especially with regard to confidence in the government which, as Wilkinson states, is crucial in the development of a successful strategy.[64] Martin's acknowledgement of the need to bridge this gap between theory and practice is somewhat undermined by his inability to discuss the impact of counter-terrorism tactics upon the civilian population.

Nevertheless, one of the great advantages of Martin's textbook format is his willingness to define the language that is common in the counter-terrorism discourse but seldom explained. This enables analysts to review the use of what have become everyday terms. For example, '[r]*esponding to terrorism* is defined as any action taken by a targeted interest in reply to a terrorist incident or terrorist environment'.[65] Useful as this is in facilitating consideration of such definitions, Martin's understanding is limited. He does not consider the actuality that the term *terrorism* tends to be bestowed upon another arbitrarily, yet is rarely adopted by a group itself. At root, questions such as who is the victim and who is the perpetrator must be scrutinised before stating that one is responding to a terrorist. For example, Benjamin Nimer argues that South Africa's African National Congress believed it was being targeted by the apartheid state through the use of terrorism from above and that its actions were a legitimate response to it. The apartheid government adopted a similar view but saw the terrorism as coming from below.[66] It would perhaps be more accurate to say that a response to terrorism is an action undertaken to counter or respond to the threat or act of terrorist violence.

Martin states that '[c]*ounterterrorism* refers to proactive policies that specifically seek to eliminate terrorist environments and groups', whereas '*antiterrorism* refers to target hardening, enhanced security and other defensive measures seeking to deter or prevent terrorist attacks'.[67] This is an interesting distinction, not because it is controversial but because it is seldom noted in the literature. Counter-terrorism, therefore, refers to the response undertaken to target a specific threat, whereas anti-terrorism measures involve the use of broad instruments of prevention. As mentioned previously, Martin's approach to discussing counter-terrorism policies is to categorise different responses. Martin states:

> Categories of responses should not be considered exact templates for every terrorist contingency, for there are no exact theories of responses of counterterrorism. The fact of the matter is that terrorist environments are in many ways idiosyncratic, as are many terrorist groups. The implications of this for counterterrorist policy are that some methods will be successful in only a few cases, whereas others will be adaptable to many cases. Significantly, some policy options often seem to make perfect theoretical sense when they are developed, but subsequently they make little practical sense.[68]

The idiosyncratic nature of both threats and responses to terrorism is key when analysing policies. Martin's approach to counter-terrorism is, however, broad. It does not deal adequately with core issues such as the balance between acceptability and effectiveness, the dilemmas of negotiation and the differing realities of counter-terrorism in relation to the ideological orientation of a state. The gulf between theory and practice can be reduced. This can be done if material is produced that deals with specific regions or areas, which thus recognises the idiosyncratic nature of terrorism and, by extension, counter-terrorism strategies, as is done here.

Wilkinson's 2007 edited study entitled *Homeland Security in the United Kingdom* is another example of this approach. This is because he not only focuses on one state, the United Kingdom, but also, and unusually, exclusively on the practice rather than the theory of counter-terrorism.[69] The authors of the various chapters within the book have, it would appear, been given unprecedented access to sources of information within the United Kingdom government. The granting of such access is generally difficult, since institutions that are responsible for counter-terrorism often fear the repercussions of letting sensitive information out into the public domain. Indeed, even if access is gained, publication of all the data gathered can sometimes be restricted if sensitive information is included in the study. The term 'Homeland Security' is one which 'originated in the United States in the wake of the 9/11 attacks to denote the numerous policies and measures undertaken by the United States Government to enhance the protection of United States territory against terrorist attack'.[70] Wilkinson's edited study adopted this phrase and applied it to the United Kingdom context. The focus of the study is much narrower than most counter-terrorism studies, as it maps out the structures, mechanisms and processes that were in place following 9/11, to cope with future terrorist attacks. As such, this is not a theoretical study of counter-terrorism methods, but focuses on the practical application of theory.

To do this, the study is divided into three sections that examine the nature of the threat, the mechanisms and structures that make up the civil contingency plans, emergency responses and the effort under way to improve the future preparedness of the United Kingdom.[71] While extremely useful, the study as a whole tends to be more of an indicative guide to what is, rather than an academic critique of how it should have been. For example, Littlewood and Simpson analyse the Chemical, Biological, Radiological or Nuclear (CBRN) threat to the United Kingdom. They use a historical methodology as a means of speculating on future possibilities regarding such threats. Based on this, they draw conclusions as to the likelihood of a CBRN attack taking place.

The problem with their methodology is that it fails to take into consideration the geopolitical context of the period to which they refer or to make suggestions about what should be done. For example, the authors note that '[t]errorist and other non-state actor interest in CBRN precedes the [emergence of the] current paradigm of Islamic jihadists', but fail to explain why other criminal groups have sought to use such weapons.[72] Instead, they provide a breakdown of what CBRNs are and a threat assessment relating to the potential for their future utilisation by terrorists in the United Kingdom.[73] Thus, they also do not provide specific ways in which such attacks can or should be prevented. This issue is in fact dealt with elsewhere in the edited study by other authors, thus underscoring a lack of consistent analysis from one author to another.

The drawback of this narrated approach is also evidenced in Frank Gregory's contribution to the same publication. He provides an assessment of the United Kingdom intelligence services role.[74] Gregory maps out the various intelligence agencies that occupy counter-terrorism roles and how these interact. He analyses the contributions of the various agencies in terms of resource allocation, paying particular attention to their budgets.[75] Throughout Wilkinson's edited study, the contributors provide some insightful information about the United Kingdom's ability to cope with terrorist threats. As this book attempts to map what are, basically, empirical facts regarding the United Kingdom counter-terrorism infrastructure, the use of multiple contributors – which might detract from the analytical consistency of the study – is not the key criticism here. The drawback to this approach is the lack of analysis and indeed contextualisation concerning how and why things are as described.

Shorter studies in peer-reviewed journals or chapters in edited books have tended to focus on specific techniques that have been used to counter terrorism.[76] This could detract from an understanding of how each policy instrument fits into the broader strategic apparatus. The post-Cold War analysis led to the inclusion of new areas of interest. For example, the role of intelligence was increasingly analysed after 9/11.[77] In his critique of the intelligence community both pre- and post-9/11, Ball states that '[t]he terrorist attacks on the World Trade Center and the Pentagon on [9/11] involved the worst intelligence failure by the US intelligence community since Pearl Harbor'.[78] Failures, Ball suggests, occurred at every stage of the intelligence cycle. Ball, however, believes that the intelligence agencies could neither have predicted nor prevented 9/11, as 'the warning signs were never explicit and [...] were drowned in a mass of confusing and contradictory information'.[79] The primary problem with the intelligence community, as is discussed in later chapters, was that it was still on a Cold War footing and was woefully unprepared for the asymmetrical threats of the twenty-first century. This was especially so in relation to terrorism.

Osama bin Laden was known to the intelligence services since 1995, when he was classified as a 'high priority', following his association with the 1993 World Trade Center bombing in New York.[80] His status was elevated by the United States intelligence services in 1999, when he was placed on the *Ten Most Wanted Fugitives List*, with a reward of US$5 million for information leading to his apprehension, by the Federal Bureau of Investigation (FBI).[81] This was 'the largest amount ever offered for a fugitive by the United States Government'.[82]

The value of human intelligence in understanding Osama bin Laden, and the al Qaeda network, was recognised after the 1998 East Africa bombings of the United States embassies in Nairobi and Dar es Salaam. Interrogations conducted following these attacks yielded intelligence on al Qaeda's 'key personalities and its communications networks, and deliberations up until around 1999–2000'.[83]

This was particularly important, since up until that point it was publicly acknowledged that the intelligence agencies of the international community had struggled to infiltrate the al Qaeda network. The difficulty in penetrating al Qaeda was probably due to their network structure, discussed further. This meant that a significant proportion of the information on al Qaeda was signals intelligence obtained by the National Security Agency. Ball suggests that the United States '[I]ntelligence [C]ommunity was taken completely by surprise on 9/11, although there were many indications during the preceding several months that [Osama] bin-Laden was planning a major operation'. There was no definitive evidence on when, how or where this would take place.[84] This conclusion is similar to that summarised in the *9/11 Commission Report* and is likely a dominant reason behind the increased allocation of funding to the intelligence community.[85]

The post-Cold War period saw an upsurge in the amount of literature relating to the more general topic of terrorism. This, post-Cold War and even more so post-9/11, extended to include publications specifically on al Qaeda.[86] In part this was due to the perceived broadening of the concept of security and the associated broadening of those considered *experts* in the field. The study of terrorism and counter-terrorism during the Cold War period was done through the lens of national security. This in effect led to authors considering the use of terrorism as a tool undertaken by state as opposed to non-state actors. Towards the end of the Cold War, when security threats were being considered in terms of individual, human security, the study of transnational terrorism became increasingly widespread. However, both during and following the Cold War, the literature continued to suffer the same drawbacks. Although examined by a broader field of scholars, it was still focused very much on the nature of terrorism, the reasons for its emergence and indeed the motivating factors of its advocates.

Very little emerged on counter-terrorism and what did emerge tended to make universal claims, rather than focusing on specific geographic areas – a significant shortcoming considering the irrevocably idiosyncratic nature of terrorism and issues relating to motivation.[87] The countering of terrorism needs, at a minimum, to appreciate the specific reasons for the emergence of a group in a particular area. A strategy needs to ask why these groups are finding a support base within a particular country and, indeed, an appropriate governing authority needs to work within the confines of its own laws and regulations to combat the terrorist threat in an acceptable manner. The need for such analytical and consistent study underpins the focus of this work.

Transnational terrorist violence

Distinguishing terrorist violence from other forms of violence is just one way in which terrorism may be characterised. Silke, for example, states that by classifying terrorism as warfare, its acts become violations of war and its practitioners 'war criminals',[88] due to their disregard for the principles of chivalry and humanity.[89] Schmidt agrees, highlighting the criminal nature of terrorist groups who do not wear distinguishing uniforms, carry their arms openly and consciously target civilians to communicate their message(s).[90] Their actions would be considered violations of the Geneva and Hague Conventions that advocate the protection of non-combatant(s) and the innocent in times of war.[91] Terrorists may argue that their disregard for 'chivalry and humanity' is in fact the price that must be paid (collateral damage) for their campaigns against perceived oppression, or injustice.[92] Adhering to the norms of conflict would place them at a tactical disadvantage, as the authorities would be in a position to act to suppress their campaign en masse. However, some groups considered terrorists, such as the Columbian Fuerzas Armadas Revolucionarias de Colombia–Ejército del Pueblo (FARC-EP), discussed further below, have adhered to the aforementioned norms and are often referred to as guerrilla fighters.

An inherent contradiction arises when considering practitioners of terrorism as war criminals.[93] Ignatieff agrees that terrorism is distinct from traditional warfare and states that those who equate warfare with terrorism fail to consider the conceptual differences between *jus ad bellum* (justice of war) and *jus in bello* (justice in war).[94] These terms refer to the reason for war and the way in which war is conducted. For example, the use of state-sponsored counter-terror may be seen as an unjustified tactic within the context of a justified cause, lending credence to the claim that the end may justify the means. In contrast, terrorism is considered to be the pursuit of an unjust cause, utilising unjust means. However, the bestowment of legitimacy rests frequently with the powerful in the international arena and, as such, this may change. For example, the Afghanistan Mujahidin, once considered freedom fighters and, according to United States President Ronald Reagan, 'the moral equivalent of [the United States'] founding fathers', were later branded as supporters of terrorism.[95] Their use of terrorist tactics, supported by the Central Intelligence Agency, to expel the Soviet Union from Afghanistan in the 1980s was considered justifiable by the United States within the wider geopolitical context of the Cold War. When the Mujahidin threatened the stability of the international community, this legitimacy was withdrawn and the group reconceptualised by the United States government as a terrorist organisation. Therefore, legitimacy will always escape those that threaten a state's stability.

Acts of terrorism, undertaken in peacetime, are most closely associated with ordinary crime. Kennedy states that terrorist violence can be distinguished from other forms of 'criminal, pathological, civil or international violence'.[96] Terrorist violence should be seen as a subset of 'political violence', as not all forms of 'political violence' are terrorist (e.g. May Day protests).[97] Hoffman suggests that 'ordinary' criminals may be driven by selfishness.[98] This is because their actions are not 'designed or intended to have consequences, or create psychological repercussions beyond the act itself'.[99] In comparison, terrorist organisations may be seen as unselfish, as their acts are 'fundamentally and inherently political'.[100]

In contrast to ordinary criminals, terrorists are aiming to advance the cause of others through asymmetric tactics that may include, for example, suicide terrorists. Therefore, terrorist violence may be seen as the combination of a 'cause, the instrument of coercion and the instrument of communication'.[101] Terrorism, therefore, is an *asymmetric* tactic that may be utilised by states, guerrilla units and ordinary criminals. Considering terrorism as a philosophical dilemma of *one man's terrorist is another's freedom fighter* detracts from the debate relating to understanding its impact upon society. The employment of tactics is often intertwined with the perceived justness of the strategic cause. Organisations that employ terrorist tactics face denunciation as terrorists, as opposed to the preferable label of freedom fighter, revolutionary or liberator.

Organisations and individuals may, on occasion, go against the grain and turn, both in terms of labelling and international political consensus, from terrorist to freedom fighter. A good example of this is Nelson Mandela and South Africa's African National Congress. Mandela is the personification of the terrorist, freedom fighter dilemma, as he went from violent activist, prisoner, to respected President of South Africa and world statesman.[102] It is useful to consider terrorist violence in the following manner. Terrorism is a means of achieving a political objective through the use of violence, force and fear. 'Terror', as noted in a 1970s Department of Defense report, 'is a natural phenomenon; terrorism is the conscious exploitation of it'.[103] This form of violence may also be considered a tactic of *asymmetric* warfare that is not ideologically orientated, as ideologically orientated violence is characteristically 'sociologically and psychologically selective'.[104] The tactic of terrorism 'is meant to produce psychological effects that reach far beyond the immediate victims of the attack'.[105] In contrast, the primary intentions of broad acts of war, as opposed to specific counter-terror, are to inhibit the enemy's ability to carry on and achieve decisive victory, in theory, within the established international rules of conduct.[106] Terrorists are driven by a political desire that may not conform to universal perceptions of reality. In order to achieve these desires, terrorists undertake violent or coercive acts that may include indiscriminate bombing campaigns and assassinations, and possibly ordinary crimes, such as bank robberies, to fund terrorist violence.[107] Terrorism, therefore, is defined here as the threat, or act of violence against a people, or infrastructure for the purpose of extracting political concessions and/or causing fear.

This book, however, is not simply concerned with terrorism but rather with a specific type of terrorism that may be described as transnational. The structure and consequent diverse objectives of al Qaeda clearly indicate that their motivations and violence are not confined to a specific state or region. They are, in essence, global. The common thread that runs through al Qaeda and affiliates is the adoption of radical, Wahhabist-Islam and a desire for the destruction of the liberal democracies in the international community.

Other objectives are more localised. A separate category of transnational terrorism is needed in order to distinguish between those terrorists with and without state-specific objectives. Martin recognises this, since he describes al Qaeda as 'a transnational movement with members and supporters from throughout the Muslim world'.[108] The al Qaeda movement is 'an international revolutionary movement that uses terrorism as a matter of routine' and may, therefore, be considered an international terrorist organisation that fits into the subcategory of international religious terrorists.[109] It is also a transnational movement that aspires to link like-minded Muslim extremist groups and expel non-Muslim influences from so-called 'Islamic' regions of the world. Reconciling these two perceptions – al Qaeda being both an international and transnational movement – involves viewing international terrorism, even though it emerged prior to transnational terrorism, as a subset of the latter type. In this sense a transnational terrorist movement, such as al Qaeda, may be seen to encompass all the hallmarks of an international group, such as the Palestine Liberation Organisation; particularly with regard to structure and motivation necessarily linked to one distinct region or state. The overarching aim of re-establishing the Caliphate, an Islamic state, is transnational. Describing al Qaeda as a transnational terrorist group becomes clearer when 'transnational' is defined.

The concept of transnationalism 'refers to forces that cut across state boundaries'.[110] Transnational relations, according to Risse-Kappen, may be defined as the 'regular interactions across national boundaries when at least one actor is a non-state agent or does not operate on behalf of a national government or an intergovernmental organisation'.[111] In discussing the differences between multinational corporations and transnational corporations, Duncan, Jancar-Webster and Swiftky state that the latter 'usually view themselves as nonnational entities' whereas the former have parent companies in one state with subsidiary units in others.[112] A transnational terrorist organisation, therefore, is one that is not affiliated to one particular state. The Provisional Irish Republican Army, which undertook terrorist violence in Northern Ireland and the mainland of the United Kingdom during and after the Cold War period, would not be a transnational terrorist group, as their focus was on the establishment of a fully unified Republic of Ireland.

In the second chapter of this book an outline of the post-9/11 counter-terrorism strategies of both the United Kingdom and the United States is provided. Intuitively, it may be argued that the responses by both states have been similar if not identical. Such an argument would, however, be misleading. Following 9/11 the United Kingdom, although supporting military actions in Afghanistan, took a much more legalistic approach to counter-terrorism. This is due primarily to an acknowledgement of a home-grown presence of terrorist practitioners. In contrast, the United States, although proposing an increase in domestic counter-terrorism policies, focused primarily on the projection of power externally – overseas. This is due to United States beliefs that a home-grown threat was minimal and that the United States needed to focus on preventing terrorists from gaining weaponry or expertise that allowed them to enter and attack the country undetected.

While Chapter 2 focuses on the intention, as shown in the published strategies of the United Kingdom and United States during the post-9/11 period, Chapters 3, 4 and 5 assess the policy implications of their use. In line with this, Chapter 3 analyses the contribution of intelligence, while Chapter 4 focuses on law enforcement and Chapter 5 on military force. The data used in these chapters are taken from previously unpublished interview data with counter-terrorism professionals, politicians and academic specialists in the areas; these are combined with primary sources, such as strategies and policy documents, to help provide a unique appraisal of both the United Kingdom and United States counter-terrorism strategies.

Researching counter-terrorism: qualitative sources

In addition to other primary and secondary data, this book utilises previously unpublished data that were gleaned from interviews with professionals and academics with a specialist expertise in counter-terrorism. The bulk of interviewees came from the United States. Interviewing individuals on areas related to terrorism and perhaps more importantly counter-terrorism was, for obvious reasons relating to security, problematic. Practitioners in the United States were more willing to discuss post-9/11 strategy than those in the United Kingdom, perhaps due to the closer links between the academy and the civil service.

Interviewees from the United Kingdom included John Jackson, who served in the British Army for twenty-seven years, mostly in the areas of education. He was a lecturer at the Royal Military Academy Sandhurst and, when we first met, a seasonal lecturer at the University of Reading. There he convened a module on terrorism while at the American College in Bath he taught Irish history. Another member of the British Army who has gone into academia is Timothy Cross. A former Major-General, he joined the British Army in 1971. Among other postings he served in Germany, Northern Ireland, the Gulf and the former Republic of Yugoslavia. In the lead-up to the 2003 Gulf conflict, Cross was deployed to Washington, then Kuwait and Baghdad, as deputy in the Office of Reconstruction and Humanitarian Affairs (later the Coalition Provisional Authority). Cross was vocal in his criticism of the preparations for post-conflict Iraq. After retiring from the British Army, he became visiting lecturer at the University of Nottingham and Cranfield Defence University.

Other interviewees involved in the implementation of United Kingdom counter-terrorism policy included Inspector Jonathon Brooke of South Yorkshire Police Constabulary. Brooke has a background in the Safer Neighbourhood schemes, both working in communities and at district level. At the time of interview, his position was that of PREVENT Delivery Manager for South Yorkshire. As PREVENT Delivery Manager he was responsible for implementing the PREVENT/counter-radicalisation strand of the United Kingdom's counter-terrorism strategy, discussed further in this book. In addition to Brooke, an interview was undertaken with Superintendent Andrew Pratt of Lancashire Constabulary. After joining the police in 1982, Pratt had two secondments. One was to work for Her Majesty's Inspectorate Constabulary on the back of the Lawrence Report, while looking into the workings of the Metropolitan Police Service. The second was a one-year secondment to London, where he wrote the Police Plan for the Prevention of Terrorism under the auspices of the Association of Chief Police Officers. In essence Pratt authored the Police response to the United Kingdom's counter-terrorism strategy and the guidelines behind its implementation.

To get a 'political' perspective on post-9/11 strategy an interview was undertaken with Patrick Mercer (MP). Mercer has a military background in the British Army in Northern Ireland, Germany, Canada, Uganda, Brunei and the Balkans. He was decorated for service in Bosnia. After 9/11 he served on the House of Commons Defence Select Committee, Conservative Defence Team and acted as Parliamentary Private Secretary to the Shadow Defence Secretary during the 2003 Gulf conflict. In December 2008 he was appointed Chairman of the House of Commons Sub-Committee on Counter-Terrorism. Between June 2003 and March 2007 he also served as the Shadow Minister for Homeland Security. In addition to Mercer, an interview, on condition of anonymity, was conducted with a clerk to the Defence Committee, who was able to offer an insight not just into the workings of the committee, but also a greater understanding of the way in which decisions are made and what kinds of oversight roles they have.

Within the United States, it was possible to gain substantially greater access to a greater mix of interviewees; although a significant proportion were interviewed under condition of anonymity. A good source of information, particularly on the workings of the Department of Homeland Security, was Robert G. Ross. A thirty-year veteran of the United States Coast Guard, he has a background in marine safety, environmental protection, and military readiness and contingency planning. As well as gaining a degree in systems management (not computer systems), Ross has been stationed in Baltimore; Washington, DC; Guam; Norfolk; Virginia; London; New Orleans; Miami; and San Juan. He has been the Federal On-Scene Coordinator for several major events, including the Exxon Valdez incident. His final position in the Coast Guard, running the Office of Strategic Analysis for the Commandant, in many ways informed his new role within the Department of Homeland Security. This is because the role involved considering potential threats in the distant future and how, if at all, the Coast Guard may tackle them. When interviewed, Ross was Chief of the Risk Sciences Branch in the Department of Homeland Security, Science and Technology Directorate. His role involved conducting and sponsoring research into homeland security decision-making for adaptive, reactive, intelligent and strategically driven adversaries.

Interviews were conducted with a number of individuals within the Department of Homeland Security which was created in the aftermath of 9/11 with the remit of protecting the United States homeland. One such source included a senior House Committee on Homeland Security staffer whose specialism related to issues concerning information-sharing and terrorism risk assessment, all within the context of the Department of Homeland Security. This individual was not part of the Department of Homeland Security, but of a committee that oversaw the Department of Homeland Security's work; basically a committee to which Department of Homeland Security is accountable.

The Department of Homeland Security, as discussed further, is home to a number of different agencies. These include, for example, the Federal Emergency Management Agency (FEMA) which primarily responds to all threats, manmade and natural. At the time of interview Corey Gruber was Executive Director of the National Preparedness Taskforce and as such works to prepare

FEMA for future threats. Gruber, a twenty-year veteran of the United States Army has worked in facilitating military assistance to other United States government agencies such as the FBI both in and out of government. Alan Cohn, Deputy Assistant Secretary for Policy (Strategic Plans) within the Department of Homeland Security, was another interviewee. Cohn has served as a Department of Homeland Security Liaison to the Homeland Security and Emergency Management Committee of the American Bar Association Section on State and Local Government Law. He started working for the Department of Homeland Security in 2006 as the Director of Preparedness of Response Policy within the Office of Development, which comes under the Office of Policy.

Other interviewees included Michael Jacobson, who served in the FBI as an intelligence analyst within the Office of the General Counsel. Jacobson also assisted the 9/11 Commission focusing on issues related to domestic intelligence policy, as well as investigating the FBI's response. Randall J. Larsen, a retired Colonel of the United States Air Force and current Director of the Institute for Homeland Security, is also the National Security Advisor to the Center for Biosecurity at the University of Pittsburgh Medical Center. As well as being the author of numerous books, Larsen has designed and led war-games, including DARK WINTER (bioterrorism, 2001), SILENT VECTOR (critical infrastructure, 2002), CRIMSON SKY (agro-terrorism, 2002), CRIMSON WINTER (food security, 2003) and TERMINAL RISK (environmental terrorism, 2003).

In February 2009 Joseph McMillan was also interviewed for this research. At the time he was working at the National Defense University. Two months later, in April 2009, he accepted a position in President Obama's administration as Principal Deputy Assistant Secretary of Defense for International Security Affairs. In this role McMillan oversaw the formulation, coordination and implementation of strategy and policy involving Africa, Europe, NATO, the Middle East and most of the former Soviet Union. He also serves as a key advisor to the Secretary of Defense on issues related to these regions. It should be noted that the comments made during the interview not only came prior to his appointment, but were his own, and did not necessarily represent any 'official' views, opinions and/or policies.

McMillan joined the Department of Defense in 1978 as a logistics analyst in the Office of the Chief of Naval Operations. Among other positions he was country director for Pakistan, Jordan, India and other countries inside the Defense Security Assistance Agency. In 1988 McMillan joined the Office of the Secretary of Defense and had regional portfolios for defence and security issues affecting the Persian Gulf, Levant, South Asia, North Africa and the former Soviet Union. In 1997 he was named Principal Director for Russia, Ukraine and Eurasia. In 1988 he was further promoted to the Senior Executive Service, where he also became Principal Director for Near Eastern and South Asian Affairs.

Another individual interviewed who has also had a long and illustrious career in public office is John B. McGowan. Before 9/11, McGowan had spent thirty-three years working for United States Customs. He served as Director of the Office of Inspectional Enforcement Liaison, Assistant Regional Commissioner for all Customs operations in the states of Texas, New Mexico, Arizona and

Oklahoma, Executive Director of Passenger Programs and Executive Director for Enforcement Programs. After 9/11 his extensive career in the area of border security made him the ideal candidate to develop *homeland security* policy. Thus he became Director of Cargo and Port Security, Office of Homeland Security within the Executive Office of the President, and Director for Cargo and Trade Policy within the Border and Transportation Security Directorate, Department of Homeland Security. This latter position made him responsible for providing advice·on the national direction, development and implementation of the federal government's organisation, planning and response to perceived and real threats to homeland security, as well as guiding Department of Homeland Security policy on international trade issues.

McGowan was also Executive Director for the Radiation Dispersal Device/ Improvised Nuclear Device Preparedness Working Group across the federal sector; Executive Director of the Interagency Commission on Crime and Security in United States Seaports; served on the Aviation Safety Advisory Committee to the Federal Aviation Administration and the National Chamber Foundation blue ribbon review of United States seaport capacity; he also served on the Interagency Committee on the Maritime Transportation System. Currently, he is a member of the American Association of Port Authorities, serving on the Port Security Committee and on the Traveller and Immigration Policy Committee and the Import Export Procedures Committee of the Border Trade Alliance.

Randy Beardsworth, similar to McGowan, had a distinguished career in government. He served in two Presidential administrations as Director for Defense Policy on the National Security Council staff. Previous roles included Assistant Secretary for Strategic Plans, where he created long-range plans for the Department of Homeland Security and oversaw counter-terrorism strategic planning as well as the creation and initial oversight of the Program Management Office for the Secretary's Secure Border Initiative. In 2002 he helped develop and integrate the Border and Transportation Security Directorate's functional structure within the newly formed Department of Homeland Security and then became its Director of Operations. This was followed by his being named Acting Under-Secretary for Border and Transportation Security Directorate. In this particular role he oversaw the four agencies that make up the directorate: Customs and Border Protection, Immigration and Customs Enforcement, Transportation Security Administration, and the Federal Law Enforcement Training Center.

The above interviewees are just some of those who have been consulted in this research. Others are cited throughout the book. As mentioned above, with regard to the United Kingdom but also to a lesser extent the United States, interviewees did not serve as the only source of information for this publication. Documents such as the National Security Strategy, the counter-terrorism strategies and PREVENT implementation documents are also assessed here. Although names have been mentioned in the above sample, some other interviewees, for obvious reasons, have had to be kept anonymous while as much information as possible about their roles is given.

Notes

1 Anonymous Source B, interview conducted by the author, held in Washington, DC in February 2009.
2 United States government (December 1976), 'Report of Task Force on Disorders and Terrorism', p. 3.
3 Samuel M. Makinda, 'Human Security Between Terrorism and Counter-terrorism – Eclectic Perspective', *The Human Security Gateway* (1 July 2004), www.humanse-curitygateway.com/data/item700486941/view, accessed on 1 December 2005, p. 11.
4 Alex P. Schmid, 'Terrorism and Democracy', in Alex P. Schmid and Ronald D. Crelinsten (eds) *Western Responses to Terrorism* (London: Frank Cass, 2003), pp. 14–15.
5 Paul Wilkinson, *Political Terrorism* (Essex: The Macmillan Press, 1974), p. 136.
6 Ibid.
7 Schmid, 'Terrorism and Democracy', p. 15.
8 Beatrice de Graaf, *Evaluating Counter-Terrorism Performance* (Abingdon: Routledge, 2011).
9 United Kingdom government (July 2006), 'Countering International Terrorism: The United Kingdom's Strategy'.
10 United Kingdom government (March 2009), 'Countering International Terrorism: The United Kingdom's Strategy'.
11 Ibid., p. 6.
12 United States government (September 2006), 'National Strategy for Combating Terrorism'.
13 United States President Barack Obama, 'Executive Order 13492 of January 22, 2009 Review and Disposition of Individuals Detained At the Guantanamo Bay Naval Base and Closure of Detention Facilities'; and United States President Barrack Obama, 'Executive Order 13491 of January 22, 2009 Ensuring Lawful Interrogations' (27 January 2009).
14 David McKeeby, 'Analysis: Obama Offers New Approach to Counterterrorism – Emphasis on American Values Central to Struggle Against Extremism' (23 January 2009), *America.gov – Engaging the world*.
15 The concept of transnationalism 'refers to forces that cut across state boundaries'. Transnational relations may be defined as the 'regular interactions across national boundaries when at least one actor is a non-state agent or does not operate on behalf of a national government or an intergovernmental organisation'. A transnational terrorist group, therefore, is one that is not affiliated with any one particular state. W. Raymond Duncan, Barbara Jancar-Webster and Bob Swiftky, *World Politics in the 21st Century*, 3rd edn (London: Pearson Longman, 2006), p. 321; and Thomas Risse-Kappen, 'Bringing transnational relations back in: introduction' in Thomas Risse-Kappen, *Bringing Transnational Relations Back In – Non-State Actors, Domestic Structures and International Institutions*, 3rd edn (Cambridge: Cambridge University Press, 1999), p. 3.
16 Schmid and Crelinsten (eds), *Western Responses to Terrorism*.
17 See Grant Wardlaw, *Political Terrorism – Theory, Tactics and Counter-measures*, 2nd edn (Cambridge: Cambridge University Press, 1989).
18 See General Sir Frank Kitson, *Low Intensity Operations – Subversion, Insurgency, Peace-keeping* (London: Faber and Faber, 1971); Admiral Stansfield Turner, *Terrorism and Democracy* (Boston, MA: Houghton Mifflin); and Colonel Michael Dewar, *War in the Streets – The Story of Urban Combat from Calais to Khafji* (Newton Abbot: David & Charles, 1992).
19 For more information on British experiences in Malaya see Phillip Deery, 'Malaya, 1948 Britain's Asian Cold War', *Journal of Cold War Studies*, 9 (winter 2007), 1, pp. 29–54.

20 Kitson, *Low Intensity Operations*, pp. 13–63.
21 Ibid., p. 50.
22 Wilkinson, *Political Terrorism*, p. 139.
23 Kitson, *Low Intensity Operations*, p. 53.
24 Wilkinson, *Political Terrorism*, p. 137.
25 Ibid.
26 R. Moss, quoted in Paul Wilkinson, *Political Terrorism*, p. 137.
27 Wilkinson, *Political Terrorism*, p. 138.
28 Ibid.
29 Ibid., pp. 137–138.
30 Ibid., p. 138.
31 G. Davidson Smith, *Combating Terrorism* (London: Routledge, 1990), pp. 27–32.
32 Ibid., p. 27.
33 Ibid.
34 Ibid.
35 Ibid.
36 Ibid., pp. 99–231; pp. 47–48; and pp. 66–85.
37 Ibid., p. 66.
38 The 1970 'October Crisis' was triggered by the kidnap of the British Trade Commissioner, James Cross, on 5 October. This was swiftly followed by the kidnap on 10 October and subsequent execution of the Labour Minister and Vice-Premier of Quebec, Pierre Laporte. Davidson Smith, *Combating Terrorism*, p. 66.
39 Davidson Smith, *Combating Terrorism*, p. 50.
40 Ibid., pp. 66–85.
41 Wilkinson, *Political Terrorism*.
42 Davidson Smith, *Combating Terrorism*.
43 Simon Dalby, 'Contesting an Essential Concept: Reading the Dilemmas in Contemporary Discourse', in Keith Krause and Michael C. Williams (eds) *Critical Security Studies – Concepts and Cases* (Abingdon: Routledge, 1997), p. 4.
44 Ibid.
45 Stephen M. Walt, 'The Renaissance of Security Studies', *International Studies Quarterly*, 35 (1991), 2, p. 213.
46 Ibid., pp. 211–239.
47 Dalby, Contesting an Essential Concept, pp. 3–31.
48 Ibid., p. 9.
49 Barry Buzan, 'Is International Security Possible?', in Ken Booth (ed.) *New Thinking About Strategy and International Security* (London: Harper Collins Academic, 1991), p. 31.
50 Paul Rogers, *Global Security and the War on Terror – Elite Power and the Illusion of Control* (London: Routledge, 2008); Jessica Stern, *The Ultimate Terrorists* (London: Harvard University Press, 1999), p. 84.
51 For example, see Paul Wilkinson (ed.), *Homeland Security in the United Kingdom – Future Preparedness for Terrorist Attack since 9/11* (London: Routledge, 2007); Lawrence Freedman (ed.), *Superterrorism – Policy Responses* (Oxford: Blackwell Publishing, 2003); and Grant Wardlaw, *Political Terrorism*.
52 Kenneth Christie, *America's War on Terrorism – The Revival of the Nation-State versus Universal Human Rights* (Ceredigion, Wales: The Edwin Mellen Press, 2008), p. 255.
53 Gus Martin, *Understanding Terrorism – Challenges, Perspectives, and Issues*, 2nd edn (London: Sage), p. 246.
54 Michael Ignatieff, *The Lesser Evil – Political Ethics in an Age of Terror* (Edinburgh: Edinburgh University Press, 2005).
55 Ibid.
56 Ibid., p. 40.

57 Byman also discusses what he calls targeted killings within the context of Israeli management of the terrorist threat. Byman argues that such a policy tactic can be effective so long as it is undertaken within a 'broader counterterrorism program with better defences and improved intelligence'. Daniel Byman, 'Do Targeted Killings Work?', *Foreign Affairs*, 85 (March/April 2006), 2, p. 111.

58 Tamar Meisels, *The Trouble with Terror – Liberty, Security, and the Response to Terrorism* (Cambridge: Cambridge University Press, 2008), p. 130.

59 Ibid.

60 Other examples of single-authored studies on terrorism that adopt this *afterthought* approach when discussing counter-terrorism include Dipak K. Gupta, *Understanding Terrorism and Political Violence – The Life Cycle of Birth, Growth, Transformation, and Desire* (Abingdon: Routledge, 2008), pp. 181–206; James M. Lutz and Brenda J. Lutz, *Global Terrorism*, 2nd edn (Abingdon: Routledge, 2008), pp. 261–282; Michael Chandler and Rohan Gunaratna, *Countering Terrorism – Can We Meet the Threat of Global Violence* (London: Resktion Books, 2007), pp. 201–220; Randall J. Larsen, *Our Own Worst Enemy – Asking the Right Questions about Security to Protect You, Your Family, and America* (New York: Grand Central Publishing, 2007), pp. 269–279; and Richard English, *Terrorism – How to Respond* (Oxford: Oxford University Press, 2009), pp. 118–143.

61 Martin, *Understanding Terrorism*, p. 345.

62 Ibid.

63 Ibid.

64 Wilkinson, *Homeland Security in the United Kingdom*, p. 137.

65 Martin, *Understanding Terrorism*, p. 345.

66 Benjamin Nimer, 'Terrorism and Southern Africa', *Terrorism*, 13 (1990), 6, pp. 447–453.

67 Ibid.

68 Martin, *Understanding Terrorism*, p. 345.

69 Wilkinson, *Homeland Security in the United Kingdom*.

70 Ibid., p. 3.

71 Ibid., pp. 23–114, pp. 331–368 and pp. 115–330.

72 Jez Littlewood and John Simpson, 'The Chemical, Biological, Radiological and Nuclear Weapons Threat', in Wilkinson, *Homeland Security in the United Kingdom*, p. 60.

73 Ibid., pp. 71–75.

74 Frank Gregory, 'An Assessment of the Contribution of Intelligence-led Counter-terrorism', in Wilkinson, *Homeland Security in the United Kingdom*, pp. 181–282.

75 Ibid., p. 190.

76 For example, see Lawrence Freedman (ed.), *Superterrorism – Policy Responses* (Oxford: Blackwell Publishing, 2002); Steve Tsang (ed.), *Intelligence and Human Rights in the Era of Global Terrorism* (Stanford, CA: Stanford University Press, 2008); Yonah Alexander (ed.), *Counterterrorism Strategies – Successes and Failures of Six Nations* (Virginia: Potomac Books, 2006); and Stephen J. Flanagan and James A. Schear (eds), *Strategic Challenges – America's Global Security Agenda* (Virginia: Potomac Books, 2008).

77 For numerous articles on the role of intelligence in the United Kingdom, for example, see *Review of International Studies*, 35 (October 2009), 4, pp. 887–1009.

78 Desmond Ball, 'Desperately Seeking Bin Laden: The Intelligence Dimension of the War Against Terrorism', in Ken Booth and Tim Dunne (eds) *Worlds in Collision – Terror and the Future of Global Order* (Basingstoke: Palgrave Macmillan, 2002), p. 60.

79 Ibid., pp. 87–109.

80 Ibid., pp. 60–61.

81 Ibid., p. 61; see also United States government (June 1999), 'FBI Ten Most Wanted Fugitive: Usama Bin Laden', Federal Bureau of Investigation, www.fbi.gov/wanted/topten/usama-bin-laden, accessed 10 November 2007.

82 Ball, 'Desperately Seeking Bin Laden', p. 61; see also United States government (June 1999), 'FBI Ten Most Wanted Fugitive: Usama Bin Laden'.

83 Ball, 'Desperately Seeking Bin Laden', p. 62.

84 Ibid., p. 64.

85 Thomas H. Kean, The 9/11 Commission Report – Final Report of the National Commission on Terrorist Attacks Upon the United States – Authorised Edition (London: W.W. Norton, 2004).

86 See John K. Cooley, Unholy Wars – Afghanistan, America and International Terrorism, 3rd edn (London: Pluto Press, 2002); Jason Burke, The True Story of Radical Islam, 2nd edn (London: Penguin Books, 2004); Christopher C. Harmon, Terrorism Today, 2nd edn (London: Routledge, 2008); Paul Rogers, Global Security and the War on Terror; Jessica Stern, The Ultimate Terrorists; and Giles Kepel and Jean-Pierre Milelli (eds), Al Qaeda in its Own Words (Cambridge, MA: Harvard University Press, 2008).

87 See Laura K. Donohue, The Cost of Counterterrorism – Power, Politics, and Liberty (Cambridge: Cambridge University Press, 2008).

88 Andrew Silke, 'Terrorism and the Blind Men's Elephant', Terrorism and Political Violence, 8 (1996), 3, p. 18.

89 Robert Kennedy, 'Is One Person's Terrorist Another's Freedom Fighter? Western and Islamic Approaches to "Just War" Compared', Terrorism and Political Violence, 1 (1999), 1, pp. 8–15.

90 Alex P. Schmid, 'The Response Problem as a Definition Problem', in Schmid, 'Terrorism and Democracy', p. 12.

91 Unknown author (12 August 1949), 'Geneva Convention Relative to the Treatment of Prisoners of War', United Nations Office of the High Commissioner for Human Rights; and unknown author (18 October 1907), 'Hague Convention Respecting the Laws and Customs of War on Land', Law of War.

92 Silke, 'Terrorism and the Blind Men's Elephant', p. 18.

93 Ibid.

94 Contemporary debate on the distinctions between jus ad bellum (justice of war) and jus in bello (justice in war) highlights the existence of cultural variances. Western perspectives can be traced to the 1139 'Second Lateran Council's Treuga Dei'. The Treuga Dei banned certain weapons from the battlefield and guaranteed the safety of 'travellers, pilgrims, merchants, and peasants and their animals'. Another example is the Medieval 'Code of Chivalry' that existed between feuding European powers. Similarly, Western rules did not apply to those 'from beyond the shared cultural domain' who were considered barbarians and infidels. Walter Laqueur, The New Terrorism – Fanaticism and the Arms of Mass Destruction (London: Phoenix Press, 2001), p. 279; Robert Kennedy, 'Is One Person's Terrorist Another's Freedom Fighter? Western and Islamic Approaches to "Just War" Compared', pp. 8–15; and Michael Ignatieff, 'The Lessons of Terror: All War Against Civilians is Equal', New York Times (17 February 2002).

95 Eqbal Ahmad, 'Terrorism: Theirs and Ours – A Presentation at the University of Colorado', The Wisdom Fund (12 October 1998).

96 Kennedy, 'Is One Person's Terrorist Another's Freedom Fighter?', p. 4.

97 'Unknown author (1 May 2002), 'Skirmishes Mar May Day Protests', BBC News, http://news.bbc.co.uk/1/hi/uk/1963069.stm, accessed 15 January 2009.

98 Bruce Hoffman cited in David J. Whittaker, The Terrorism Reader (London: Routledge, 2001), p. 9.

99 Ibid.

100 Ibid., p. 5.

101 Ahmad, 'Terrorism'.
102 Nimer, 'Terrorism and Southern Africa', pp. 447–453.
103 United States government (1976), 'United States National Advisory Committee on Criminal Justice Standards and Goals', *Report of the Task Force on Disorders and Terrorism*, p. 3.
104 Ahmad, 'Terrorism'.
105 Bruce Hoffman, 'The Logic of Suicide Terrorism', *The Atlantic Monthly*, 291 (2003), 5, www.rand.org/pubs/reprints/2005/RAND_RP1187.pdf, 12 August 2010, p. 6.
106 Unknown author (12 August 1949), 'Geneva Convention Relative to the Treatment of Prisoners of War'.
107 Superintendent Andy Pratt, Lancashire Police Constabulary, interview conducted by the author, held in Preston, United Kingdom, 22 November 2009.
108 Martin, *Understanding Terrorism*, p. 293.
109 Ibid.
110 W. Raymond Duncan, Barbara Jancar-Webster and Bob Swiftky, *World Politics in the 21st Century*, 3rd edn (London: Pearson Longman, 2006), p. 321.
111 Thomas Risse-Kappen, 'Bringing Transnational Relations Back In: Introduction', in Thomas Risse-Kappen, Bringing Transnational Relations Back In – Non-State Actors, Domestic Structures and International Institutions, 3rd edn (Cambridge: Cambridge University Press, 1999), p. 3.
112 Duncan et al., World Politics in the 21st Century, p. 243.

2 Threat and response post-9/11

Transnational terrorism continues to represent a significant threat to both the United Kingdom and United States' ability to provide security for the citizenry and their interests at home and abroad. The evolved methodology of al Qaeda has reduced the effectiveness of traditional prevention and detection techniques with regard to ongoing terrorist operations. The flat network structure further decreases the state's traditional counter-terrorist *modus operandi* when, for example, it comes to gaining human intelligence. The adoption and manipulation of Wahhabism, a radical form of Islam adopted and promoted by the late Osama bin Laden, is used simply but effectively as a means of recruiting Muslim sympathisers of terrorist causes with a view to transitioning them into practitioners of terrorist violence.

The objectives of the al Qaeda movement on a global level have been easily identifiable since the early 1990s.[1] If the rationality of a terrorist is judged by whether they hold politically motivated – even if, from the perspective of the targeted state, politically unacceptable – objectives, then the al Qaeda movement is, for all intents and purposes, rational. This is because they have the traditional political undertones relating to territory and influence.

The threat of transnational terrorism is not an indicator of a 'clash of civilisations'; nor is it a case of the West versus the rest as proposed by Samuel Huntington.[2] Indeed, the very religious identity to which al Qaeda subscribes is a complicated one. Sunni-Muslims, who make up the bulk of the al Qaeda movement's membership and Shi'a-Muslims, entertain a great deal of animosity towards each other.[3] It is for this reason, Steven Hewitt states, that

> [t]o lump together all Muslims in any respect, including the idea that there is a unitary form of terrorism connected to Islam under the label of 'Islamofascism', is grossly simplistic. It is also counterproductive in terms of developing a sophisticated response to the threat.[4]

However, it should be noted that those who purport to justify the actions of terrorists also have a tendency to consider all Muslims as one and the same, either as supporters or apostates. Speaking shortly after the 7 July 2005 (7/7) London bombings, Omar Barki Mohammed, a radical cleric, responded to a question regarding the targeting of civilians and stated: '[w]e don't make a distinction between civilians and non-civilians, innocents and non-innocents. Only between Muslims and non-believers. And the life of an unbeliever has no value. It has no sanctity.'[5] Terrorists as well as academics, therefore, take part in contentious labelling practices.

Transnational terrorism: aims, objectives, lethality and structure

A claim that is frequently put forward by scholars and supporters of the proposition that today's terrorism is new is that transnational 'religiously motivated terrorism [...] is inextricably linked to [the] pursuit of mass casualties' and that it is irrational.[6] This perceived irrationality, therefore, makes redundant traditional counter-terrorism tools such as negotiation. Terror, Captain Morgan (125th Military Intelligence Battalion) states, 'has evolved from being a means to an end, to becoming the end in itself'.[7] Traditionally, religion has played little part in the 'political and social aims' that terrorists want to achieve.[8] The link between religion and terrorism, although nothing new or exclusively linked to Islam (e.g. Christian Crusades), has rarely become a prominent feature within the campaign of a non-state terrorist movement.[9] Exhibiting a religious trait gives the impression that there is no peaceful means of conflict resolution, short of complete capitulation by the targeted state(s), as 'violence is itself the objective'.[10] Jonathon Stevenson agrees, noting that al Qaeda's 'apocalyptic vision of the United States and its allies internationally disseminated by radical Islam is not amenable to political negotiation'.[11] As a consequence, Simon argues, '[t]raditional strategies of deterrence by retaliation are unlikely to work because the jihadists have no territory to hold at risk, seek sacrifice, and court Western attacks that will validate their claims about Western hostility to Islam'.[12]

The late Osama bin Laden, a leading inspirational figurehead in the al Qaeda movement, stated, through a Fatwa,[13] that Muslims have suffered in places such as Chechnya, Somalia, Palestine, Iraq and Bosnia-Herzegovina in a 'clear conspiracy between the United States and its allies under the cover of the iniquitous United Nations'.[14] He therefore called for the destruction of economic, financial and societal institutions as well as the expulsion, at any cost, of the United States' presence and influence from the Middle East – in addition to the destruction of Israel.[15] Osama bin Laden also argued that it was the duty of all Muslims to kill Americans in order to pressurise them into leaving 'the land of Islam', again a reference to the United States' support for Israel and wider presence in the Middle East.[16]

Religiously motivated terrorism, while not being the only form of transnational terrorism, is sometimes regarded as the most likely kind to employ weapons of mass destruction. Today's terrorists are seldom 'constrained by the fear that excessive violence will offend some constituency'.[17] Driven by a 'desire for a new [world] order' their wish is not to pressure or persuade, but for the destruction of the old order.[18] Proponents of the new terrorism proposition further argue that today's terrorists are likely to acquire and utilise high-yield weapons if they believe they would attract more attention, damage economies, or influence enemies to do their will.[19] Indeed, today's terrorists are perceived as being more lethal due to their belief that they need to undertake more destructive violence in order to attract the attention of the mass media. The ability of transnational terrorists to undertake destructive acts of violence is made easier by the accessibility of civilian targets, as demonstrated by the 2008 hotel attacks in Mumbai. Furthermore, the shift in prominence, from political mind-sets to vengeful, hard-line thoughts, also appears to make transnational terrorists significantly more dangerous than *traditional* ones.[20] Terrorist movements undertaking acts on behalf of the economically poorer regions of the world (Africa, the Middle East, South and Southeast Asia) are more likely to feel lesser degrees of moral self-restraint.[21] These restraints may continue to erode as the availability of Chemical, Biological, Radiological, or Nuclear (CBRN) materials increases.

Political aims in these areas are becoming entwined with aspirations for increased fatality figures as a 'high number of corpses is also a desirable aim' for today's terrorist movements.[22] This point is particularly applicable to religious fanatics' 'central objective[,] of killing as many people as possible', is motivated by the desire to create a new world order and is spurred by the perception of their instrumental role in completing a divine plan.[23] Walter Laqueur believes that it is only a matter of time before fanatics or 'deranged' terrorists, who are already financially and logistically secure and, due to their structure, harder to detect, acquire the technological know-how to produce catastrophic results.[24]

The contemporary threat of terrorism emerged at a critical time when communications and the availability of information had evolved, particularly with reference to increased speed. Coupled with apocalyptic rhetoric and what are, from the perspective of the targeted state, unacceptable aims, transnational terrorists have the potential to be more lethal. Aum-Shinrikyo, a contemporary but arguably non-transnational organisation founded by Shoko Asahara, utilised a crude chemical weapon in 1995 when they carried out a Sarin gas attack on the Tokyo subway in Japan.[25] The delivery platforms were primitive and, despite twelve killed and fifty-four seriously injured with a further 1,000 feeling the effects, the attack failed to reach its full lethal potential. The actual and the desired use of CBRN materials has added a further reason for states to desist from supporting terrorist organisations. This is because if traced back to a state, the repercussions could be severe.

In the post-Cold War market, gaining the necessary components can therefore present a problem for terrorist organisations. David Claridge discusses the plausibility of a terrorist organisation acquiring and using weapons of mass destruction. Claridge suggests that the notion of 'superterrorists' using weapons of mass destruction is supported by proponents of the new terrorism proposition for five reasons.[26] First, data show an increased number of fatalities and potentially fatal events throughout the 1990s.[27] Second, terrorists always want to increase their technological prowess; therefore, proliferation is inevitable. This leads to the third and fourth assumptions: that CBRN materials are more readily available in the post-Cold War era and that, within this same time frame, information on the creation of weapons of mass destruction has become more readily available through the internet. Finally, terrorists are constantly trying to 'out gun one another' in terms of technology and lethality, to gain media attention.[28] Terrorists also feed into this by highlighting their apocalyptic intentions. For example, in 1998 at a memorial service organised by Hamas, Asaid Al-Tamini, a prominent figure in Middle Eastern politics, spoke of the inevitability of a mass casualty attack due to the increased availability of CBRN materials.[29] Asaid Al-Tamini further indicated that Hamas had acquired such materials and would be in a position to *weaponise* them.[30] In the same year the United States' Federal indictment of Osama bin Laden suggested the existence of evidence that the al Qaeda leader had attempted to acquire chemical weapons.[31] Following the 1993 World Trade Center bombing, Ramzi Yousef, a suspected al Qaeda operative, confessed to experimenting with and considering the use of CBRN components in his bomb. He decided against their inclusion due to the prohibitive financial costs. Claridge argues that transnational terrorists are not suddenly about to emerge or switch from conventional arms to CBRN-based weapons.[32]

If today's groups are to be characterised by the increased availability, proliferation, development and use of weapons of mass destruction, then the proposition of the existence of a new, more lethal terrorism is false. The financial cost alone, as pointed out by Yousef, reduces significantly the potential for their wide-scale use. It should be noted though that cost is 'dependent on the desired effect required', as demonstrated by Aum-Shinrikyo.[33] Kidnappings, bombings, attacks on infrastructure, hijackings, hostage-taking and assassinations have remained the preferred *modus operandi* of traditional and transnational terrorists.[34] The 9/11 attacks were undertaken using conventional (insofar as they had frequently been used by terrorist groups of the past) means of attack in lethal combination – hijackings and suicide bombers – but not weapons of mass destruction.

Transnational terrorists have up until this point been unable to effectively utilise weapons of mass destruction due, in part, to the inherent problems of acquisition and, perhaps more notably, *weaponisation* of CBRN materials. The above is frequently pointed to as evidence of the new terrorists' ambition to obtain CBRNs, but in actuality 'can hardly be described as the use of weapons of mass destruction' on a large scale or even at all, as they have not been responsible for staggering casualty figures that proponents of the new terrorism proposition predicted.[35] This is not to say that terrorists have not used weapons of mass destruction. There have been sporadic 'low-grade' attempts by white supremacists in the United States as well as the Sarin attack in 1995.[36] Laqueur states that CBRN material and its increased availability 'are a fact of life' and therefore the *weaponisation* and deployment of weapons of mass destruction should be considered plausible.[37] Weapons of mass destruction will not, however, be used by traditional groups, such as the Provisional Irish Republican Army, who are still restricted by 'psychological and moral constraints'.[38]

Gus Martin indeed confirms that 'the potential now exists for methods to include high-yield weapons [...] all that is required is the will to do so'.[39]

The aims and objectives of contemporary transnational movements may, when compared with traditional ones, still be considered political in nature. However the desire of transnational movements to utilise the latest technologies when carrying out terrorist attacks remains similar, albeit, with the introduction and availability of advanced technologies, potentially more destructive. Transnational terrorists have evolved significantly beyond the traditional structural model. The structure of transnational movements has made detection and penetration considerably harder for global counter-terrorism, particularly intelligence services. This has been due to the necessity for human assets to have a close association and cultural understanding that is difficult to acquire through formal training. The structure of today's terrorist groups is, in comparison to traditional organisations, complicated. Traditional terrorist organisations, such as the Red Army Faction, Baader-Meinhoff and the Provisional Irish Republican Army, were organised along hierarchical lines similar to an inverted pyramid depicted in Figure 2.1.

In theory, for counter-terrorism services, this meant that the severing of the head of the organisation would cause its collapse or significantly hinder their operations. Contemporary terrorist organisations are structured in a more linear fashion, meaning that the interdiction of one cell would not affect the broader movement to quite the same extent.

The change and interconnectedness of transnational terrorist movements goes further than the network of hierarchical structures depicted in Figure 2.2. Wilkinson describes al Qaeda as 'a transnational network of "ism" rather than a traditional highly centralised and tightly controlled terrorist organisation'.[40] This shift caused a number of interesting anomalies that, in part, support the theory that al Qaeda rather than being an organisation per se is more of an idea or movement to which smaller units subscribe. The network formation means, first, that there is an absence of a 'central authority or control'.[41] This, as Sookhdeo states, is intentional because affiliates of the al Qaeda network are encouraged to structure themselves in a manner similar to 'a cellular organisation so that if one link fails,

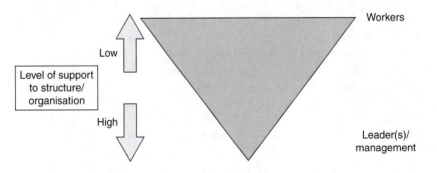

Figure 2.1 Traditional structure of terrorist organisations.

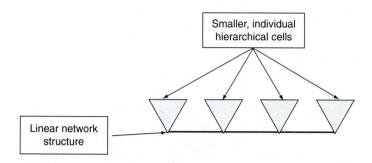

Figure 2.2 Network of hierarchical structures.

the organisation as a whole does not suffer a lethal blow'.[42] Consequentially the removal of any leader will not stem the campaign in the same way as traditional groups, as each entity is able to act independently. As each cell consists of few members, they are difficult to infiltrate. Within each cell, however, there is inevitably some form of hierarchical structure. It is more accurate, therefore, to look at the system as a large network of small hierarchies or, as Wilkinson suggests, a 'network of networks'.[43] (See Figure 2.3.)

A spin-off of the network structure and argument proposed by supporters of the idea of an emergence of a new form of terrorism is the apparent rise of amateur terrorists. Amateurs are considered to deploy, or advocate, tactics that

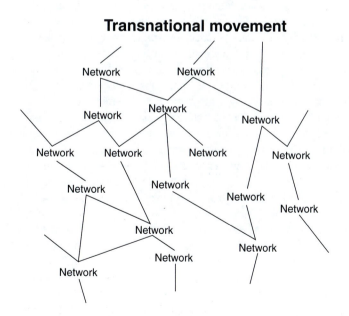

Figure 2.3 Network of networks.

are crude or overzealous. Amateurs are further seen as having a 'darker' attitude and an 'apparent increased willingness [...] to inflict casualties'.[44] The end of the Cold War made it easier for terrorists to gain lethal technologies and was the sustaining factor of this new attitude. A further factor may also be seen in the absence of a restraining force, previously instigated by states. The *new* terrorists were seeking more destructive means to draw attention to their cause.[45] Tucker, however, believes that it was a mistake to attribute the network structure of terrorist groups to the rise of amateurs.[46] The re-emergence of amateur international Islamic terrorists occurred due to the relative youth of the international Islamic movement. This is in contrast to domestic or nationalist movements such as Hamas and Hezbollah that had been operating significantly longer. Therefore, given enough time to learn from successes and failures, such terrorists would become professionals, as all 'are amateurs when they begin'.[47]

Towards a working definition of transnational terrorism

The link between terrorism, religion and the pursuit of mass casualties can, according to Wilkinson, be expressed as follows: 'al Qaeda believes that the use of the weapon of mass casualty and the belief that Allah is "on their side" will ensure that they win ultimate victory.'[48] Systematic, transnational, terrorist violence, in this sense, is seen as a tool for achieving political goals. The use of Islam is as a driving force to unite Muslims behind the cause to establish a new Caliphate across the Middle East. 'New' and 'old' terrorism, therefore, are rooted in disputes over land and influence. The fact that rhetoric is interlaced with religious undertones does not detract from the political underpinning of transnational terrorism campaigns. This is not to say that Islam has not been manipulated as a means of justifying violence, but rather to highlight that at heart this violence does have clear political, even if unacceptable, objectives.

Can it be said that there is in fact a new kind of terrorism? Terrorism has historically been extremely difficult to define. It is perhaps a characteristic of the word that no consensus exists on its exact meaning. It is possible, as at the start of this chapter, to identify some general characteristics associated with terrorism. These may include links with political objectives, employment of violence by non-uniformed personnel (indicative of terrorism from below), as well as the crude use of weaponry. There are, however, exceptions, such as rogue military or policing units doubling up as terrorists, as has happened frequently in Iraq.[49] Terrorist actions can be found in history from religious wars to assassinations of heads of state. Terrorist methods have been viewed as virtues of the state, weapons against oppression and a means to achieving a justifiable end. Terrorism and its activities transcend the boundaries and classifications of violence, with actions such as murder, robbery, assassinations, hijackings and kidnappings, to name but a few, all considered past examples of terrorism in action. Terrorism has been an integral part of humanity's evolution.

Contemporary terrorism, this book argues, continues this evolution. Just as anti-colonial terrorism (or insurgency) derived a label from a supposed objective, perhaps it would be more accurate to name contemporary terrorism *techno-terrorism*, due to the utilisation (albeit not exclusively) of high technology for intelligence and communications. Today's terrorists are transnational, making them harder to identify. The post-Cold War era has changed the nature of the world. The increasingly plausible acquisition of CBRN materials and deployment of weapons of mass destruction are considered an indicator of the emergence of today's terrorism that makes it *new*, when compared to other terrorism types.[50]

Contemporary transnational terrorism is a largely Islamic phenomenon, as it can be traced to the Middle East and those identified as perpetrators of this type of terrorism utilise this religion in order to justify their deeds. Its actions and repercussions, however, are global in magnitude and not restricted to one particular state, region or community. Motivated by apocalyptic visions, or a hatred for non-conformers, such terrorists aim to inflict mass casualties and destruction, although they remain politically orientated and restrained by the tools that are available to them. This political orientation undermines the new terrorism proposition of 'vaguely articulated political objectives', as they are only vague due to a lack of understanding on the part of analysts and policymakers.[51] Indeed, as Ahmad notes, governments are reluctant to gain an understanding of terrorist grievances, through fear that they may confer some form of legitimacy upon their cause.[52] The emergence of transnational terrorism arguably began in the latter half of the Cold War period and coincided with the re-emergence of fundamentalist, radical, Wahhabism Sunni-Islam, as well as the acceleration of globalisation and the spread of liberal democratic, capitalist ideas.[53]

Assisted by the information technology revolution, terrorists today are independent of the state, instead looking for online information or other cells for support. As successful non-governmental organisations, terrorists have transnational objectives. In addition to gaining a greater level of agility, resilience and efficiency, the network structure makes it harder for law enforcement agencies to keep track of terror cells. Terrorists of this nature will seek weapons of mass destruction as a means of fulfilling their objectives, but have to this point struggled with the technological problems of acquiring and deploying such weapons. Terrorists, although aiming for a long-term objective, are satisfied – for the moment at least – with short-term victories, which are generally seen as causing disruption to normal society through the spreading of panic, as well as achieving publicity for their cause.

Raufer states that something is new when its nature is changed.[54] How do you know when something's nature has changed? Is it quantifiable? Terrorism is quantifiable, insofar as it is possible to count how many reported events and casualties have occurred. When and where the count starts and, furthermore, what kinds of parameters are used to refine the selection of violent acts, would be key questions in a quantitative analysis. Moreover, describing today's terrorism as new brings us back once again to the question of definition. There is no way of knowing whether today's terror is new or not, as there is no benchmark indicating where terrorism begins or ends, or how terrorist acts can be identified and categorically distinguished from other forms of violence as discussed in Chapter 1.

United Kingdom–United States threat assessment

Regardless of the academic debate on whether today's terrorism is new or not, each of the states under analysis in this work assess the threat posed by transnational terrorism in their own distinct way. The United Kingdom state that the primary threat is described as coming 'from radicalised individuals who are using a distorted and unrepresentative interpretation of the Islamic faith to justify violence'.[55] The 2006 United Kingdom counter-terrorism strategy, CONTEST-2006, identifies recent Islamic terrorist activity ranging from the World Trade Center bombing in the United States on 26 February 1993 to the 7/7 London transport bombings. 'Terrorism is not a new phenomenon,' it states, but 'the threat that we currently face does have certain distinct characteristics'.[56] First, in contrast to traditional terrorist organisations, the threat posed today 'is genuinely international'.[57] The statement that accompanies this claim suggests that the basis for this assertion is that terrorist attacks have been occurring overseas and that those that commit such attacks 'make maximum use of the freedoms and possibilities of modern life' specifically with regard to travel, information availability and money flows.[58] Second, the threat, 'comes from a variety of groups, networks and individuals'.[59] To complicate matters further, although with regard to transnational, al Qaeda-type terrorism, the overarching aim might be similar. Each cell may 'often also pursue separate goals' at the operational or tactical level.[60] Third, practitioners no longer require state sponsorship. The conflict in Afghanistan following 9/11, coupled with the continued violence inflicted by al Qaeda affiliates, demonstrates the resilience and adaptability of the movement despite declining state sponsorship. Moreover, the 7/7 attacks in London underscored the notion that terrorists of this sort may well be British-born, *homegrown* citizens.

The desire to undertake mass, indiscriminate casualty events, whereby citizens and government alike are targets, is itself not new: 'Other terrorist groups have done this in the past, but not on such a scale.'[61] The uniqueness of the current threat to the United Kingdom is also evidenced by the use of suicide bombers. Suicide bombing, the strategy states, is not new. However, 'it has not been a feature of previous threats that the United Kingdom has faced'.[62] The fourth characteristic of the contemporary threat is the religious element. '[T]he people involved in these terrorist attacks are driven by particular violent and extremist beliefs.'[63] This is the common thread that has linked some of the most devastating attacks and threats in the post-9/11 era.

The level of detail provided in the United Kingdom's 2006 counter-terrorism publication contrasts greatly with that presented by the United States in the same year, which is shorter and, conceptually speaking, broader. A 'significantly degraded but still dangerous al-Qaida network' is the clear threat to the United States and its partners, and thus represents the principal enemy.[64] The al Qaeda movement is seen as being one that has an inspirational role among its affiliates but that also remains 'the most dangerous manifestation of the enemy'.[65] A distorted version of Islam is utilised to achieve 'a violent political vision'.[66] Indeed, this recognition of political demands is also acknowledged as 'a host of other groups and individuals also use terror and violence against innocent civilians to pursue their political objectives'.[67] Although the United States strategy talks throughout about the threat from al Qaeda, this section clearly makes a distinction between this specified principal enemy and other terrorist organisations which also target civilians. This ties closely into United States President George W. Bush's speech, in which he stated that '[o]ur war on terror begins with al Qaeda, but it does not end there. It will not end until every terrorist group of global reach has been found, stopped, and defeated.'[68] This taken into consideration, the key objective of the United States' Global War on Terror is the defeat of the al Qaeda movement, with other threats originating from overseas.

✶ Today's terrorism has emerged as a result of an evolutionary process and is not new. Just as following the Second World War a promotion of democratic principles and rights to self-determination led to anti-colonial terrorism, the changing nature of the world today, spurred by the globalisation of technologies, has led to an evolved breed of terrorists. The end of the Cold War, facilitated by the economic collapse and breakup of the Soviet Union and its spheres of influence, led to an increase in the amount of CBRN materials available on the black market which contemporary transnational terrorists have attempted to exploit. Information technology has not caused today's terrorists to emerge but it has supported their existence. Terrorists, like businesses, have utilised communication and information-gathering technologies to help achieve their objectives. Violence and use of these technologies have increased the ability of terrorists to conduct mass casualty attacks.

The response

Countering terrorist violence from the perspective of a state can prove extremely problematic. Terrorist violence and the responses to it sit at a kind of half-way point on the spectrum of ordinary crime through to military violence bordering on war. States face a balancing act between the social acceptability – particularly with regard to individual rights – and the effectiveness of that strategy in stemming the threat of terrorism. Policy discussions such as whether to develop 'special' rules and/or laws or indeed the level of military involvement need to be tackled while avoiding a knee-jerk reaction to terrorist atrocities.

The United Kingdom is no stranger to terrorist violence. Overseas, the Mau Mau rebellions and, closer to home and more recently, Northern Irish terrorism, have formed the bedrock of responses to terrorist events. The threat posed by the al Qaeda network was, however, considered unique among the senior echelons of counter-terrorism professionals. Al Qaeda demonstrated through the 9/11 attacks, in addition to the attempted bombing of the World Trade Center in the early 1990s, the United States embassy bombings in Tanzania and Kenya and the attack on the United States warship *USS Cole*, that they were an international force to be reckoned with. Not only could they pull off multiple simultaneous terrorist attacks, but they had left a trail of evidence that indicated a desire to seek and deploy nuclear, biological, chemical and/or radiological weapons to cause as many casualties as possible. For Dame Eliza Manningham-Buller, the then Director-General of the United Kingdom Security Service (also known as MI5) and her team, the events of 9/11 acted as a 'major catalyst that led to a paradigmatic change in the way that the United Kingdom perceives its national security'.[69] It was on the back of this that the United Kingdom began to reconsider its policies for countering transnational terrorist violence.

For the United States the threat and nature of al Qaeda-type violence had been known to them for some time. The events of the 1990s highlighted the very real threat that al Qaeda and its affiliates represented. Prior to September 2001, however, the threat was largely seen as being one directed towards assets and citizens overseas and not the Homeland. From the mid-1990s to the early 2000s, the United States publicly and annually released three main assessments on terrorism activity. These were the Significant Incidents of Political Violence Against Americans; Patterns of Global Terrorism; and released biannually Foreign Terrorist Organization Designations. Produced by the United States Department of State these three reports formed the primary assessment of terrorist threats against the United States emanating from overseas. The FBI, charged with domestic law enforcement operations that transcend state boundaries, began producing, for public consumption, annual reports on terrorism in 1996. Titled *Terrorism in the United States – Counterterrorism Threat Assessment and Warning Unit National Security Division*, these reports formed a summary of incidents, preventions and accomplishments. The reports provided in unparalleled detail terrorist events and responses. They outlined both the broader threat of terrorism and other, so-called, topical issues. In a 1996 report one such issue was the changing face of terrorism. The report suggested that terrorism largely originated from outside the United States and as such the role of the FBI, as a law enforcement organisation, could be seen to 'include the protection and safety of American citizens from terrorist acts within the United States, as well as the application of its extraterritorial jurisdiction in instances where Americans are harmed by terrorists'.[70] The reality as picked up further in this book was that the FBI, due to its role, acted largely in a responsive fashion, initiating investigations where crimes were in evidence.

United Kingdom: overview of post-9/11 response

For both states, the events of 9/11 may be considered to be a watershed moment not just in the way in which the threat of terrorism was conceptualised but the realisation that the 'traditional' methods of countering it needed to be re-examined. Such an assessment had been ongoing in both states since the mid-1990s. The 9/11 attacks provided a new impetus.

A year after al Qaeda's first terrorist attack on the United Kingdom, the government for the first time published its counter-terrorism strategy. The 2006 publication of what was known as CONTEST recognised a new counter-terrorism environment in which states had to be prepared to face the possibility of multiple, simultaneous suicide attacks similar to those that occurred on 7 July 2005

(7/7) in London.[71] In 2009 and 2011 subsequent, more detailed editions that drew on the experiences of the United Kingdom's counter-terrorism agencies as well as those from other states were published.[72]

The strategy is based on the United Kingdom's previous experiences of terrorism.[73] Broadly speaking, the CONTEST strategies embody long-term approaches to countering the threat of terrorism. All editions of CONTEST highlight the fact that terrorism does not originate from one particular quarter. That said, earlier editions, particularly the 2006 version, were, as was to be expected due to the geopolitical climate, focused primarily on al Qaeda-type terrorism. While this was still a key factor in 2011, by this time the al Qaeda network had been substantially weakened and a rise in other, such as Northern Irish-related, terrorism had increased. The core of al Qaeda had in essence been replaced by a number of affiliates that worked broadly towards similar overarching objectives; but prioritising local grievances for which they fought.

Although not publicly available until 2006, the aim of CONTEST has, since 2003, been to reduce the risk to the United Kingdom and its interests overseas from terrorist violence. In order to achieve this, governments have worked towards the successful implementation of short- and long-term objectives. These objectives are divided into four principal areas known as strands: PREVENT, PURSUE, PROTECT and PREPARE. It is important to note that there is a considerable amount of overlap between the different strands. That said, the PREVENT strand is focused on preventing terrorism by tackling the radicalisation of individuals. In many respects, as discussed further in this book, this has been not only one of the most controversial but also the one strand that has been subjected to most change, particularly following the 2010 General Election that saw a change in government. In contrast to PREVENT, PURSUE does not tackle the route course. This strand is focused very much on the detection of those who have committed terrorist violence, are planning to or have sponsored them. The PROTECT strand is closely related insofar as it is focused on responding to threats by increasing broad security measures around the public, key national services and United Kingdom interests. Finally, the PREPARE strand requires that plans be set to respond to a 'successful' terrorist attack. This is primarily focused at government level but encouragement has been given to the private sector to consider how they would respond to such events. The PROTECT strand is about setting up not just an element of resilience to a terrorist attack but also making sure that the continuation of key services, such as those related to health, law and order and the economy, occurs.

Variants of this four-pronged model may be found in other counter-terrorism strategies. The 2005 European Union Strategy, for example, is divided between protect, prepare, pursue and respond, and the 2010 Australian model is divided between analysis, protection, response and resilience.[74] This model aims to approach all areas of terrorist activity. These include countering the threat of radicalisation, tackling those that plan, undertake or support terrorist violence, ensuring that broad, preventative measures are taken, and preparing for the aftermath of a terrorist attack.

The United Kingdom's counter-terrorism strategy embodies principles that guide its implementation. These may be summarised as respect for international law and human rights standards; the promotion of good governance; equality, social inclusion and community cohesion; and partnerships between government and the public, private, voluntary and individual sectors of society. There are a number of different institutions that have an input and ownership of elements within the CONTEST strategy.

In detailing the institutions responsible for CONTEST, it is clear that the strategy as a whole is geared primarily towards domestic as opposed to international counter-terrorism – in contrast to the United States discussed further. Figure 2.4 shows the agencies with responsibilities for the implementation and delivery of aims and objectives for the strategy. The 2006 edition of CONTEST stated and this continues to be the case, that '[d]eveloping and delivering the Government's counter-terrorism strategy involves all parts of Government acting together and taking a joined-up approach to dealing with this complex and wide-ranging threat. Delivery depends upon partnerships with many others.'[75] Others,

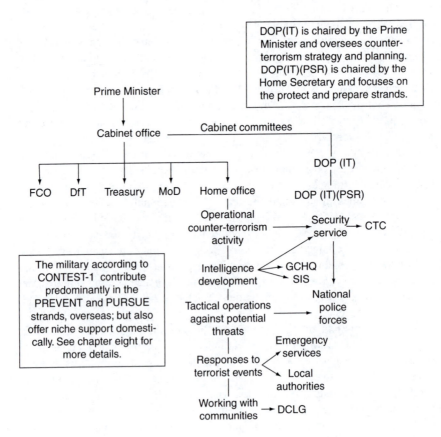

Figure 2.4 CONTEST accountability.

as discussed further below, refer to links between the United Kingdom's and United States' counter-terrorism agencies, in addition to partnerships in the private and voluntary sectors within the United Kingdom.

In 2011, the counter-terrorism strategy and planning in the United Kingdom was overseen by a Cabinet committee and chaired by the Prime Minister (also known as DOP(IT)). The Home Secretary chaired another Cabinet-level committee (also known as DOP(IT)(PSR)), which was concerned primarily with the PROTECT and PREPARE strands of CONTEST-2006. The Security and Intelligence Coordinator, based in the Cabinet Office, is responsible for providing strategic direction and cross-government delivery of CONTEST. A number of other government departments, including the Foreign and Commonwealth Office, the Department for Transport, the Treasury and the Ministry of Defence, have counter-terrorism roles in specific areas, for which they are specialists. The overarching lead department for counter-terrorism strategy, and as a consequence the department responsible for the implementation of CONTEST, is the Home Office. Under the Home Office, a number of different agencies are responsible for delivering different parts of the short- and long-term objectives of CONTEST.

A frequent issue both in CONTEST and other counter-terrorism strategies is how effectiveness, and in turn success, is measured. The definition of success beyond the aim of reducing the risk of terrorism to the United Kingdom and its interests overseas is not immediately clear. Certainly success is bound to be conceptualised in a manner that acknowledges achievement of the overarching aim but what metric is to be used has not always been outlined.

The meaning and attainment of success varies between the aims and the objectives that are implemented to achieve success. Even within these specific objectives (or the strands) success is conceptualised in a different manner, in order to fulfil the requirements of that specific section of the strategy. For example, the PREVENT strand of the United Kingdom's counter-terrorism strategy aims to stop terrorist violence by hindering the radicalisation of individuals, whereas the PURSUE strand aims to track down practitioners of terrorist violence and those that sponsor them. Indeed, the success criteria of one strand may well indicate the failure of another, for example, the need to prepare and ensure that government, the private sector and individuals are ready for the aftermath of a terrorist attack. The processes in the PREPARE and PURSUE strands are only implemented and the criteria of success tested following the failure of the PREVENT strand to hinder terrorist activity.

In the 2006 edition of CONTEST a summary of progress and by inference success was provided (an extract of which is shown in Table 2.1). In 2010 an update (as opposed to a new edition) to CONTEST was published which outlined the threat and – to a limited extent – the progress that had been made.

The full annex from the 2006 edition of CONTEST lists a total of twelve points that have been looked at and are seen as areas of progress within CONTEST-2006.[76] These points were presented by then United Kingdom Prime Minister Tony Blair in August 2005. Their development had followed two weeks of

Table 2.1 Extract of Annex A of CONTEST-2006 (summary of progress)

2	Create an offence of condoning or glorifying terrorism.	Actioned	Section 1 of the Terrorism Act 2006 made it a criminal offence to encourage terrorism. This offence includes statements or publications that glorify terrorism and came into force on 13 April 2006.
8	Expand court capacity to deal with control orders.	Actioned	The Courts are ensuring that the capacity required is available for terrorism cases. The appropriate judicial resources are allocated accordingly and the matter is being kept under review.
9	Proscribe Hizb ut Tahrir and the successor organisation of Al Mujahiroun.	Under review	Section 21 of the Terrorism Act 2006 widened the criteria for proscription. The list of proscribed organisations is currently being reviewed on the basis of these new criteria. Forty international and fourteen domestic terrorist organisations are currently proscribed in the United Kingdom.

'intensive meetings and discussions across government to set a comprehensive framework for action in dealing with the terrorist threat in Britain' in the aftermath of 7/7.[77] Those areas that have been *actioned* serve as an indication of a very specific perception of success. The United Kingdom government, taking the example from point eight above, set out to increase court capacity and achieved it. In this example, the measure of success is quantifiable. However, no indication is given as to how the United Kingdom government intended to measure success in its objectives which are less quantitative, such as the prevention of terrorist activity.

United States: overview of post-9/11 response

The United States counter-terrorism strategy since September 2001 has been largely implemented overseas, most notably in Afghanistan. Incursions into Pakistan, particularly the border regions with Afghanistan, and the necessity to undertake counter-insurgency/counter-terrorism actions in Iraq have also been undertaken. In the early post-2001 years there was a perception that al Qaeda-type terrorism was a phenomenon that necessitated an outwardly facing response. It was for this reason that the military and agencies with remits involving border security took the lead. The establishment of the Department of Homeland Security which bought under it a number of different agencies and is discussed further in this book also lends support to this assertion.

In 2006, under the George W. Bush administration, the United States published its first post-2001 counter-terrorism strategy known as the *National Strategy for Combating Terrorism* (NSCT-2006).[78] Published by the Executive Branch, this short document provided a succinct appraisal of the threat posed by al Qaeda and its affiliates, and the response undertaken by the administration. The strategic campaign was outlined as being to win the Global War on Terror. In the first instance this was envisioned as being achievable by seeking and/or killing terrorists and preventing the proliferation of weapons of mass destruction. In the long term the administration outlined their desire to advance liberal democratic ideals, such as the establishment of 'effective democracy' and adherence to 'freedom of religion, conscience, speech, assembly, association, and press'.[79] Liberal democracy, therefore, was considered to be the 'antithesis of terrorist tyranny'.[80] Consequently, it is inevitable that in the long run, in order to win the Global War on Terror, the empowerment of peoples, the resolution of conflicts or grievances, the facilitation of free speech within states and universal respect for human rights, must be achieved.[81] The realisation of such ideals was said to be achievable via the successful attainment of four short-term priorities which would serve as a kind of temporal buffering zone, put in place to allow for the long-term objectives to develop and take shape. These four 'priorities of action' were: prevent attacks by terrorist networks; attack terrorists and their capacity to operate; deny weapons of mass destruction to rogue states and terrorist allies who seek to use them; and deny terrorists control of any nation they would use as a base and launching pad for terror.[82] The phrasing throughout NSCT-2006 is one of clear conviction. The strategy does not state what *may* occur when referring to potential outcomes, but outlines what *will* happen when the various long- or short-term objectives are implemented. For example, when detailing the first priority, the prevention of attacks by terrorist networks, the strategy states:

> The hard core among our terrorist enemies cannot be reformed or deterred; they will be tracked down, captured, or killed. They will be cut off from the network of individuals, institutions, and other resources they depend on for support and that facilitate their activities. The network, in turn, will be deterred, disrupted, and disabled.[83]

This unwavering confidence in the justification, process of implementation and consequences of those processes is seen throughout the NSCT-2006. As stated above, the four priorities of action are subdivided into more defined categories which help provide a deeper understanding of what the *National Strategy for Combating Terrorism* seeks to achieve. The presentation of these priorities is not in any particular order. One priority does not, it appears, need to be achieved before the next can be worked upon. For the priority regarding the prevention of terrorist attacks by networks, it is made clear that the first duty of government is the protection of 'the lives and livelihoods of its citizens'.[84] Targeting the support base of terrorists, which is the first subcategory, is described as a key method by which to facilitate the destruction of their associated networks. Consequentially, the NSCT-2006 focuses on targeting the capacity of terrorists to operate, focusing particularly on leaders, foot soldiers, weapons, funds, communications and propaganda operations. These targets are described at a level beneath that of the earlier mentioned subcategory. This particular level of detail is unique to this first priority. Overlap between differing categories is seen when considering the distinction between the targeting of leaders and foot soldiers.

Up until 2009 when Barack Obama took over the presidency of the United States, what constituted success was not immediately clear. In NSCT-2006, success was seen as the advancement of effective democracies. This was considered to be the long-term antidote to the ideology of terrorism. Success was also considered to include the prevention of attacks by terrorist networks; denial of weapons of mass destruction to rogue states and terrorist allies who seek to use them; denial of terrorists the support and sanctuary of rogue nation-states; denial of terrorists control of a nation they would use as a base and launching pad for terror; and laying of the foundations to build the institutions and structures needed to carry the fight forward against terror and help ensure our ultimate success. The broad statements are not out of keeping with the audience for which this strategy was published: the mass public. The absence of a specific metric, either quantitative or qualitative, in which each of these is judged or measured was unfortunate.

Leaders of terrorist organisations were considered to be those 'who provide the vision that followers strive to realize' as well as 'operational leaders and managers who provide guidance on a functional, regional, or local basis'.[85] Such individuals included Osama bin Laden, who had been both the direct planner and instigator of terrorist attacks, as seen with the August 1998 bombings of the United States embassies in Tanzania and Kenya; and a motivational figurehead, as seen, for example, with 7/7 and the 2004 attacks in Madrid, Spain.[86] Leaders, therefore, are seen as those who have either an inspirational role or a coordinating function within a network or movement. In contrast: '*Foot soldiers*, which include the operatives, facilitators, and trainers in a terrorist network', do not have such a role.[87] The slight overlap in the manner in which leaders and foot soldiers are conceptualised and distinguished may be seen readily in the description of the latter as being those that are facilitators and those that are foot soldiers. Foot soldiers, this book suggests, are those that undertake tactical-level operations. In contrast to leaders who inspire, plan and coordinate terrorist events, foot soldiers follow the directions, either vague (as would be delivered by inspirational figureheads) or specific (as would be seen with those who coordinate) of terrorist leaders.

When President Barack Obama took office in January 2009 he promised a reassessment of the Global War on Terror. Among other proposals, Obama sought to close the controversial interrogation camps at Guantánamo Bay through the use of Presidential Executive Orders. Obama sought clarity over the objectives of the Global War on Terror, a reduction/withdrawal of combat troops in Iraq and Afghanistan, and greater international cooperation in combating the threat of transnational terrorism.

In assessing the Canadian response to terrorism during the 1960s and 1970s, the strength and robustness of institutional mechanisms was noted by Smith to be critical to the success of a counter-terrorism strategy.[88] Ultimately, the success of any strategy is, in large part, dependent upon the institution(s) that are charged with its implementation. The institutionalisation of a strategy is particularly crucial with regard to policies that are likely to be undertaken over a protracted period. The process of institutionalising the counter-terrorism response in the United States post-2001 is comparable to the manner in which the United States government restructured during the Cold War period to meet the communist threat. The process of institutionalisation has been most visible in the United States due, as is noted below, to the establishment of new, and the reorganisation of old, counter-terrorism agencies. The purpose of institutionalisation is to embed the counter-terrorism strategy, not just in domestic institutions but also in international ones, such as the United Nations (UN) and the Group of Eight (also known as G-8) richest states. Doing this, especially with the latter, helps provide a legitimate foundation for counter-terrorism strategies. It also provides a justification for the development, but more importantly the use, of policy instruments within the strategy.

In both the George W. Bush and Obama administration's strategies the establishment and maintenance of international standards of accountability is considered critical. The post-9/11 strategies redefine the interactions between the state, the international community and the domestic population of states. The Westphalia system of states, upon which international interactions are based, suggests that domestic issues, namely those within a state, should not be a concern for the international community. This position alters when such a dispute spills over international borders. The responsibility for its resolution then falls into the purview of the international community. The United States approach suggests that sovereign states have responsibilities including countering terrorism. In NSCT-2006 the UN Security Council's Resolution 1373 is quoted as an indication of what shape such responsibilities should take in relation to counter-terrorism. The Resolution provides 'binding obligations on all states to suppress and prevent terrorist financing, improve their border controls, enhance information sharing and law enforcement cooperation, suppress the recruitment of terrorists, and deny them sanctuary'.[89]

Since 2001 countering transnational terrorism has been done in conjunction with other states and multilateral organisations – such as the International Maritime Organisation, International Civil Aviation Organization, Asia-Pacific Economic Cooperation and the African Union. A continuation of this *modus operandi* is considered critical to winning the Global War on Terror. In some areas the strengthening of coalitions, particularly in reference to states, may take the form of providing practical support via the provision of training, funds or military equipment.

One of the most visible initiatives undertaken as a means of institutionalising the United States counter-terrorism strategy was the establishment of a fifteenth Federal Executive Department, the Department of Homeland Security, which encompassed twenty-two different agencies. The Department is not only responsible for the countering of terrorist violence, but is also charged, through the Federal Emergency Management Agency (FEMA), with responding to man-made and natural disasters. Enhanced coordination, especially among agencies that have an intelligence role, is part of the reason why the Department of Homeland Security was created. This is discussed in later chapters. The establishment of the post of Director of National Intelligence, the National Counterterrorism Center, enactment of the United States Patriot Act, the cultivation of international human intelligence sources through the Central Intelligence Agency and the establishment of the Treasury's Office of Terrorism and Financial Intelligence, which investigates financial resources that may be used by terrorist organisations, may all be seen as institutional-level responses to the threat of terrorism post-2001. The restructuring of the Department of Defense to fight a new type of asymmetric conflict against transnational terrorists and the use of diplomatic initiatives through the Department of State are all examples of strengthening government architecture and interagency collaboration.

In considering both the United Kingdom's and United States' responses to post-9/11 terrorism the aims and objectives may be considered to be strikingly different. For the United Kingdom the aim is to reduce the threat of terrorist violence, whereas for the United States it was to defeat global terrorism under the Bush administration. Under the Obama administration it has been made clear that the United States is 'not at war with the tactic of terrorism'.[90] This ties into another observation which is the focus of each of the strategies. For the United Kingdom the focus is domestic, which links into the conceptualisation of threat as originating both overseas and domestically. For the United States which still to a certain extent conceptualises the threat in terms of terrorism coming from overseas, the strategy has been one that is focused on international policy. Domestic policy has been restricted primarily to border management. The United Kingdom's strategy is, therefore, very practical in its overarching approach. In contrast to the United Kingdom the United States' strategy, although through its short-term priorities of action is very practical, has an idealistic foundation in its long-term objectives. Put another way, the United Kingdom looks to achieve its overarching aim through established international and domestic legal norms and, where these norms need to be changed, it suggests partnership, collaboration and diplomacy. On the other hand, the United States strategy wants to achieve its aim by re-orientating the international community in line with its approach. This is evidenced by United States President George W. Bush's speech shortly after 9/11 in which he stated that states around the world were either with the United States or 'with the terrorists'.[91]

The response: strategic observations

Both the United Kingdom's and the United States' counter-terrorism approaches are not just interesting for what they include and the similarities that they have but also for what they miss out. Three observations may be made regarding these approaches. The first is the difference in how each conceptualises the *international* and the *transnational* threat and the impact this has on identifying where terrorists come from. The second observation made is the difficulty in identifying the policy instruments within the strategies and the third and final observation is the notable lack of consideration for what is known as cross-fertilisation – *traditional* and transnational terrorist organisations working together.))

A key observation to be made is the differing orientations of the post-9/11 counter-terrorism strategies. The United States' approach was to counter the transnational threat, which by virtue of its title contrasts with CONTEST. This contrast, beyond labelling practices as discussed earlier between transnational and international, is worth dwelling on briefly, as it highlights either an error in the wording of the strategies or a significant gulf in their approach. The origin of where each state sees the threat as coming from varies. This has in turn had a significant impact on the way in which each state has responded. Up until 2011, the United Kingdom considered the threat as one that was both *home-grown* and international in origin. For the United States, the threat of terrorism is considered to be one that originates, almost exclusively, from outside its borders.

Another distinguishing observation may be seen in the response undertaken by both states. It is important to note at this juncture that the United States has not always considered terrorist activities as being the purview of law enforcement. It is for this reason that policy instruments other than law enforcement are considered critical to success in the Global War on Terror. The second point to note is that all of the suggested policy instruments may be used both domestically and internationally. The circumstances under which these policy instruments are implemented are not stated. The emphasis on collaboration, underscored throughout the post-9/11 years, is indicative of the overlapping or perhaps interconnecting nature that each of the counter-terrorism policy instruments has. Indeed, a further indication of this may be seen in the identification of the institutions that are responsible for implementing the United States' counter-terrorism strategy. The primary structure, which was formed following 9/11, is the Department of Homeland Security. This acts as a coordinating body between federal agencies, to counter and respond to terrorist violence. The fact that the Department of Homeland Security is a coordinating agency supports the notion that countering terrorist violence involves a combination of various policy instruments of national power, not independently but in collaboration with one another. This point was also noted in the *9/11 Commission Report*.[92]

Even less explicit, the United Kingdom's approach has rarely discussed the policy instruments used to counter the threat of terrorist violence. One reason for this is emphasised at the beginning of the document as 'our counter-terrorist strategy comprises both open elements (which can be freely publicised and discussed) and classified elements (which are kept secret), this paper gives only a partial account of the strategy and omits those secret aspects'.[93] It is clear, from the structure of CONTEST, that the United Kingdom government's response is, by and large, intelligence and police led. The lead department is the Home Office under which the Security Service, an intelligence agency, operates in conjunction with the police. National police forces, particularly the Metropolitan Police Service's Counter Terrorism Command, are responsible for countering potential threats using both intelligence and anti-terrorist measures. The use of a diplomatic approach, although mentioned in an international sense, via the provision of aid and intelligence to other states, is discussed primarily and briefly, in a transnational manner, insofar as the state discusses working with non-state actors. Work in this area is undertaken by the Foreign and Commonwealth Office, and includes the promotion of UN and European Union sanctions and, similar to the United States, the endorsement of the rule of law and respect for human rights. In pursuing those that have threatened or undertaken terrorist violence, CONTEST suggests a legislative instrument that focuses on issues concerning deportations, control orders, financial orders and the seizing and freezing of assets.

The primary policy instruments used by both states are intelligence, law enforcement and military force. What varies between them, as is discussed over the next three chapters, is the degree to which each instrument is used. The use of these three policy instruments, in a counter-terrorism capacity, is interlaced with the location from which both states see the threat as originating. For the United Kingdom, as mentioned above, the threat is both domestic and international. Consequentially the emphasis is on intelligence and law enforcement. For the United States the threat is international, and therefore the response is military force. Both states can claim to tackle the root causes in their counter-terrorism strategy. For the United Kingdom this is done through the presentation of a PREVENT strand that aims to tackle radicalisation. For the United States it is through the desire to seek collaboration through international organisations, in an effort to spread democratic ideals and liberal values.

The 9/11 attacks, while increasing government interest in al Qaeda-type terrorism, led to a decline in traditional terrorist groups. The publication of CONTEST-2011 and a recent upsurge in writings regarding domestic terrorism threats has triggered a reappraisal of 'traditional' terrorist threats. Studies in terrorism and counter-terrorism literature following the demise of the Cold War, but particularly following 9/11, tended to make a distinction between traditional terrorist groups, such as the Irish Republican Army and *Euskadi Ta Askatasuna* (more commonly known as ETA), and new, apocalyptic terrorist groups, such as Aum Shinrikyo and al Qaeda. Stevenson argues that it is a mistake to assume that these types are completely different agencies. Stevenson states that both traditional and contemporary transnational terrorist groups 'share a methodology: to cow public support for legitimate government objectives by instilling fear in the civilian population'.[94] The 9/11 attacks in the United States increased the perceived distance between traditional and new groups. However, according to Stevenson, 'new terrorists and old terrorists could cross-fertilise'.[95] At first glance such a suggestion seems illogical, as traditional terrorist groups are more interested in getting people, particularly governments, to notice their actions. This contrasts with new groups that seemingly focus on killing as many people as possible with a view to forcing government(s) to capitulate. Stevenson makes a compelling argument:

al Qaeda's aims diverge thoroughly and qualitatively from the [Irish Republican Army] and those of most other 'old' terrorist groups. They would not make a ready fit. At the same time, if most terrorists remain fanatically ded-icated, they will also forge highly pragmatic and flexible alliances to attain the results they seek. That a politically frustrated ETA [*Euskadi Ta Askatasuna*], say, would accept attenuated al Qaeda assistance – for example, weapons, training or financial assistance rather than actual over-sight – should not be ruled out. In this vein, it is sobering to recall the [Irish Republican Army's] long and intimate relationship with Libya and Colonel Muammar Gaddafi.[96]

If, for argument's sake, post-Second World War terrorism can be split into two camps, nationalistic and religious, then the United States' counter-terrorism strategy after 9/11 is focused wholly on the latter. Cross-fertilisation, as Steven-son notes, would be most effective in the areas of support for a terrorist organ-isation, financing, training, and possibly reconnaissance and refuge. The United States' counter-terrorism strategy specifically targets the financing, support and sanctuary undertaken by rogue states, not necessarily nationalistic terrorist groups. Moreover, new terrorist groups have, in many ways, been born out of the successes and failures of nationalistic terrorist groups. The resort to violence as a means of achieving a political objective has been seen in some cases as suc-cessful (South Africa, Algeria and the anti-colonial movements that the United Kingdom confronted in the post-Second World War period such as that in Malaya). Furthermore, it is the unresolved grievances which led those traditional groups to take up arms that have, in part, formulated the justifications of *trans-national* terrorists to undertake violence, most notably with regard to the Arab–Israeli conflict. The point, however, should not be understated. The absence of any broad commitment to deal with nationalistic terrorism highlights a signi-ficant shortcoming in both states' post-9/11 counter-terrorism responses.

Notes

1 Osama bin Laden (1996), 'Declaration of War against the Americans Occupying the Land of the Two Holy Places'.
2 Samuel P. Huntington, 'The Clash of Civilizations', *Foreign Affairs*, 72 (1993) 3, pp. 22–49; and Samuel P. Huntington, 'The West: Unique, Not Universal', *Foreign Affairs*, 75 (1996) 6, pp. 28–46.
3 The divisions within the Muslim community date back to the civil wars triggered by the assassination of the third caliph – supreme ruler of the Muslim community – Uthman ibn 'Affan in 656. The power struggle regarding the succession to his posi-tion resulted in the emergence of the Shi'a and Khariji divisions in the Muslim Community. Patrick Sookhdeo, *Global Jihad – The Future in the Face of Militant Islam* (Virginia: Isaac Publishing, 2007), pp. 216–218.
4 Steve Hewitt, *The British War on Terror – Terrorism and Counter-Terrorism on the Home Front Since 9/11* (London: Continuum, 2008), p. 58.
5 Unknown Author (12 July 2005), 'Al Muhajiroun leader Bakri told press "Al Qaeda in Europe was planning inevitable attacks" still not arrested', *Militant Islam Monitor. org*, www.militantislammonitor.org/article/id/784, accessed 15 January 2009.
6 Steven Simon, 'The New Terrorism: Securing the Nation Against a Messianic Foe', *The Brookings Institution*, 21 (winter 2003), p. 18.

7 Captain Matthew J. Morgan, 'The Origins of the New Terrorism', *Parameters* (spring 2004), http://carlisle-www.army.mil/usawc/Parameters/04spring/morgan.htm, accessed 10 March 2006, p. 30.
8 Walter Laqueur, *The New Terrorism: Fanatics and the Arms of Mass Destruction* (London: Phoenix Press, 2001), p. 81.
9 Ibid., p. 128.
10 Morgan, The Origins of the New Terrorism, p. 34.
11 Jonathan Stevenson, 'Pragmatic Counter-terrorism', *Survival*, 43 (winter 2001–2002) 4, p. 35.
12 Simon, 'The New Terrorism', p. 18.
13 A Fatwa is an Islamic legal pronouncement.
14 bin Laden, op. cit.
15 It should be noted that, according to Mendelsohn, al Qaeda have been unsuccessful in gaining a foothold with regard to the Arab–Israeli conflict. This is in spite of 'increasing numbers of statements dedicated to the Palestinian issue'; al Qaeda have been unable to find common ground with Hamas or other dedicated Palestinian groups. Barak Mendelsohn, 'Al Qaeda's Palestinian Problem', *Survival*, 51 (August–September 2009), p. 71.
16 bin Laden, op. cit.; and United States President George W. Bush (20 September 2001), 'Address to a Joint Session of Congress and the American People', *United States Department of Homeland Security*, p. 26.
17 David Tucker, 'What's New About New Terrorism and How Dangerous Is It?', p. 2.
18 Ibid., p. 3.
19 Martin, op. cit., pp. 250–251.
20 David Claridge, 'Exploding the Myths of Superterrorism', *Terrorism and Political Violence*, 11 (1999), 4, pp. 133–138.
21 Laqueur, op. cit., p. 160.
22 Ibid.
23 Gus Martin, Understanding Terrorism – Challenges, Perspectives, and Issues, 2nd edn (London: Sage, 2004), p. 251.
24 Laqueur, op. cit.
25 Since 2000 known as 'Aleph'; Born Chizuo Matsumoto. Claridge, op. cit., pp. 133–147.
26 Ibid.
27 Ibid.
28 Ibid., p. 137.
29 Ibid., p. 135.
30 Ibid.
31 United States government (5 November 1998), 'United States District Court Southern District of New York: United States – v. – Usama Bin Laden', Federation of American Scientists, www.fas.org/irp/news/1998/11/indict1.pdf, accessed 15 January 2003, p. 7.
32 Claridge, op. cit., p. 140.
33 Ibid., p. 135.
34 Bruce Hoffman and Donna K. Hoffman, 'The Rand – St Andrews Chronology of International Terrorist Incidents – 1995', *Terrorism and Political Violence*, 8 (1996), 3, pp. 89–90.
35 Claridge, op. cit., p. 136.
36 Ibid., p. 136.
37 Laqueur, op. cit., p. 254.
38 Ibid., p. 260.
39 Martin, op. cit., p. 250.
40 Paul Wilkinson, 'The Threat from the Al Qaeda Network', in Paul Wilkinson (ed.) *Homeland Security in the United Kingdom – Future Preparedness for Terrorist Attack since 9/11* (London: Routledge, 2007), p. 25.

41 Tucker, op. cit., p. 2.
42 Patrick Sookhdeo, *Global Jihad – The Future in the Face of Militant Islam* (Virginia: Isaac Publishing, 2007), p. 297.
43 Wilkinson, op. cit., p. 25.
44 Tucker, op. cit., p. 2.
45 Martin, op. cit., p. 250.
46 Tucker, op. cit., p. 4.
47 Ibid.
48 Wilkinson, op. cit., p. 226.
49 For examples see Unknown Author (16 February 2006), 'Iraq Death Squad Caught in the Act', *BBC News*, http://news.bbc.co.uk/1/hi/world/middle_east/4719252.stm, accessed 20 January 2009; and Aleisha Scott (28 September 2009), 'Iraq Hostage Had Been Shot in Head', *Independent*, www.independent.co.uk/news/world/middle-east/iraq-hostage-had-been-shot-in-head-1794488.html, accessed 15 October 2009.
50 Morgan, op. cit., pp. 41–42.
51 Martin, op. cit., p. 250.
52 Ahmad, op. cit.
53 For more information on the different variants of Wahhabism see Sookhdeo, op. cit., pp. 276–278.
54 Xavier Raufer, 'New World Disorder, New Terrorism: New Threats for Europe and the Western World', *Terrorism and Political Violence*, 11 (1999), 4, p. 35.
55 United Kingdom government (July 2006), op. cit., p. 6.
56 Ibid.
57 Ibid., p. 7.
58 Ibid.
59 Ibid.
60 Ibid.
61 Ibid.
62 Ibid.
63 Ibid.
64 United States government (2003), 'National Strategy for Combating Terrorism', p. 5.
65 Ibid.
66 Ibid.
67 Ibid.
68 United States President George W. Bush (20 September 2001),'Address to a Joint Session of Congress and the American People', p. 4.
69 Bradley W.C. Bamford, 'The United Kingdom's "War Against Terrorism"', *Terrorism and Political Violence*, 16 (winter 2004), 4, p. 740.
70 Federal Bureau of Investigation, 'Terrorism in the United States – Counterterrorism Threat Assessment and Warning Unit', www.fbi.gov/stats-services/publications/terror_96.pdf, p. 19.
71 Bamford, op. cit., p. 740.
72 In 2010 an update to CONTEST was published that outlined what was happening both in terms of threat and response.
73 Alex P. Schmid and Ronald D. Crelinsten, 'Western Responses to Terrorism: A Twenty-Five Year Balance Sheet', in Schmid and Crelinsten (eds), *Western Responses to Terrorism* (London: Frank Cass, 1993), p. 309.
74 European Union Counter-Terrorism Strategy, 30 November 2005, http://register.consilium.eu.int/pdf/en/05/st14/st14469-re04.en05.pdf; and Australian Government, Counter-Terrorism White Paper, 24 February 2010, www.dpmc.gov.au/publications/counter_terrorism/3_strategy.cfm.
75 United Kingdom government (July 2006), op. cit., p. 28.
76 Ibid., pp. 30–32.

77 Prime Minister's Press Conference: Anthony Blair, 'PM's Press Conference – 5 August 2005', Number 10.gov.uk, www.number10.gov.uk/Page8041, accessed 25 January 2009.
78 United States government (September 2006), op. cit.
79 Ibid., p. 9.
80 Ibid., p. 10.
81 Ibid.
82 Ibid., pp. 11–17.
83 Ibid., p. 11.
84 Ibid.
85 Ibid.
86 United States government (June 1999), 'FBI Ten Most Wanted Fugitive: Usama Bin Laden', *Federal Bureau of Investigation*, www.fbi.gov/wanted/topten/usama-bin-laden, accessed 10 November 2007.
87 United States government (September 2006), op. cit., p. 12.
88 G. Davidson Smith, *Combating Terrorism* (London: Routledge, 1990), pp. 27–32.
89 United States government (September 2006), op. cit., p. 19.
90 United States government (June 2011), 'National Strategy for Counterterrorism', p. 2.
91 United States President George W. Bush (20 September 2001), 'Address to a Joint Session of Congress and the American People', *United States Department of Homeland Security*.
92 Thomas H. Kean (Chair), *9/11 Commission Report* (London: W.W. Norton, 2004), p. 408.
93 United Kingdom government (July 2006), op. cit., p. 1.
94 Stevenson, op. cit., p. 37.
95 Ibid.
96 Ibid.

3　Intelligence

Intelligence, although not as public as the application of military force, formed what may be considered to have been the backbone of the strategic direction of both the United Kingdom's and the United States' counter-terrorism strategy after 9/11. Both states sought to improve their knowledge of al Qaeda's objectives, methods and personnel.[1] Indeed, it was, as is argued below, a fundamental failure of intelligence that contributed to the success of the 9/11 attacks, and as such it was developments in this area that arguably should have taken priority.

Intelligence and the United Kingdom: a qualitative assessment

Intelligence was central in the thinking surrounding the development and implementation of the United Kingdom's first publicly released counter-terrorism strategy in September 2006. The main intelligence agencies are the Security Service, the Secret Intelligence Service and General Communications Headquarters (GCHQ) – collectively known as the Security and Intelligence Agencies

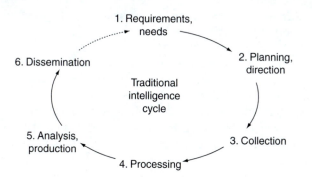

Figure 3.1 The traditional intelligence cycle.

Note
The dotted line, between stage 6 and 1, represents the transition from one cycle to the next, during which consumers review the products and formulate new requirements and needs.

(or the Agencies). The role of the Agencies in countering this transnational threat is to gather 'covert' intelligence on terrorists and their supporters by using specialist clandestine methods.[2] The Agencies, therefore, gather information and formulate intelligence assessments that, in turn, inform the decisions of policymakers as to the intentions of those that threaten or have perpetrated acts of terrorism against the state, or its interests. The United Kingdom's intelligence structure, known as the National Intelligence Machinery, may be broadly split into four categories: tasking, collection, analysis and oversight.

The 2001 publication of the National Intelligence Machinery states that the United Kingdom's Prime Minister, through the Cabinet Office and other relevant ministries, is ultimately responsible for stating strategic requirements or needs.[3] This is indicative of an inductive approach whereby evidence is collected and evaluated prior to a hypothesis or theory of action being decided upon. The Joint Intelligence Committee then instructs collectors and assessors, within the National Intelligence Machinery, to undertake tasks that help achieve the strategic requirements or needs.[4] Requirements, or needs, as identified in stage one of the traditional intelligence cycle, depicted in Figure 3.1, are traditionally undertaken by policymakers and senior ministers. Although this in theory means that members of the National Intelligence Machinery are answerable to the Joint Intelligence Committee, in practice much of the day-to-day decision-making is done by the Agencies through their associated Secretaries of State, namely the Home Secretary and Foreign Secretary.[5]

Initial analysis is frequently undertaken within the Agencies and easily shared between them. In line with the requirements that are set, broader analysis, which takes into consideration sources of information beyond that gathered by the immediate agency, is undertaken by the Joint Intelligence Committee, Defence Intelligence Staff, Assessment Staff, Central Intelligence Groups and the Joint Intelligence and Analysis Centre.[6] Unlike the United States, no definitive divide exists in the United Kingdom with regard to areas of operations among the Agencies. The primary function of the Security Service is the domestic realm and for the Secret Intelligence Service it is the international realm. However, the Regulation of Investigatory Powers Act states that

> [i]ntrusive surveillance in relation to any premises or vehicle in the British Islands shall be capable of being authorised by a warrant issued under this Part on the application of a member of the [Secret Intelligence Service] or GCHQ only if the authorisation contained in the warrant is one satisfying the requirements of section 32(2)(a) otherwise than in connection with any functions of that intelligence service in support of the prevention or detection of serious crime.[7]

This indicates that, with prior authorisation, the Secret Intelligence Service may operate domestically within the United Kingdom.

When looking at the structure of a strategy, three levels may be identified. These, as depicted in Figure 3.2, are strategic, institutional and operational. The

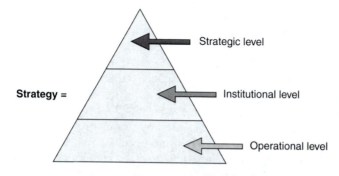

Figure 3.2 Levels of strategic control in the UK NIM.

lead counter-terrorism agencies at each level have historically varied within the United Kingdom's system. Prior to the 1990s, the lead counter-terrorism agency was the police at both the institutional and operational level, with the Home Office taking command at the strategic level.[8] Domestic terrorist actions were therefore considered a wholly criminal affair for which the police had jurisdiction.[9] This did not prevent the police from calling on other agencies, such as the Armed Forces' bomb disposal teams, for specialist help.

The publication of the 1989 Security Service Act put, for the first time, the Security and Intelligence Agencies on a statutory footing. The Act described the domestic role of the Security Service and GCHQ as being

> the protection of national security and, in particular, its protection against threats from espionage, terrorism and sabotage, from the activities of agents of foreign powers and from actions intended to overthrow or undermine parliamentary democracy by political, industrial or violent means.[10]

The police were responsible for providing the response capabilities to terrorist threats and events, while the Security Service and GCHQ were given a broader remit of countering all (man-made) threats to national security. The key difference between the powers of the police and Agencies was that neither the Security Service nor GCHQ could arrest people. This crucial, but purposeful, omission from the powers held by the Security Service and GCHQ, who operate domestically, confirmed without debate within and between United Kingdom government agencies that the police were the lead agency in areas concerning counter-terrorism at the operational and institutional levels.

This changed after 9/11 and more so after 7/7, when a process ensued that resulted in the affirmation of the Agencies as the lead at the institutional level on issues concerning terrorism. This was due in large part to the downsizing of the threat posed by the Provisional Irish Republican Army and the increase in prominence of transnational terrorism from the 1990s onwards. These events triggered a reconsideration of the hierarchical relationship between the Agencies and the police. By 2008 it was 'the dominance of the intelligence services in all of this, at all levels' that represented the single biggest shift in counter-terrorism thinking since the end of the Second World War.[11]

The establishment of the Security and Intelligence Agencies as the lead counter-terrorism institution in the United Kingdom had a profound impact on the decision-making process concerning counter-terrorism initiatives. 'Operational decisions', it states in the United Kingdom's 2006 counter-terrorism strategy, 'on whether and how to conduct counter[-]terrorist operations are a matter for the police'.[12] Domestically, '[c]overt operational counter-terrorist activity in the United Kingdom is conducted by the Security Service' who have the lead 'in close collaboration with police forces across the country and the Anti-Terrorist Branch of the Metropolitan Police'.[13] Without the power of arrest, the role of the Agencies was considered, certainly prior to 9/11 and perhaps more so between then and 7/7, to be that of a provider of intelligence, a role that Hastedt suggested was to 'inform and warn policy makers' and aid them in reaching decisions.[14] This, discussed further below, was not always possible, due to restrictions placed by the Agencies on how and when such intelligence could be shared.

Terrorist-related intelligence can help provide data on suspects identified by the police.[15] The promotion of the Agencies over the police when it came to counter-terrorism suggests that the Agencies, after 9/11, began to inform the police of suspects and, crucially, instruct them on when to act. Not having the power of arrest implies that the success of counter-terrorist-related activity is dependent upon the relationship between the Agencies and the police which, as is discussed further below, appeared difficult due to competing roles and objectives of both agencies in the early post-9/11 years. This reinforces the view that the Agencies were, during this period, expected to undertake more and more decisions and responsibility that were within the traditional purview of the police, an aspect discussed later in this book.

Another area of concern regarding the contribution of intelligence during this period centres on the roles and objectives of the Security and Intelligence Agencies when compared to other counter-terrorism agencies such as the police. A crucial tension that seems to have existed between the Agencies and the police concerned the manner and extent to which data, particularly that generated by the Agencies, was shared. The Agencies, as has already been discussed, had the institutional lead in counter-terrorism activities within the United Kingdom post-9/11. The police, on the other hand, taking their lead from the Agencies, were responsible for operational-level matters. The establishment of the Agencies as the lead in counter-terrorism matters, in the early 1990s, did not appear to diminish their desire to keep as much data as possible secret from other interested, indeed critical partners, including decision-makers.

In an interview with Superintendent Pratt, responsible for writing the Police Response to the United Kingdom's counter-terrorism strategy, a suggestion that much of what the Agencies wanted to keep secret after 9/11, but really did not need to be so, was made. Pratt states that progress, within the PREVENT strand of the United Kingdom's counter-terrorism strategy, was hindered by the Agencies' refusal to share what was considered by the police to be pertinent information, that posed no security risk, with other agencies, such as local authorities.[16] Put another way, the Agencies were willing to share intelligence with law enforcement, but were not happy with law enforcement sharing that intelligence with other bodies.

The role of local authorities was especially important during this period, as they were the authorising body for community police programmes, such as the counter-radicalisation Channel Project. Local authorities formed the lead authority for the PREVENT strand of the United Kingdom's counter-terrorism strategy. This was until the implementation of the new policies outlined in PREVENT 2011. In PREVENT 2011 the coupled notions of counter-radicalisation and community cohesion were split by the Coalition government.[17]

There was a constant trade-off between what the police wanted to share and what they were allowed to share. One consequence expressed by Professor Bruce Hoffman of Georgetown University was that it led to local authorities having to make strategic decisions without always being in possession of all the facts regarding the threat.[18] It should be noted that, in the opinion of Pratt, and of Brook, the PREVENT Delivery Manager with South Yorkshire Police Constabulary, restrictions placed on the police, while inconvenient, did not endanger life, as when an imminent threat did exist the Agencies passed on all pertinent information to enable the police to act decisively.[19] This potentially had a negative impact on the manner in which the police and local authorities responsible for the PREVENT strand operated.

A shift occurred during this period that may be characterised as moving away from the idea of states arresting their way out of threats of terrorism, to operating on pre-emptive intelligence.

One possible consequence of this, depicted in the simplistic illustration in Figure 3.3, is the divergent points at which the Agencies and the police interrupted and interdicted known terrorist-related threats to the state. Moving from left to right the first, outer threshold, furthest away from the target, represents the point at which the police may attempt to render the ability of terrorists to undertake an attack inoperable. The second, closer threshold is the point where the Agencies would possibly intervene. In essence, the Agencies are, it is argued, more inclined to allow a terrorist to move closer to their target not because of a cavalier disregard for the security of the state, or preservation of life, but due to the historical function for which the Agencies have operated for so long; a function based on gaining intelligence and passing it on to others to make operational decisions.[20] Operating in their previous role, the Agencies were able to retain knowledge and gain a long-term understanding of terrorist operations.

This, of course, continued after 9/11 but with a fundamental difference. In making intelligence at the institutional level, the lead in counter-terrorism, the Agencies were required to dictate when operations took place by choosing when to divulge pertinent information to the police. What is not clear is the extent and

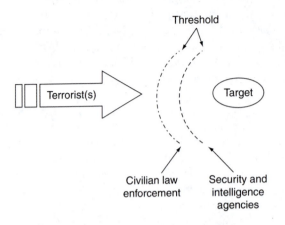

Figure 3.3 Law enforcement and Security and Intelligence Agencies.

associated impact this may have had. Indeed, even with unimpeded access to relevant documents, the number of possibilities with regard to the reasons for a failed or even successful terrorist attack makes such an assessment unfeasible.

It should also be noted that in an interview with Gary Hindle, the former Head of Research in Security and Counter-Terrorism at the Royal United Services Institute, it was suggested that the police were in no hurry to bring people to trial.[21] In Hindle's opinion, the police had a high level of understanding and appreciation for the value of gaining good intelligence.[22] The transition in lead and increase in threat after 9/11 and certainly after 2006 resulted in intelligence agencies being required to operate in an environment more suited to the police. Adversely, operational requirements necessitated an increase in the intelligence capabilities of the police.[23]

In positioning the Security and Intelligence Agencies as the lead counter-terrorism agency at the institutional level, problems did arise. These appear magnified, if the purpose of intelligence is considered to be the gathering and analysis of data and not the taking of direct or indirect operational control. Intelligence agencies being required to perform duties akin to those of the police potentially increased the frequency with which the traditionally publicity-averse Agencies appeared in public forums, particularly in relation to giving evidence in open court. The Agencies and the police provide the bulk of domestic protection advice at the operational level. This advice is based primarily on intelligence passed from the Agencies. As discussed above, there was a view that problems existed in the provision of timely intelligence to the police, particularly with regard to that which was considered non-pertinent. One of the main problems noted was the lack of desire for the Agencies to give permission for that intelligence to be shared with other stakeholders such as local authorities. Intelligence was, according to this view, late in arriving or did not provide enough information to paint an accurate picture of the perceived threat.[24] This highlights the teething problems in the arrangement of counter-terrorism agencies. These were inevitable, but did not appear to have led to any major incidents.

In assessing the contribution of intelligence it is important to note some positive factors in the post-9/11 era. The change in lead also had a positive impact on counter-terrorism activity in the United Kingdom. A key example of this was the policy of regionalisation. Prior to 9/11 the Security Service (responsible for domestic national security) had its only base in London. The recognition of a *home-grown* threat, underscored by the events of 7/7, highlighted the fact that not all would-be terrorist attackers originated from London. Indeed, the 7/7 perpetrators came from Leeds and Aylesbury (Buckinghamshire).

In response, the Security Service began establishing regional offices across the United Kingdom.[25] Regionalisation helped ensure the retention of operational, practical knowledge within the Security Service regarding local areas, groups and people of interest. It also increased the working proximity of members of the Security Service and the police. One interviewee noted that a Chief Superintendent of Greater Manchester Police and a senior Security Service Regional Officer found themselves sharing an office and that the arrangement 'seem[ed] to be operating quite well'.[26]

One possible consequence of this is that regionalisation, coupled with the repositioning of intelligence as the lead in countering the transnational threat, was that the broader Security and Intelligence Agencies needed to improve their ability to gather and disseminate pertinent intelligence. Furthermore, regionalisation more than likely increased the speed with which such assessments and distributions were conducted. Moreover, regionalisation overtly recognised that threats to the state did not occur solely in the capital, a point underscored by the terrorist attack in Glasgow on 30 June 2007.[27] Having too many resources in one place, according to one anonymous source, can undermine the attainment of an accurate national and even international picture of threats: situational awareness.[28] The consequence of regionalisation in the United Kingdom, it may therefore be argued, was an increased situational awareness, increasing the ability of the state to offer broad methods of protection by having a broader intelligence-gathering base.

Increasing the capabilities of the Security Service and the broader Security and Intelligence Agencies went beyond the process of regionalisation. Increased funding is evidenced by the 2004 Spending Review that resulted in the allocation of an additional £85 million 'to support a significant expansion of [the National Intelligence Machinery's] counter-terrorism capabilities' and enabled 'the early delivery of increased capacity to counter the threat of international terrorism'.[29] The Agency's need to gather an ever-increasing volume of data on potential threats led to a major recruitment campaign for further intelligence analysts after 9/11.

In a speech in 2006 by the Director-General of the Security Service (2002–2007), Dame Eliza Manningham-Buller, it was stated that out of a staff of 2,800, approximately 50 per cent had been recruited since 9/11.[30] How this increase was spread among the differing roles within the Security Service is unknown. It may be reasonably surmised that a significant portion went into increasing the number of intelligence analysts, to fill the requirement shortfall. This meant that more data could be analysed, resulting in increased potential to prevent or detect more terrorist-related threats. Consequentially, the ability of the state to increase broad protection by offering increased intelligence means that this was beneficial to the PROTECT strand of CONTEST.

As has been noted extensively throughout this chapter, the police and the Agencies had a close working relationship during this period. It may well have been the case that information that would have been beneficial to counter-radicalisation initiatives was passed on to the police who, as discussed in the following chapter, considered one of their primary roles to be counter-radicalisation.

The transition from a law enforcement- to an intelligence-institutional-level lead was characteristic of a change in the needs and requirements of the state, to counter the new transnational terrorism threat. The potentially cataclysmic nature of well-coordinated transnational terrorist events strengthened the view that reacting through responsive policing, as opposed to actively seeking intelligence on plots before they reached fruition, was no longer an option. Kevin O'Brien agrees, stating that 'a notable shift away from the attitude in some Western countries [...] that we could somehow arrest our way out of this' no longer applied.[31] He argues that increasing the number of arrests did not dispel the threat of transnational terrorism.[32] Indeed, arrest and detention without charge, as was the case in Northern Ireland under the policy of Internment, may have served more as a recruiting sergeant than as a deterrent.[33] This is because such a policy reinforces perceptions that practitioners of terrorist violence may have been trying to impress upon sympathisers – that governments are purposefully targeting groups through their actions and that, moreover, in response to this targeting, it was the duty of sympathisers to respond with violence.

The primary areas highlighted throughout centred on the use of intelligence as the lead agency at the institutional level, and the process of expansion indicated by increased funding and regionalisation. The overarching implications here were that the United Kingdom increased its ability to gather intelligence useful in countering threats of transnational terrorism. However, a disconnect regarding the sharing of intelligence generated by the Agencies meant that members of the police felt inhibited when it came to dealing with those susceptible to radicalisation.

Intelligence and the United States: a qualitative assessment

The Federal (national) intelligence agencies of the United States are collectively known as the Intelligence Community. There are seventeen members of the Intelligence Community:

- Air Force Intelligence;
- Army Intelligence;

- Central Intelligence Agency;
- Coast Guard Intelligence;
- Defense Intelligence Agency;
- Department of Energy;
- Department of Homeland Security;
- Department of State;
- Department of the Treasury;
- Drug Enforcement Administration;
- Federal Bureau of Investigation;
- Marine Core Intelligence;
- National Geospatial-Intelligence Agency;
- National Reconnaissance Office;
- National Security Agency;
- Navy Intelligence; and
- Office of the Director of National Intelligence.[34]

Agencies of the Intelligence Community can be broadly split between *inward-* or domestically focused and *outward-looking*, or internationally focused agencies.[35] Having intelligence agencies that are focused solely on the international or the domestic realm is also applicable in the United Kingdom context, as the Secret Intelligence Service's primary focus is international and the Security Services' is domestic. Prior to 9/11 these divisions were more entrenched in the United States, contributing to a lack of willingness to share intelligence among the agencies within the Intelligence Community.[36] This culture, present in the lead-up to 9/11, was one of the key criticisms made in the *9/11 Commission Report*.[37] The focus of analysis when considering the United States' Intelligence Community differs from that of the United Kingdom. The role of intelligence in the United States context is analysed here by looking at the Intelligence Community as a whole – specifically its structure and the relationships between the different agencies.

The events of 9/11 had a profound impact on United States intelligence agencies. They were, in the *9/11 Commission Report*, considered to be archaic in a manner that contributed to the inability to identify the emerging threat of 9/11.[38] The *9/11 Commission Report* stated that the complexity of the organisational structure of the intelligence agencies meant that '[e]ven the most basic information about how much money is actually allocated to or within the Intelligence Community and most of its key components is shrouded from public view'.[39]

By 2006 intelligence was considered by many both within and outside the Intelligence Community to be a critical tool for countering terrorism.[40] The primary problem with the Intelligence Community was, according to a Senior House Committee on Homeland Security Staffer, that by 2009 it was still on a Cold War footing and consequentially woefully unprepared for the asymmetrical threats of the twenty-first century, particularly transnational terrorism.[41]

Addressing the overarching concern of structure was a priority, as this had an impact on the sharing of intelligence. The fundamental issue regarding the structure was characterised by an inability within the Intelligence Community to share intelligence among other agencies, particularly between inwardly and out-wardly focused ones. The *9/11 Commission Report* stated that structural barriers to the sharing of intelligence hindered effectiveness, and that '[t]he importance of integrated, all-source analysis cannot be overstated. Without it, it is not pos-sible to "connect the dots". No one agency holds all the relevant information.'[42] An inability to collate all the relevant information in the weeks and months leading up to 9/11 was considered a systemic failure that, in the view of the *9/11 Commission Report*, necessitated an overhaul of the Intelligence Community.

This overhaul took the form of a restructuring of the Intelligence Community. The purpose of this was to facilitate the sharing of intelligence between inwardly and outwardly looking agencies, both within and outside the Intelligence Com-munity. Furthermore, this restructuring was intended to help create an area where all the agencies could see each other's intelligence, so as to help create a picture and mentality that corresponded to a single, 'joint[-]mission'.[43]

One consequence of this Cold War footing, still present in 2012, was that the Armed Forces took the lead in counter-terrorism activities, thus reducing the sig-nificance of the Intelligence Community. Furthermore, this structure was not conducive to the coordinated functions necessitated by the transnational threat of terrorism activity. As discussed below, the establishment of new coordinating authorities to tackle the archaic structure was not wholly successful.

To aid coordination between agencies of the Intelligence Community, the Department of Homeland Security was established, envisioned as being the loca-tion where all federal intelligence and policing agencies converged to share data. It was believed that the Department of Homeland Security would take the lead at the federal level in horizontal intelligence sharing. Although not officially acknowledged, this remit changed when, in 2003, the Terrorist Threat Integra-tion Center, precursor to the National Counterterrorism Center, was established. The Terrorist Threat Integration Center's primary function was to act as coordi-nator for the United States' intelligence agencies. One view is that the practical application of this new agency led to confusion as to what the Department of Homeland Security's function was.[44]

The Terrorist Threat Integration Center was able to increase the sharing of intelligence among intelligence agencies. What it could not do and what the Department of Homeland Security was set up to do was to facilitate the timely distribution of pertinent intelligence to state, local and territorial policing agen-cies. This inability to capitalise on the initial remit of the Department of Home-land Security hampered the ability of the state as a whole to counter threats of terrorist violence and also to put in place broad, blunt, defensive counter-terrorism measures.

Within the Department of Homeland Security, the Office of Intelligence and Analysis, whose establishment was heavily supported by Congress, was given wide-ranging legislated authority to drive through changes needed to force col-laboration between agencies of the Intelligence Community.[45] Moreover, the Office of Intelligence and Analysis was to collect intelligence products and distribute them to local police agencies. They could, according to a former member of the FBI, 'see each other's information, the most sensitive information, the highest classification' prior to sanitisation and distribution to the police.[46]

In early 2009 the Office of Intelligence and Analysis' ability to do this was called into question. When asked what kind of feedback had been received regarding the Office of Intelligence and Analysis' role, a Senior House Committee Staffer on Homeland Security stated:

> What I'm getting is: 'This product does not tell me what I need to do'; or 'This was an excellent product and it would have been useful to me, seven weeks ago'; or 'This is a repackaged product that another intelligence agency has created and they've simply put the [Office of Intelligence and Analysis'] letterhead on it, it doesn't tell me anything'; or 'I pass a lot of information up to the Department of Homeland Security, but I never know what happens with it'; or 'why doesn't anyone from the Department of Homeland Security talk to me about what's going on in my community, I have a lot to say'.[47]

While the Department of Homeland Security and specifically the Office of Intelligence and Analysis' intended purpose could be seen as beneficial to the overarching strategy, by late 2009 this was still very much a work in progress. The Office of Intelligence and Analysis was set up in order to improve communication between agencies of the Intelligence Community. With the quality of the data considered lower than that required, the Office of Intelligence and Analysis proved to be more of a liability than a benefit in protecting the state.

Failure to invest in the Office of Intelligence and Analysis may also be seen as symptomatic of a culture of investing excessively in visible, technologically based quick fixes. Investment in counter-terrorism technologies during this period formed the backbone of many frontline efforts to improve the ability of the state to protect itself. However, an uneven balance between technology and human assets – particularly a weakness over the recruitment and retention of intelligence analysts – may have also served to make the state more vulnerable.

The *9/11 Commission Report* findings suggested that the Intelligence Community lacked sufficient analytical capability and that this, in part, led to the failure of intelligence to see the emerging threat that came to fruition on 9/11.[48] By late 2009, five years after the *9/11 Commission Report* released its findings and six years after the establishment of the Department of Homeland Security and its sub-office, the Office of Intelligence and Analysis, investment in human assets could still be considered as lacking. This was because the George W. Bush administration chose to invest in technological solutions. One interviewee noted that the reason for this was because it is far easier to justify technologies such as metal detectors, scanners and so forth, as these are quick, easily visible projects. Recruiting, training and retaining an intelligence analyst is a substantial investment that may not yield tangible results for years. Consequently, according to one source, rather than investing in these human assets, the administration chose to look at technology.[49] Having the technology to gather data, but not the operators to interpret that data, makes such an investment questionable.

In addition to questionable decisions over the allocation of funds, the transnational threat led, from the perspective of the United States, to a fear that 9/11 might be repeated. Therefore, extra-ordinary means of 'protecting' the state were introduced. The process of extra-ordinary rendition involved the transportation of suspected *enemy combatants* to detention centres such as that in Guantánamo Bay, Cuba in an extra-judicial manner. According to Secretary of State Condoleezza Rice, the process of extra-ordinary rendition had been used for decades preceding 9/11 as a means of countering terrorist activities.[50] Post-9/11, however, those who were rendered were not subject to, or afforded the protection of, the laws of either the United States or the Geneva Conventions on Prisoners of War.

The specific role of United States intelligence agencies in the process of extra-ordinary rendition is unknown. The accusation is that agencies of the United States government abducted and moved, for the purpose of interrogation and even torture, individuals thought to be a threat to United States interests both domestically and overseas.[51] The movement of such suspects was not undertaken through ordinary judicial means, but rather in a clandestine, extra-ordinary manner. A number of these suspects rendered found themselves in one of three camps at Guantánamo Bay Detention Centre: Camp's Delta, Iguana and X-Ray, or other, so-called *black sites* that apparently existed and were run by the Central Intelligence Agency in countries including Egypt, Lithuania and Poland.[52]

Although the use of such methods is legally and morally questionable, it is not that aspect which is detrimental to United States strategy in the Global War on Terror. Rather, it is the public awareness of its use.[53] Rendering suspects for the purpose of interrogation or torture not only highlights the weaknesses of the government in dealing with this threat in a manner conducive to the laws and regulations of the land and in accordance with international law, but also serves as a recruiting sergeant for those considered sympathisers.

As discussed earlier, the United States appeared to have invested more in technologies than in recruiting and training new analysts. What also occurred was a redistribution of human assets from outwardly to inwardly focused intelligence agencies.[54] The reason for this was that, in the aftermath of 9/11, the United States Congress was eager to make sure that intelligence analysts featured prominently in new, domestic security ventures. However, recruiting and training intelligence analysts takes time. Therefore, in order to meet short-term demand, a number of intelligence analysts transferred from focusing on the international to the domestic sphere.[55] However, outward-looking agencies frequently operate under a different set of 'rules' from inwardly orientated ones. This, according to one interviewee, had serious repercussions when outward agents were transferred to the domestic arena, particularly with regard to the requirement that hey adhere to domestic law.[56]

When assessing the effectiveness of United States counter-terrorism strategy, one cannot escape, as the interviewee at the start of this book stated, the irrefutable fact that since 9/11, no major terrorist incident has occurred within the territorial borders of the United States. However, the reason for this is not clear, as there were a number of 'close shaves'.[57] Indeed, any positives in an assessment of United States counter-terrorism strategy during this period need to be made with caveats. This is due to the fact that following 9/11 and the *9/11 Commission Report*, structures, such as the Department of Homeland Security, had not bedded down and still needed time to establish themselves. Moreover, some agencies were still trying to define their role and were in need of further legislation to formalise it. For instance, the establishment of the Office of Intelligence and Analysis went a long way toward filling the gaps, procedurally speaking, within the Intelligence Community that were identified in the *9/11 Commission Report*. However, as was demonstrated by the 2009 Christmas Day attempted terrorist attack in the United States, the establishment of these mechanisms did not sufficiently encourage the agencies to share intelligence among themselves.[58]

Matters did, in the years since 9/11, get better. The Office of Intelligence and Analysis did begin to share *products* with law enforcement agencies. Intelligence gathered from other collectors such as the Central Intelligence Agency and the National Security Agency was more widely distributed. Criticisms persisted, suggesting that the intelligence was arriving late and that its format hindered the ability of police personnel to work out what they should do. Following the establishment of the Office of Intelligence and Analysis, communication did improve, but was still not operating at a high enough standard.[59]

The 2001 to 2002 *standing-up*[60] of the Department of Homeland Security represented the institutional response to the threat posed by transnational terrorism.[61] The role of the Department of Homeland Security was key. For the establishment of the Department of Homeland Security, the fifteenth federal department, solidified the notion that countering the threat of terrorism was a task to which all branches of the United States government was committed for a prolonged period. As Deputy Assistant Secretary Alan Cohn noted: 'significant Congressional pressure for the creation of a national cabinet department that would be responsible for homeland security' was present in the immediate aftermath of the 9/11 attacks.[62]

The idea for a Department of Homeland Security, however, actually came about prior to 9/11 as a means of collating the overlapping roles of immigration, transportation and border management. The post-9/11 version of such a department was quite apart from this. Consisting of no fewer than twenty-two agencies of which half possessed policing powers, the Department quickly became known as an 'all hazards' agency of the federal government.[63] Yet, as discussed earlier, there appeared to be a failure to capitalise on the remit for which the Department of Homeland Security was created. The establishment of this Department served as a template for how counter-terrorism was to be carried out. The Department of Homeland Security highlighted the importance of communication, sharing and undertaking coordinated operations in countering the threat of terrorism.

In addition to promoting collaboration among different agencies, the task of the Department of Homeland Security was also to safeguard civil liberties. Counter-terrorism, especially when related to the collection and retention of data since 9/11, coincided with a rise in concern for civil liberties, not only by civil liberty groups, but also by oversight committees and other members of the Intelligence Community.[64] Perhaps counter-intuitively, concern from the state tended to focus not so much on the collection and retention of such data – and, by extension, the use of intelligence in this area – but on how it was *operationalised* by the police and Armed Forces.

In the case of the United States, the greatest advocates for civil liberties when it came to domestic policy formulation were, 'surprisingly', law enforcement agencies.[65] 'Americans', according to Gruber (Executive Director of the National Preparedness Taskforce within the Federal Emergency Management Agency or FEMA), 'are rightfully suspicious of reorganisations that touch on Civil Rights and Civil liberties[; t]hat touch on security, in particularly the homeland'.[66] It is for this reason, Gruber adds, that the Department of Homeland Security was created with an Office for Civil Rights and Civil Liberties.[67] The Office's mission was, in accordance with Title 6 of the United States Code, to review 'information concerning abuses of civil rights, civil liberties, and profiling on the basis of race, ethnicity, or religion, by employees and officials of the [Department of Homeland Security]'.[68] Furthermore, they were tasked with implementing and reviewing policies that safeguard civil liberties.[69] Thus, this Office's statutory duty was not just to respond to areas of note that arose, but also to take a proactive role in preventing such issues from arising.

A report published in 2004 by the Senate Committee on Governmental Affairs reaffirmed that

> [i]n enacting the Homeland Security Act, Congress understood the importance of providing checks and balances to protect Civil Rights and civil liberties. To this end, Congress created within the Department of Homeland Security, three positions devoted wholly, or in part, to ensuring respect for civil liberties as the agency carried out its mandate to protect the homeland. These positions are the Officer for Civil Rights and Civil Liberties, the Privacy Officer, and the Department's Inspector.[70]

The report, however, stipulated that 'the Act only generally described the role and responsibility of the Officer for Civil Rights and Civil Liberties' and did not 'provide for statutory guidance on how these offices should work together to address issues related to Civil Rights and civil liberties'.[71] The Office had, when Daniel W. Sutherland (Officer for Civil Rights and Civil Liberties from 2003 to 31 December 2011) took over, developed a broad strategic plan that lacked a statutory basis but, nevertheless, provided an outline of how its roles and responsibilities could develop.

The Office, therefore, had a broad statutory obligation to safeguard civil liberties. Similarly to other areas discussed in this chapter, this continued to be work in progress. Questioning by civil libertarians was considered by a Homeland Security expert, with Congressional and Executive Branch experience, to be welcome. 'Congress,' he suggested,

> is a check and that's wonderful but there's no greater check than having the privacy and civil liberties community questioning what you're doing; because it forces us to say 'wait a minute, do they have a point or not and if they do, what do we do to make sure we're doing this the right way'. It's a very healthy thing.[72]

It is clear that the United States recognised the need to preserve civil liberties in order to hinder the transition of sympathisers of terrorist causes into active practitioners of violence. The Office for Civil Rights and Civil Liberties was a positive starting point but was somewhat counterbalanced by the ongoing process of extra-ordinary rendition.

Summary

The United Kingdom and United States intelligence agencies experienced different sets of issues after 9/11. The United Kingdom's intelligence structure, made up of the Security and Intelligence Agencies, had already begun a restructuring process that saw the counter-terrorism lead move from law enforcement to intelligence at the institutional level. Furthermore, the Agencies began a process of regionalisation so as to increase domestic knowledge beyond the capital. Another key feature of the contribution of intelligence during this period was the relationship between the police and the Agencies. As mentioned, the institutional lead was that of the Agencies while operational responsibility remained the purview of the police. Sharing intelligence between these two counter-terrorism agencies was on balance effective – especially in cases which posed an immediate threat to life. Where problems did emerge was in the police's desire to share information that they regarded as non-pertinent with other partners – particularly local authorities which had the authoritative lead in the PREVENT strand of the United Kingdom's counter-terrorism strategy. A substantial investment in the Agencies meant that their ability to protect the state and prevent radicalisation from occurring significantly increased during this period.

When considering the contribution of intelligence in the United States, a broader approach was employed. This was because many of the concerns regarding the Intelligence Community during this period centred on relationships between agencies and non-agencies of the Intelligence Community, particularly with regard to the sharing of intelligence. These distinctions, as well as those characterised by inwardly and outwardly focused agencies, created an artificial institutional divide. This in turn led to the inability of agencies of the Intelligence Community to share information that might have prevented 9/11 from occurring. Consequentially, the Commission recommended, and Congress demanded, the setting up of mechanisms that would increase intelligence sharing within the Intelligence Community and between them and law enforcement agencies. With the former, the Terrorist Threat Integration Center was set up and worked effectively. With the latter, the Office of Intelligence and Analysis was created within the Department of Homeland Security, but struggled to get pertinent information, in a manner required by law enforcement agencies, out into the field in an understandable, actionable format. This is an issue considered further in this book. Another key issue during this period was an investment programme that favoured technology over intelligence assets. This meant that the Intelligence Community was, even after the *9/11 Commission Report* recommendations, lacking in experienced analysts.

Notes

1 This chapter forms the first of three assessing the contribution of counter-terrorism policy instruments used by both the United Kingdom and United States during the post-9/11 period. It focuses on the contribution of intelligence, with law enforcement and military force covered further in this publication. It should be noted that publicly available primary information, such as documents, regarding the contribution of intelligence during this period is extremely sparse. There are two main reasons for this. First, if a government was to reveal such data it may also identify the extent to which intelligence assets have penetrated either individual cells or overarching terrorist organisations. Second, revealing such information may aid the enemy in understanding the methods used to observe and infiltrate such groups. All the data used in this chapter has been gathered from publicly available documents, articles and interviews undertaken for this publication.

2 United Kingdom government (July 2006), 'Countering International Terrorism', pp. 16–17.

3 United Kingdom government (September 2001), *National Intelligence Machinery*, 2nd edn, Cabinet Office.

4 The Joint Intelligence Committee had multiple roles in 2005 to 2009. Their primary duty was the provision of timely intelligence to ministers and senior officials through a process of collating information submitted by different analytical agencies. It also 'periodically scrutinizes the performance of the Agencies in meeting the collection requirements placed upon them'. See United Kingdom government (8 October 2009), 'The Joint Intelligence Committee (JIC)', Cabinet Office, www.cabinetoffice.gov.uk/security_ and_intelligence/community/central_intelligence_machinery/joint_intelligence_committee.aspx, accessed 12 November 2009.

5 The Security Service reports to the Home Office while SIS and GCHQ report to the Foreign and Commonwealth Office.

6 In order to see how the different agencies of the NIM interconnect, see United Kingdom government (September 2001), op. cit. In order to see those regulations that put elements of the Security and Intelligence Agencies on to a statutory footing see United Kingdom government (2000), 'Regulation of Investigatory Powers Act', Office of Public Sector Information; United Kingdom government (1994), 'Intelligence Services Act', Office of Public Sector Information, www.opsi.gov.uk/ACTS/acts1994/pdf/ukpga_19940013_en.pdf; and United Kingdom government (1989), 'Security Service Act', Office of Public Sector Information.

7 United Kingdom government (2000), op. cit., p. 48.

8 John Jackson, Royal Military Academy Sandhurst, interview conducted by the author, held at Royal Military Academy Sandhurst, 30 July 2008.

9 Alex P. Schmid and Ronald D. Crelinsten, 'Western Responses to Terrorism: A

Twenty-Five Year Balance Sheet', in Schmid and Crelinsten (eds), *Western Responses to Terrorism* (London: Frank Cass, 1993), p. 309.

10 United Kingdom government (1989), op. cit.

11 Jackson, op. cit.

12 United Kingdom government (July 2006), op. cit., p. 17.

13 Ibid.

14 Glenn Hastedt, *Controlling Intelligence* (London: Frank Cass, 1991), p. 16.

15 Kevin A. O'Brien, 'Managing National Security and Law Enforcement Intelligence in a Globalised World', *Review of International Studies*, 35 (October 2009), 4, p. 904.

16 Superintendent Andy Pratt, Lancashire Police Constabulary, interview conducted by the author, held in Preston, United Kingdom, 22 November 2009.

17 The 2004 Spending Review, *Stability, Security and Opportunity for All: Investing for Britain's Long-term Future – New Public Spending Plans 2005–2008*, published by Her Majesty's Treasury, allocated an extra £20 million per year from the financial year 2005 to 2006. This was done in order to 'allow local authorities to carry out emergency planning in response to the threat from international terrorism'. See United Kingdom government (12 July 2004), '2004 Spending Review, *Stability, Security and Opportunity for All: Investing for Britain's Long-term Future – New Public Spending Plans 2005–2008*', Her Majesty's Treasury, www.hm-treasury.gov.uk/d/sr2004_ch5. pdf, accessed 2 December 2009, p. 76.

18 Bruce Hoffman, Georgetown University, interview conducted by the author, held in Oxford, UK, 3 December 2009.

19 Pratt, op. cit.; Inspector Jonathan Brook, South Yorkshire Police Constabulary, interview conducted by the author, held in Sheffield, UK, 19 August 2009.

20 O'Brien, op. cit., p. 904.

21 Gary Hindle, Head, Security and Counterterrorism, Royal United Services Institute, interview conducted by the author, held at the Royal United Services Institute, London, 24 November 2009.

22 Ibid.

23 Hoffman, op. cit.

24 Anonymous Source H, interview conducted by the author.

25 For instance, those offices located in Greater Manchester and Northern Ireland. In addition to improving local situational awareness, the proliferation of offices outside London also meant that the Security Service could add to the diversity of their personnel.

26 Anonymous Source C, interview conducted by the author.

27 For further information on the attack see Mark Townsend, Jo Revill and Paul Keilbe (1 July 2007), 'Terror Threat "Critical" as Glasgow Attacked', *guardian.co.uk*, www. guardian.co.uk/uk/2007/jul/01/terrorism.world2. For further information on its repercussions see Office of Intelligence and Analysis: Department of Homeland Security and Federal Bureau of Investigation (2 July 2007), 'Joint Homeland Security Assessment – Glasgow Airport Illustrates Varied Terrorist Tactics to Attack Transportation Infrastructure', NEFA Foundation, www.nefafoundation.org/miscellaneous/Featured-Docs/dhs-fbi_glasgow.pdf.

28 Anonymous Source B, interview conducted by the author, held in Washington, DC, February 2009.

29 Security Service (n.d.), 'Funding', *Security Service – MI5*, www.mi5.gov.uk/output/ funding.html.

30 Dame Eliza Manningham-Buller (9 November 2006), 'The International Terrorist Threat to the United Kingdom – Speech by The Director General of the Security Service – At Queen Mary's College', Security Service – MI5, www.mi5.gov.uk/ output/the-international-terrorist-threat-to-the-uk-1.html.

31 O'Brien, op. cit., p. 904.

32 Ibid.

33 Jackson, op. cit.; see Philip B. Heyman, 'Dealing with Terrorism – An Overview', *International Security*, 26 (2001/2002), 3, p. 26.

34 United States government (n.d.), 'Seventeen Agencies and Organizations United Under One Goal', intelligence.gov, www.intelligence.gov/about-the-intelligence-community/.

35 Inward looking refers to those agencies of the intelligence structure for which the primary purpose is the domestic realm. Outward looking refers to those agencies that are concerned primarily with the international arena.

36 Anonymous Source B, op. cit.

37 Thomas H. Kean (Chair), *9/11 Commission Report* (London: W.W. Norton, 2004), p. 408.

38 As one interviewee notes, no one component of the IC or any other branch of the Federal government had responsibility for 9/11: 'A lot of people kind of had responsibility and kinda sort of passed the buck, didn't connect the dots. It's never the fault of one person. It's a systemic failure that caused us to sort of miss 9/11.' Anonymous Source B, interview conducted by the author, held in Washington, DC, February 2009.

39 Kean, op. cit., p. 410. The Commission's dim view of a lack of transparency in funding allocations to the IC contrasts greatly with the United Kingdom. In the United Kingdom, the allocation of funds to the Security and Intelligence Agencies is considered a matter of national security and is not made public. See United Kingdom government (12 July 2004), '2004 Spending Review, *Stability, Security and Opportunity for All: Investing for Britain's Long-term Future – New Public Spending Plans 2005–2008*', Her Majesty's Treasury, www.hm-treasury.gov.uk/d/sr2004_ch5.pdf, accessed 2 December 2009.

40 Robert G. Ross, Department of Homeland Security, interview conducted by the author, held in Washington, DC, 9 February 2009.

41 Senior House Committee on Homeland Security Staffer, interview conducted by the author, held in Washington, DC, February 2009.

42 Kean, op. cit., p. 408.

43 Ibid.

44 Senior House Committee on Homeland Security Staffer, op. cit.

45 Homeland Security Expert with Congressional and Executive Experience, interview conducted by the author, held in Washington, DC, September 2009.

46 Michael Jacobsen, Senior Fellow Stein Program on Counterterrorism and Intelligence, interview conducted by the author, held in Washington, DC, 11 February 2009.

47 Senior House Committee on Homeland Security Staffer, op. cit.

48 Kean, op. cit.

49 Anonymous Source B, op. cit.

50 Suzanne Goldenberg and Luke Harding (9 December 2005), 'Detainee Flights Have Saved Europe, Says Rice', *guardian.co.uk*, www.guardian.co.uk/world/2005/dec/09/ciarendition.lukeharding.

51 Homeland Security Expert with Congressional and Executive Experience, op. cit.

52 See Unknown Author (22 December 2009), 'Lithuania Hosted Secret CIA Prisons', *BBC News*, http://news.bbc.co.uk/1/hi/world/europe/8426028.stm; and Jim Barnett and Matthew Chance (23 December 2009), 'Lithuania Denies Report it Hosted Secret CIA Prisons', *CNN World*, www.cnn.com/2009/WORLD/europe/12/23/cia.lithuania/index.html.

53 Homeland Security Expert with Congressional and Executive Experience, op. cit.

54 Ibid.

55 Colonel Randall J. Larsen, Retired; Director, Institute for Homeland Security, interview conducted by the author, held in Washington, DC, 10 September 2009.

56 Homeland Security Expert with Congressional and Executive Experience, op. cit.

57 Randy Beardsworth, former Assistant Secretary for Strategic Plans; former Director of Operations; former Under-Secretary for Border and Transportation Security Dir-

ector; former Director for Defence Policy on the National Security Council, interview conducted by the author, held in Washington, DC, 10 September 2009.

58 United States government (January 2010), 'Summary of the White House Review of the December 25, 2009 Attempted Terrorist Attack', White House, www.whitehouse. gov/sites/default/files/summary_of_wh_review_12–25–09.pdf; and United States President Barack Obama (7 January 2010), 'Memorandum – Intelligence Screening, and Watchlisting System Corrective Actions', White House, www.whitehouse.gov/ sites/default/files/potus_directive_corrective_actions_1–7–10.pdf.

59 Homeland Security Expert with Congressional and Executive Experience, op. cit.

60 '*Standing up*' is the verb of the frequently used (certainly in interviews with American specialists and practitioners) term '*stood up*'. Similarly to its colloquial usage, it is used throughout this chapter to refer to the establishment of the Department of Homeland Security.

61 Alan D. Cohn, Deputy Assistant Secretary for Policy, Strategic Plans, Department of Homeland Security, interview conducted by the author, held in Washington, DC, 12 February 2009.

62 Ibid.

63 Jonathan R. White, *Terrorism and Homeland Security*, 5th edn (USA: Thomas Wadsworth, 2006), p. 279; and Corey Gruber, Executive Director, National Preparedness Task-Force, Federal Emergency Management Agency, Department of Homeland Security, interview conducted by the author, held in Washington, DC, 11 February 2009.

64 One interviewee states that the House Committee on Homeland Security prioritise civil liberties in their deliberations:

> I mean there's always a concern about civil liberties [...] and it should be at the top of our list of concerns frankly; because you know when you begin to violate people's rights, you've lost something. Something's lost, here in the United States; and I think you're going to fail to win the battle in the long term to an extent that the terrorists win, when we violate our own rights is I think a valid one.
>
> (Anonymous Source B, interview conducted by the author, held in Washington, DC, February 2009)

65 Senior House Committee on Homeland Security Staffer, op. cit.

66 Gruber, op. cit.

67 Ibid.

68 United States House of Representatives (5 May 2009), 'Title 6 (Domestic Security), Chapter 1 (Homeland Security), Sub-chapter VII (Management), Section 345 (Establishment of the Officer for Civil Rights and Civil Liberties), Paragraph a, Clause 1', United States Code: Office of the Law Revision Counsel U.S. House of Representatives, http://uscode.house.gov/.

69 Ibid.

70 Susan M. Collins (20 September 2004), 'Homeland Security, Civil Rights and Civil Liberties Protection Act of 2004', Committee on Governmental Affairs, United States Senate, http://frwebgate.access.gpo.gov/cgi-bin/getdoc.cgi?dbname=108_cong_reports& docid=f:sr350.108.pdf.

71 Ibid., p. 2.

72 Homeland Security Expert with Congressional and Executive Experience, op. cit.

4　Law enforcement

The use of law enforcement to counter terrorist threats is the traditional approach adopted by both states. For the United Kingdom, law enforcement has been utilised over the years to counter the threat of Northern Irish-related terrorism. For the United States, the Federal Bureau of Investigation fully utilised their remit in order to investigate terrorist crime both domestically and overseas. In the post-9/11 period a number of issues, as discussed below, emerged concerning the role of law enforcement in both states.

Law enforcement and the United Kingdom: a qualitative assessment

Inspector Brook, the PREVENT Delivery Manager of South Yorkshire Police Constabulary, stated in an interview that the role of the police is minor when compared against the wider counter-terrorism strategy of the United Kingdom and that when assessing their role this must be taken into consideration.[1] The role of the police is actually quite significant in all strands of the United Kingdom's strategy, primarily because their remit is not only responsive but also preventative.[2] Indeed, the Metropolitan Police Service's Statement of Purpose says in the first line that '[t]he purpose of the Police Service is to uphold the law fairly and firmly; to prevent crime; to pursue and bring to justice those who break the law'.[3] What is noticeable is that the prevention of crime comes prior to the pursuit of perpetrators.

Furthermore, under Public Service Agreement 26, the police and local authorities are statutorily obligated to 'Reduce the *risk* [emphasis added] to the United Kingdom and its interests overseas from international terrorism'.[4] Reducing risk, as is the obligation of the police and local authorities, meant acting in a preventative fashion. Public Service Agreements were introduced in 1998 as a means of setting consistent delivery targets across the United Kingdom government and delivery partners. The police played a central role in providing security, planning for future events and also liaising closely with local authorities in community engagement projects. This latter role was in order to facilitate counter-radicalisation under the PREVENT strand of the United Kingdom's counter-terrorism strategies.

In the previous chapter, it was noted that the Security and Intelligence Agencies (or the Agencies) had, since the end of the Cold War, taken over from the police as the institutional lead in counter-terrorism. The Agencies, focused on gathering intelligence, had a lower threshold when it came to the question of when to act than that of the police. Nevertheless, and as will be discussed further below, the relationship between the two organisations worked well in the years following 9/11.[5] The police were privy to a pool of intelligence and received, when requested, regular updates.[6] The potential tension identified between the Agencies and the police, therefore, was not in relation to the manner, or time, in which intelligence was shared. Rather it was with regard to the restrictions placed upon that intelligence which, in turn, prevented the police from sharing it with other, mostly critical, stakeholders.[7]

Sir Richard Dearlove, former Chief of the Secret Intelligence Service (1999–2004), described this state of affairs as adherence to the third-party rule.[8] With reference to interactions between the United Kingdom's National Intelligence Machinery and the United States Intelligence Community, Dearlove said that the third-party rule means that intelligence should not be shared by those to whom it has been disseminated without the express permission of those who collected it.[9] One probable impact that the third-party rule had within the United Kingdom context comes in the provision of knowledge to those responsible for agreeing to police requests to extend their powers. The police, it is argued, found themselves unable to share what some, such as Pratt – who was responsible for writing the Police Response to the United Kingdom's counter-terrorism strategy – considered to be pertinent information, with those in decision-making positions.[10] A case in point is the July 2008 proposal to extend the period of pre-charge detention from twenty-eight days to forty-two days.[11] The proposal required that Members of the House of Commons and the House of Lords pass legislation that was not based on their own interpretation of evidence supporting the presence of a threat, but on that of those who had seen the intelligence reports. The plans were subsequently dropped in October 2008 after a number of high-profile officials, such as Attorney General Lord Goldsmith and the former Director-General of the Security Service (2002–2007) Eliza Manningham-Buller, who were privy to the intelligence, publicly questioned the need for the extension.

In her critique, Manningham-Buller stated that the 'law would actually harm the counter-terrorism effort rather than assisting it, and [that] this demonstrates only too clearly that it is an action motivated by politics rather than the nation's security'.[12] The argument upon which the then Labour government founded their request for an extension of pre-charge detention was that intelligence, which could not be divulged, indicated it was needed. As discussed above, one view that exists about the restrictions placed upon who could and could not access data gathered and shared with the police by the Security and Intelligence Agencies is that the restrictions not only impacted upon the state's ability to provide protection to the state, but also on its ability to counter radicalisation.

Pratt, whose position afforded him an overarching appreciation of the United Kingdom's counter-terrorism strategy and the police's response to it, states that one of the perhaps informal roles of the police during this period was to facilitate the movement of secret intelligence into the public domain. Only about 10 per cent of what was collected, in Pratt's view, needed to be kept secret.[13] Keeping low-priority counter-radicalisation intelligence secret meant that those in decision-making positions, such as local authorities, may have been pressured into authorising, or refusing as the case may be, measures, without the benefit of fully understanding or appreciating their necessity. This arguably occurred nationally, in relation to the debate surrounding pre-charge detention and also within local authorities which were responsible for the implementation of the PREVENT strand of the United Kingdom's counter-terrorism strategy.[14] Local authorities, given the position they held, frequently needed to give the go-ahead to activities for which the police needed their support.[15]

As the decision on whether to keep something secret is subjective, it is difficult to see how this could have been resolved. The Agencies, understandably, always erred on the side of caution when deciding what and with whom to share information. Therefore, one possible knock-on effect of this was that local authorities frequently found themselves in the position of approving, or not approving, actions relating to counter-radicalisation without fully knowing the reason(s) why.[16] This impacted upon transparency in the counter-terrorism process. Further, it added to a perception that particular members of the wider community, specifically Muslims, were being targeted.

The police during this period did not only rely on intelligence gained from the Security and Intelligence Agencies. In conjunction with local government authorities, the police instigated a number of community programmes. The lack of transparency and community understanding identified above was not, therefore, just an issue of sharing intelligence but also of how it was used. Concerns regarding the perception of the extension of pre-charge detention periods were seen as potentially damaging to the image of the Agencies and the police.[17]

Following the development, publication and implementation of the United Kingdom's counter-terrorism strategy, a number of community engagement programmes were introduced. Operation Nicole, for example, was run by Lancashire Constabulary.

> The exercise [was] designed to explore community concerns, giving the police greater understanding of the community and the community greater understanding of counter-terrorism operations. The participants [made] decisions and [were] provided with legislative guidance by a specialist senior investigating officer.[18]

Another, the Black Country Imams Project, involved thirty-six imams from Dudley, Wolverhampton, Sandwell, Walsall and Birmingham.[19] This project allowed Imams to take part in training that made them 'not only more effective as teachers and community leaders but also more accessible to young people by improving their communication skills'.[20] The Channel Project, perhaps more significant due to its national standing, 'centred on the identification of those individuals at risk through a MAPPA [Multi-Agency Public Protection Arrangements][21] type process, developing a partnership intervention strategy and then delivering interventions'.[22] The Channel Project worked by identifying those considered to be vulnerable to radicalisation and, if necessary, diverting them away from perceived *radicalisers*.

The purpose of programmes such as these was to facilitate the sharing of information between the police and the wider community. The police and local authorities relied on partners in communities, especially in areas where young people congregated frequently, such as schools, to feed them intelligence.[23] The police and the United Kingdom government during this period continually emphasised the need for partnerships, both in the PREVENT agenda and the wider counter-terrorism strategy.[24] From a policing perspective this involved developing and distributing information to partners that would increase their awareness of ongoing radicalisation.[25] This proved to be controversial, as criticisms were made of the police to the effect that the programmes led to the deliberate targeting of Muslims. These criticisms were further supported by the manner, or criteria, through which funding was made available.[26]

A June 2007 report produced by Buckinghamshire County Council states that eligibility for funding from the 2007/2008 *Prevent*ing Violent Extremism Pathfinder Fund of £6 million 'was based on concentrations of Muslim population, with 5% used as a starting point'.[27] Moreover, the report states,

> [c]rudely, each eligible local authority with a minimum Muslim population of 4,000, using 2001 census data, will receive baseline funding of £85k [*sic*] and an additional £20k [*sic*] for every 5,000 Muslims in their local area in Year 1, rising to £25k [*sic*] and £31k [*sic*] in years 2 and 3.[28]

The allocation of funds based on concentrations of Muslim peoples would have no doubt added to the perception that they were being deliberately targeted by law enforcement which, with local authorities, played a significant role in the PREVENT strand.

While this criticism did not significantly hamper the ability of the police to engage through the PREVENT agenda, it did appear to make communities less trusting and indeed provoked some into becoming more closed off.[29] The impact this potentially had on the state was profound. This is because part of the reason for continued Islamic self-disenfranchisement with regard to established political processes, and also for the justification for such community programmes, was a sense of victimisation by the state. Community-based projects, from the perception of the state and indeed many of the non-marginalised participants, were aimed at increasing awareness of mainstream Islamic thought and at identifying radicalisers, those who have been radicalised and those susceptible to radicalisation. However, one conclusion that may be drawn is that this process of community engagement also increased perceptions of alienation, by focusing primarily on those of Islamic faith and those irrevocably, rightly or wrongly, associating this religion with acts of terrorist violence. This increased and linked focus on Islam and terrorism may have increased the rhetoric that could be used by radicalisers. In essence, PREVENT focused more on the effectiveness of its implementation as opposed to how acceptable it was in terms of community perceptions.

Further criticism may be levelled at the funding arrangements for early PREVENT work. There appeared to be a disconnect between where investment was said to be going and where it actually went. In outlining this, it is clear that ascertaining exactly how much money was spent on United Kingdom counter-terrorism during this period is challenging, due to the dual purpose of many tools, techniques and/or programmes. For example, the Channel Project, although focused on identifying those vulnerable to radicalisation, had at its heart professionals, such as teachers and social workers, who simply looked for disturbing trends in young people and as such would identify many symptoms consistent with vulnerability.[30] It is possible to make a rough estimate of thinking on the importance of counter-radicalisation, based on available primary data. The last PREVENT strategy published under the then Labour government stated that in the financial year 2007 to 2008 approximately £6 million was spent on activities. Local authorities received anywhere from £15,000 to £500,000 to run PREVENT initiatives.[31] In the same period the Security and Intelligence Agencies[32] received approximately £1.4 billion.[33]

An unbalanced allocation of financial resources, that did not favour the PREVENT strand of CONTEST, potentially misses the point that some in law enforcement recognised. This was that if PREVENT was done correctly it reduced the need for the other strands. One possible consequence of reduced funding to the state was that the short-term gain in terms of pursuing those suspected of terrorist-related activity, or establishing physical barriers to terrorist violence, came at the expense of achieving the long-term goal of reducing the threat of terrorism to the United Kingdom by tackling the reasons for radicalisation.

Precisely what covers PREVENT, it is argued in PREVENT 2011, changed – significantly so with the transition from Labour to the Conservative-Liberal Democrat Coalition government. In 2008 PREVENT was broadly described as having the 'aim of stopping people becoming or supporting violent extremism'.[34] In 2011, PREVENT, the meaning of, was explicit: 'to stop people becoming terrorists or supporting terrorism'.[35] PREVENT, in essence, aims to engage with those individuals who have a low probability of committing terrorist violence but who have demonstrated a potential for it.

It was therefore against a backdrop of mistrust and confusion surrounding funding, aims and objectives that the Coalition government undertook a broader review of PREVENT and CONTEST. In addition to the publication of a new strategy, the review allowed for an analysis of PREVENT initiatives to date. This enabled the development and implementation of the new strategy to be based on fact as opposed to perception. The new PREVENT strategy was based on three objectives. The first objective was to respond to the ideological challenge. Previous PREVENT work had struggled to reach those most susceptible to radicalisation, due in part to a broad as opposed to a targeted approach. Indeed, work in this area had 'sometimes given the impression that Muslim communities as a whole [were] more "vulnerable" to radicalisation than other faith or ethnic groups'.[36] As a consequence, the new review sought to improve communication of the rationale behind government initiatives both at home and abroad. More projects in education, communities and the criminal justice system would be undertaken; and support would be given to experts to counter misinterpretations and/or representations of theology. The second objective centred on preventing people from being drawn into terrorism, by building on the Channel Project. The review noted that previously involvement by the police was perceived as being facilitated by such programmes, which were considered to be intrusive, resulting in disproportionate actions. The new PREVENT strategy would seek to make sure that programmes would 'pre-empt and not facilitate law enforcement activity'.[37] The third objective was a continuation and increase in intensity of work with sectors and institutions to prevent radicalisation. Radicalisation is a process as opposed to a single, specific event. Working with institutions, the 2011 strategy argues, can help identify and stop, at various points, this process. As such, priority areas included education, faith, health, criminal justice, charities and the internet.

The delivery of PREVENT would no longer be based on demographics. It would instead be based on 'different information and policing indicators of terrorist activity'.[38] The new strategy allocated funding for PREVENT programmes based on police indicators of where the threat of terrorism was most likely to come from. It is not clear, therefore, where the difference in terms of the areas in which funding was allocated to lay, since both funding arrangements were based on perception as well as closed and open source intelligence estimates.

This particular point also highlights another glaring contradiction within this review. PREVENT 2011 went to great lengths to state that it was not a policing programme – rather, the police were stakeholders within the PREVENT strategy – but that the allocation of funding was based on police indicators of terrorist activity. So perhaps more so now even than previously, PREVENT is about preventative police work.

The theory behind community engagement programmes, such as the Channel or Black Country Imams Project, was to fit in with the police's ethos of being a preventative in addition to being a responsive service, as noted in the Metropolitan Police Service Statement of Purpose discussed previously. As Pratt and Brook note, engaging in the community in a social as opposed to a law enforcement manner was considered critical to this remit. This view was not reflected in the limited funding arrangements for this particular strand of the United Kingdom's counter-terrorism strategy and as such hindered law enforcement's approach to countering the threat of radicalisation and more broadly of terrorism.[39]

In addition to the aforementioned discussion regarding perceptions associated with community engagement projects and also the disproportionate lack of funding for such ventures and the impact this had, particularly with regard to perceptions of targeting Muslims, other concerns became apparent. It is important to note that counter-radicalisation projects depend on trust and understanding between those in authority and the local population.[40] Members of the community needed to feel that, should they approach the police or other counter-terrorism agencies with information relating to suspicious activity, this information would be investigated in a fair and proportionate manner.[41] Further, a level of fairness was needed more broadly in implementing counter-terrorism initiatives.

This perception of fairness was significantly undermined following the introduction of stop-and-search powers. Part five, section 44 of the Terrorist Act, 2000 provided authorisation for uniformed officers to stop and search vehicles, individuals and their belongings in designated areas if the person initiating the search 'considers it expedient for the prevention of acts of terrorism'.[42] Lord Carlile stated at a conference, in April 2010, that up until 2009, 156,000 people had been stopped in the London area alone, while 180 had been stopped in Scotland during the same period.[43] Hewitt quotes the Metropolitan Police Authority who note that in the first six months of 2006, 22,700 stops occurred which led to twenty-seven terrorist-related arrests and that the programme was 'doing "untold damage" to community relations and also to perceptions of the police'.[44] The perceptions of victimisation, or deliberate targeting through the use of section 44, were compounded by Home Office Minister (with responsibility for crime reduction, counter-terrorism and policing) Hazel Blears' 2005 comments that as the threat from terrorism is associated with Islam, 'some of our counter-terrorism powers will be disproportionately experienced by the Muslim community'.[45]

One law enforcement observation is that counter-terrorism activity should be conducted in a just and cordial manner. The use of techniques that appear unfair inevitably provokes those susceptible to radicalisation into becoming practitioners of terrorist violence. This clearly has an impact on the state, which has opted for short-term effectiveness even if this is questionably acceptable. The argument is not that the United Kingdom should abandon counter-terrorism measures, but that their presentation and indeed usefulness should be re-evaluated. For instance, in the argument surrounding the extension of pre-charge detention, the rhetoric could have been framed so as to take into account all serious crimes, not just terrorism, thus underscoring the police's desire to see terrorism in the same frame as other types of *ordinary* crime.[46] This perception of deliberate targeting resulted in reduced trust and cooperation between members of the community and the police.

Four key points stand out, all of which, as Peter Clarke, former Metropolitan Counter-Terrorism Commander, stated, suggest the presence of a 'deficit of trust' between law enforcement and segments of the population.[47] First, funding for PREVENT initiatives was originally based on demographics. This increased feelings of political disenfranchisement and perceptions of victimisation. This leads on to the second point. Perceptions of alienation were exacerbated by the perceived targeting of individuals based on ethnicity and creed. Third, poor funding arrangements meant that in contrast to other strands of the United

Kingdom's counter-terrorism strategy, PREVENT was receiving comparatively little funding. Finally, trust in PREVENT was lacking. Individuals needed to feel that if they were to report something of a suspect nature to law enforcement, this would be investigated in a fair and proportionate manner.

The role of the police, as discussed above, is in part preventative, but also highly responsive to events. One of the biggest criticisms faced by the United Kingdom's law enforcement agencies has been the lack of a single, unified lead for terrorist-related investigations.[48] When considering the structure and function of law enforcement it is necessary to note that the United Kingdom still does not have a wholly national police force similar to the United States' FBI.

Police forces in the United Kingdom are geographically bound, in that they operate within specific territorial areas. There were forty-three police forces by the end of 2009, each governed by a policing authority.[49] When considering arrest powers, it is interesting that in addition to the constabularies that were tied to specific geographic areas, for example, Greater Manchester Constabulary and South Yorkshire Constabulary, the United Kingdom had a number of smaller non-territorial police forces. These included British Transport Police; Central Motorway Policing Group; Civil Nuclear Constabulary (formerly United Kingdom Atomic Energy Authority Constabulary); the Ministry of Defence Police; Port of Dover Police; Port of Liverpool Police; The Serious Organised Crime Agency; and Scottish Drug Enforcement Agency.[50] All but the last had arrest powers that cut right the way across the United Kingdom's territory but were, in other ways, restricted in what they could investigate.[51] For instance, the Civilian Nuclear Police Constabulary could undertake investigations, or arrests, away from nuclear facilities so long as it was related to their speciality – nuclear issues. The Ministry of Defence Police who presented themselves as 'the United Kingdom's only truly national police force' were different in that they could invoke powers of arrest in the United Kingdom without territorial restriction or specific specialisation.[52] However, during this period the Ministry of Defence Police were not structured in such a manner as to form a viable, national, counter-terrorism policing entity.

The primary counter-terrorism law enforcement agency in the United Kingdom is the Metropolitan Police Service' Counter-Terrorism Command (CTC, also known as SO15). The Metropolitan Police Service CTC was established on 2 October 2006 through the merging of Special Branch and the Anti-Terrorism Branch. The CTC has various responsibilities relating to terrorism within London and throughout the United Kingdom. These responsibilities are, however, with regard to coordination only and as such lack the power to instruct other police forces on how to conduct operations.[53] The West Midlands Police Constabulary and Greater Manchester Police Constabulary also have their own CTCs to supplement the work of the Metropolitan Police Service.

Former Assistant Commissioner in charge of Specialist Operations for the Metropolitan Police Service, with counter-terrorism responsibilities, Andy Hayman (2002–2005), said that the United Kingdom police structure meant that the Metropolitan Police Service CTC was dependent upon the 'goodwill' of other forces.[54] They cannot force other constabularies to abide by the decisions of the Metropolitan Police Service CTC. Furthermore, independence of other forces can sometimes prove detrimental during fast-moving pursuits. For example, in July 2007 a car was discovered in central London and later found to contain explosives.[55] Specialist firearms units were needed in the pursuit of suspects which left the jurisdiction of the Metropolitan Police Service and ended a day later in Cheshire. Hayman noted that even at this time prior authorisation was needed, before the units in pursuit could continue through other jurisdictions with their firearms.

The lack of a single police lead that could instruct, rather than request, measures by other forces impacted upon the United Kingdom's ability to pursue and apprehend those suspected of terrorist-related activity. This is because within the United Kingdom the police have the operational lead in countering the threat of terrorism. In practice this means that they are responsible for pursuing those suspected of planning, or who have undertaken, acts of terrorism. In fast-paced pursuits, such as the one outlined above, the lack of central control reduces the ability of police forces to undertake these duties across territorial boundaries. Although the actual potential of a suspect being lost, or missed, due to this is limited, it may, in times when the police require coordination across boundaries, prove an additional hurdle in countering the threat of terrorism and so increase the threat to the state.

The United Kingdom's law enforcement agencies were, it should be noted, faced with threats that they were not accustomed to, including suicide bombers and fast-paced pursuits associated with failed attacks, as demonstrated by the attempted terrorist attacks in London on 21 July 2005. The responses, such as stop-and-search and extension of pre-charge detention, were viewed as controversial.

The increasing intelligence role of the police, Jackson argues, is relatively new to law enforcement within the United Kingdom.[56] Traditionally, intelligence was passed by the Security Service to the Police as and when required. Although police forces had their own, basic intelligence capabilities the Security Service was clearly the lead in this area. A notable exception to this is Northern Ireland. This is because up until the late 1960s intelligence in Northern Ireland was gathered by the police force there. The quality of that intelligence was so low, however, that when the Army took over law enforcement duties in 1969 they had to establish their own intelligence network.[57] This highlights the inherent difficulties the police faced not just in the United Kingdom, as will be considered further, but also in the United States, when trying to simultaneously act as a policing and intelligence-gathering body. With the development of transnational terrorism and the transition, at the institutional level, from a police- to an intelligence-led approach, it would be reasonable to assume that intelligence gathering was firmly out of the police's purview. This was not the case.

As Hoffman suggests, both in the United Kingdom and United States the police were increasingly developing viable and sustainable intelligence capabilities that operated independently from national intelligence-gathering agencies.[58] Within the United Kingdom, the intelligence capabilities of individual police constabularies, although able to work independently, operated closely with the Security and Intelligence Agencies through mechanisms such as the Joint Intelligence Committee. This allowed the police, who worked nearer to local communities, to develop broader responses to threats that presented themselves. This potentially improved community relations and by extension facilitated the provision of intelligence so as to aid the state as a whole in countering the threat of transnational terrorism.

It has been pointed out already that community engagement programmes and stop-and-search legislation created the perception that the police, representatives of the state, were deliberately targeting Muslims. Such perceptions, as was illustrated, were further compounded by the revelation that some community engagement programmes appeared to have had their funding decided based on the population of the local Muslim community. This had a negative impact on the implementation of the PREVENT strand of CONTEST and, along with other measures, such as stop-and-search, led to a further disenfranchisement of sympathisers of terrorist causes.

The drawbacks and distinct problems in communicating the purpose of what amounted to counter-radicalisation programmes led to many of the problems they encountered. However, both Pratt and Brook conclude that, on balance, intelligence, whether through such programmes or not, did improve in the aftermath of 9/11.[59] This improvement in the garnering of intelligence from different communities in all likelihood aided in reducing the threat of terrorism to the state. This would have been done by helping the state, through the police, to identify individuals or groups who might be susceptible to radicalisation and as such to terrorist-related activity, particularly violence. It is interesting to note that Pratt considered PREVENT to be about educating, albeit not necessarily through formal training courses, the general public about terrorism, radicalisation and how to counter them.[60]

Having discussed the relationship between intelligence and law enforcement it is necessary, at this juncture, to discuss the relationship between the latter and the Armed Forces. After 9/11, significant debate involving law enforcement and military force occurred within the context of capabilities – what the police and the Armed Forces were able to do.[61] There were two features of this discussion: augmentation and niche.[62] Niche capabilities may be described as those that are deployable only by the Armed Forces due to their specialist training or capabilities, such as aircraft interception, typically undertaken when an aircraft enters United Kingdom airspace and does not identify itself. Augmentation refers to the substantial number of quickly deployable troops that the Armed Forces can deliver in times of need. While this is not their primary function, the fact that they retain the numbers and a rapid deployment capability means that they can provide the obvious reserves when required.[63]

The 2001 bout of foot-and-mouth disease that swept the United Kingdom and involved the deployment of the Armed Forces brought to the attention of the United Kingdom government that the Ministry of Defence had a lot of trained manpower and logistical expertise and that a structure needed to be developed that planned for civil-military operations. The Joint Doctrine Publication, as is discussed later, formed the foundation of the relationship between the police and the Armed Forces.[64]

In evidence given to the House of Commons Defence Committee a diagram highlighted the changing relationship between the civilian sector and military forces.[65] It was this model and thinking that informed both sides of the debate regarding whether law enforcement and the civilian sector, more broadly, should retain more of those capabilities currently tasked to the military, through a process known as *pull-through*.[66] The term 'pull-through' was used in the Defence Contribution to United Kingdom National and Security Resilience published by the Committee in 2009. It describes the process through which technologies and tactics that were previously undertaken by the military have moved into the civilian sector.[67] The report suggests that this pull-through occurred because military commitments meant that assets were not always available. Consequentially a duplication of functions was necessitated.[68]

The kinds of functions that were duplicated included bomb disposal, explosive rapid entry and the ability to board suspect ships. In his evidence to the Committee, Chief Constable Hogan-Howe stated that the pull-through of these capabilities did not signify a full-scale retention of any specific niche capabilities by the police. Hogan-Howe, using explosive rapid entry as an example, made a distinction between terrorist and criminal activity. The police, he stated, were capable of dealing with criminal threats or violence that required rapid, explosive entry. The police, however, fell back on the military when it came to dealing with terrorists, due to their specialist training.[69] Furthermore, the provision of Standing Home Commitments, discussed in Chapter 5, meant that military assets for situations requiring specialist expertise were always available in the United Kingdom.[70]

The police had developed the ability to deal with incendiary devices of a type commonly used in Northern Ireland and were also able to undertake explosive rapid entry.[71] This is certainly the case in the capital, where the CTC, among other duties, provide 'an explosive ordnance disposal and CBRN [Chemical, Biological, Radiological and Nuclear] capability in London'.[72] An anonymous source, Mercer and Brook[73] acknowledging that this had occurred, took the view that this was not needed.[74] Mercer emphasises the roles played by the Special Boat Section, Special Air Service and the less publicly acknowledged Special Reconnaissance Regiment which all provide counter-terrorism capabilities.[75] As such, they argue that there has been no real need post-9/11 to increase the ability of the police, in terms of specialist niche capabilities, beyond that already in place.

The relationship between law enforcement and the Armed Forces was of a good standard during this period and indeed may have been considered to have improved in recent years.[76] In spite of the increased niche capability that emerged with regard to bomb disposal within the Metropolitan Police Service, there appeared to be no broad acceptance that the police needed to widen their specialist capabilities. One source commented that there were always going to be assets that the Ministry of Defence retained within the territorial boundaries of the United Kingdom at a heightened state of readiness, despite commitments overseas.[77] It should also be noted that requests for niche capabilities are relatively infrequent and as such sustainable. This also means, as will be considered later, that the Armed Forces avoid having control or responsibility in domestic counter-terrorism actions.[78]

Another reason for the continued beneficial relationship between the police and the Armed Forces is the presence of Joint Regional Liaison Officers (or Liaison Officers). These facilitate the continued development of improved communication and collaboration between the police and the Armed Forces (Figure 4.1).

In order to maintain a consistent relationship between the Armed Forces and key partners such as law enforcement, military Joint Regional Liaison Officers exist in each area of the Army Regional Command Structure. These Liaison Officers were supported by Single Service Liaison Officers who represented each of the three Armed Forces. Furthermore, Joint Regional Liaison Officers in remote areas have other Military Liaison Officers.[79] The role of Joint Regional Liaison Officers is to interact with all partners (not only the police) with whom they would need to work in the event of an emergency.[80]

Liaison Officers help to provide a constant stream of communications between the Armed Forces and other agencies, particularly the police and Fire and Rescue Services. They assist in the solidification of policies and processes, particularly in the area of command and control, and provision of information regarding the amount and availability of assets and capabilities. It is worth remembering that '[a] core principle of the Police command chain, is that the Police are operationally independent of Government (a position diametrically opposed to that of the Armed Forces for whom an operation must be approved by a Defence Minister)'.[81]

This ties in with a condition of the provision of military aid to the civilian authority being that civilian authorities retained control of and responsibility for any deployment. Knowledge of what is happening on the intelligence front is also secured by there being a representative from the Ministry of Defence on the Joint Intelligence Committee.[82] Traditionally, this representative is the Chief of Defence Intelligence.[83] These additional factors impacted upon the nature of the

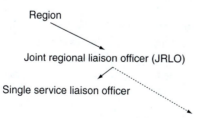

Figure 4.1 Liaison officers.

relationship between law enforcement and military force due to the increased capability it provided the state in countering those who threaten or undertake transnational terrorism.

Law enforcement and the United States: a qualitative assessment

Law enforcement jurisdiction and responsibilities have always been a complicated and vast affair in the United States.[84] The primary reason for this is that the structure of the United States is based on the idea that each of the fifty states (e.g. Alabama, South Carolina, Ohio) are independent and come together in a union. Consequentially each state, in theory, has its own Armed Force (National Guard) and a series of law enforcement agencies that are answerable to the Governor of that particular state.[85] This means that there are at least 18,000 law enforcement agencies spread throughout the United States.[86] These range from State Troopers, Highway Patrols, Metropolitan Police, through to City Police and Sheriffs' departments. Furthermore, a number of federal law enforcement agencies operate nationally but are, due to restrictions imposed by the United States Constitution, limited or constrained in the manner in which they can intervene in state affairs.

The Department of Justice is perhaps the largest law enforcement agency at the federal level, incorporating the FBI; Drug Enforcement Administration; Bureau of Alcohol, Tobacco, Firearms and Explosives; and the United States Marshal Service. This is closely followed by the Department of Homeland Security, which has under its administration Customs and Border Protection; Immigration and Customs Enforcement; United States Secret Service; and Transportation Security Administration. Most states have a State Police Force. There may also be capital police, local Sheriffs or county law enforcement departments. This is by no means an exhaustive list.

When assessing, side-by-side, the law enforcement capabilities of the United Kingdom and United States one overarching observation can be made. Within the United States context, little changed in the first decade after 9/11. As argued earlier, this was because in the early post-9/11 years, counter-terrorism was largely seen as about military deployments and border control. In essence, the threat from the perspective of the United States was an existential one. McMillan, formally of the National Defense University and, shortly after interview, Principal Deputy Assistant Secretary of Defense for International Security Affairs within the Obama administration, stated his belief that *home-grown* transnational terrorists were not a problem that existed in the United States.[87] By late 2009, as Hoffman noted, this view was beginning to change.[88]

The multiple tasks that law enforcement agencies are expected to undertake are in many respects what distinguish them from the Armed Forces. The Armed Forces are either preparing to execute (i.e. training) or executing (i.e. undertaking an action). These two roles generally do not run consecutively. One would end before the next began. On the other hand, law enforcement has multiple roles, some of them simultaneous commitments.[89] The main roles include the following:

1   Executing Statutory Obligations.

   a A twenty-four hour, seven days per week commitment to protect and serve citizenry within a specific geographically bound jurisdiction.

2   Preparing to Execute Contingent Capabilities.

   a Developing contingent capabilities.
   b Considering contingent factors.

3   When Required: Executing Contingent Capabilities.

   a Fulfil demand by executing contingent capabilities, while continuing to execute statutory obligations (point 1).[90]

Point 2 is further complicated by the need to continue with point 1 while committing personnel for training exercises. The problem that remains unresolved is the dual requirement that law enforcement agencies undertake routine duties while simultaneously preparing for other eventualities, or contingent demands. This results in fewer personnel being available for training and preparation for contingent demands.

So the police, whose primary overarching duty is to provide continuous law enforcement capabilities, struggle to simultaneously provide constant training in preparation for terrorist attacks. By extension, this inability hampers the ability of the state not just to introduce new technologies, but to maintain a constant number of personnel trained in their use.

In order to cater for this, a number of federal programmes reached fruition. One of these initiatives is the Commercial Equipment Direct Assistance Program (CEDAP) which was developed by the National Preparedness Directorate within the Department of Homeland Security.[91] The purpose of the CEDAP is to provide additional funding 'to enhance regional response capabilities, mutual aid, interoperable communications by providing technology and equipment, along with the training required to operate that equipment'.[92] This programme focused on both law enforcement and non-law enforcement agencies that serve a population of under 50,000.[93] In the 2007 to 2008 financial year the budget for the CEDAP was US$17.6 million. From this, 3,573 applications were made, 1,045 were accepted and of those, 830 were from law enforcement agencies.[94] Some of the equipment purchased through the CEDAP included fifteen gas and vapour detection kits and 216 night-vision goggles.

Two distinct views exist regarding the usefulness of such programmes. The first view, similar to the saturation of technologies when considering the contribution of intelligence, is that there was too much purchasing, especially of detection equipment.[95] Having a radiation detector at every metro stop and outside every key building is a waste, one interviewee stated.[96] By the time a device gets that close, serious casualties should be expected wherever detonation occurs.[97]

The second view relates to the issue of training and an associated presence of significant shortcomings regarding the provision of training during this period.

Ross and an anonymous source believe that during this period training was too limited.[98] They argue that the provision of funding was primarily for the purchasing of equipment and not for the training needed to use it. This view contrasts with Gruber, who believes that federal authorities had always been 'very attentive to the fact that [...] it's inappropriate to give somebody a piece of equipment or technology and not provide them with training'.[99] In February 2009 there were sixty-four training institutions offering approximately 600 courses.[100] Indeed, the necessity of providing funding for training as well as equipment could be seen in the CEDAP literature, which highlighted the provision of finance to train individuals on equipment purchased.[101]

These two positions are reconciled by taking a long-term view. Funding for training on these courses is available, as Jackson from the United States-based Homeland Security Program at the RAND Corporation states, only for a set period.[102] Frequently the case was that finance was provided for the initial two to three years immediately after purchase. After that period, agencies either had to find room in their budgets or allow equipment to become obsolete.[103]

Another problem was choosing where to deploy the technology that was purchased. Technology, in the aftermath of 9/11, was seen as a quick way of boosting security. The reality, as many of the interviewees pointed out, was that this provided a visible indication to the general public that security had increased, but was in fact less effective than portrayed. Placing a machine capable of picking up nuclear devices outside Congress, said former United States Air Force Colonel Larsen, Director of the Washington, DC-based Institute for Homeland Security, was redundant due to the extent of the damage likely to be caused by the proximity of any form of detonation.[104]

A second problem that existed regarding equipment and training was with the training provided. The police, it was suggested earlier in this chapter, had problems in simultaneously providing the statutory obligation of continuous law enforcement and attending training for new technologies. Furthermore, the structure of the police meant that staff trained in specific technologies frequently moved on to other positions, necessitating further training for their replacements. Moreover, as noted here, it seems that funding for training in new technologies ceased, after a relatively short period, to be provided by the federal government, placing financial responsibility on police departments, some of which could not meet the costs. One consequence of this was that either training that could aid in countering the threat of transnational terrorism did not occur, leaving equipment idle, or new innovations were not introduced due to problems with meeting financial responsibilities.[105] This, of course, was not always the case. Major hubs, such as the New York City Police Department, had a lot of financial resources, so that their law enforcement capabilities and indeed their intelligence assessments were on a par with national agencies.

Explaining the above involves the adoption of one of two positions. Either the state saw the defeat of terrorism as achievable in a short time frame or, perhaps more likely, perceived the threat to the state originating outside United States territorial boundaries. The latter would therefore explain the heavy investment in military solutions and border controls. Either way, the provision of funding for equipment and training in the short term gave the impression that law enforcement within the United States was not considered to be a critical partner in countering the threat of transnational terrorism in the long term. Beyond issues relating to equipment and training it is important to note that law enforcement officers were of the opinion that terrorism should be framed as a form of 'ordinary' crime.[106] This view was not meant to imply that law enforcement did not need to adjust in order to meet this new threat both in the adoption of new laws and techniques.

Changes were identified as being required in the relationships between law enforcement and other agencies in the federal system. Relationships post-9/11 changed significantly at two levels. The first level was within states and localities, due to the development and proliferation of the idea of Fusion Centers discussed further in this chapter. The second level was perhaps more pertinent and was that of a relationship alteration between law enforcement at the state, local and tribal levels and federal intelligence agencies.[107] The role of the Department of Homeland Security, through the Office of Intelligence and Analysis, in disseminating pertinent intelligence to agencies and law enforcement officials has already been considered. It is worth reiterating, at this stage, that the Department of Homeland Security saw one of its roles as being the provider of a link between the intelligence world and that of law enforcement.

Officials in the Department of Homeland Security believed that they could facilitate the sharing of intelligence from the former to the latter.[108] This had been identified as an area of significant concern by the *9/11 Commission Report* and as such was seen as one of the primary functions of the Office of Intelligence and Analysis.[109] By 2009, this objective of the Department of Homeland Security was not realised, as significant problems regarding the quality of the intelligence existed. Problems included evidence not being written in a format that helped law enforcement officials and intelligence that did not provide enough information, arrived too late and no feedback being forwarded regarding the quality of information passed up to the Department of Homeland Security.[110]

Law enforcement agencies and, by extension the state, were hindered in their ability to provide broad protective measures against the threat of transnational terrorism. Relationships between the police and other federal agencies, such as the Department of Homeland Security, were considered essential in the early years post-9/11. Relationships were improving since the criticisms of the *9/11 Commission Report* were made public, but still had significant problems.[111]

Law enforcement agencies were also under no obligation to purchase or operate compatible equipment, such as radios, that facilitated communication with other agencies/departments. This meant, as Jackson notes, that law enforcement agents in one jurisdiction could not always communicate with others in an adjacent one.[112] This, historically speaking, had not been a problem. Rarely did a jurisdiction need to communicate with others in a fashion that was not prearranged. Problems arose when unforeseen large-scale events (such as 9/11) or even predicted but underappreciated ones (such as Hurricane Katrina[113]) occurred, necessitating a wide, coordinated response that overlapped jurisdictions.[114] Federal programmes during this period operated, effectively, to bridge these communication gaps.

It is important to note that, similar to the United Kingdom, law enforcement officials were partial to framing terrorism in a manner conducive to prosecution.[115] Creating a distinction between terrorist acts and other crimes that may be considered 'ordinary' led to many of the problems that the United States faced with regard to international law – particularly with reference to the detention of prisoners.[116] Indeed, conceptualising terrorism as a form of *ordinary* crime does make the possibility of a prosecution more feasible. This, however, was not a universally accepted view and a lack of clarity as to whether terrorism should be considered an ordinary crime, or an act of war, existed and indeed continues to exist within the United States.[117]

Following the 9/11 attacks the primary method of response, as aptly demonstrated by the action undertaken in Afghanistan, was military force; whereas the traditional counter-terrorism policy instrument was law enforcement for which the FBI had the lead, both domestically and internationally.[118] Indeed, the phrasing of the response as a 'War' by senior members of the George W. Bush administration was indicative of a re-categorisation of terrorism, away from the traditional law enforcement conceptualisation to that of a more military-based one.[119]

McMillan, in acknowledging that this occurred, supports the notion that this brand of terrorism should not be considered a law enforcement issue.[120] A strong, tough response, he argues, was the best way forward as a means of demonstrating the United States' determination to prevent such acts from occurring in the future.[121] The question of whether to consider terrorist-related activity as an ordinary crime or an act of war had significant repercussions for how the United States responded to the threat. Considering, as it did in the international domain, terrorism as an act of war inevitably led to a military response. Domestically, the situation was more complicated, as the Posse Comitatus Act prohibits the domestic deployment of armed personnel.[122]

Law enforcement, as McMillan points out, traditionally has the lead in this area.[123] The after-the-fact methodology under which they operated meant that law enforcement agencies, particularly from the FBI under the Department of Justice, were in a good position to investigate, charge and prosecute perpetrators. Discussion in this category needs to be broken into two components. First is the identification or apprehension of those caught or interdicted in the preparatory phase of a terrorist attack. Law enforcement was required to increase its abilities in this regard. This increase involved the application of broad techniques, such as scanners, to detect suspects, and an increase in intelligence. In order to achieve this, agencies, such as the Office of Intelligence and Analysis and the Interagency Threat Assessment and Coordination Group (ITACG), were established to facilitate the sharing of intelligence between the Intelligence Community and law enforcement agencies. These agencies did not reach the ideal as required by law enforcement. The second component is the apprehension and identification of those who have committed acts of terror. The belief that transnational terrorists were a foreign problem with them interdicting United States territory underscored the notion that it was the role of the Armed Forces, primarily, to identify, capture or kill those considered to have perpetrated acts of terrorist violence. The United States law enforcement does still have a role, particularly in the identification phase, but as was seen by the process of extra-ordinary rendition and internment without trial at Guantánamo Bay, the operational level requirements shifted to an Armed Forces response.

The perception that transnational terrorist-related activity was beyond the capabilities incumbent upon the traditional purview of law enforcement and was considered to be related to war served, primarily, to facilitate the transition of sympathisers of terrorist causes towards becoming practitioners of violence. In considering the countering of transnational terrorism as a role for the Armed Forces, the state was not only aiding the rhetoric used to encourage sympathisers of terrorist causes into practitioners of violence, but was also suggesting that this form of violence was beyond the traditional law enforcement capabilities of the state. Put another way, the state could not provide security through normal means and so was resorting to extra-ordinary measures. This was particularly so due to the seemingly disproportionate responses, particularly with regard to internment at Guantánamo Bay, authorised by the United States government.

Debate during this period focused very much on the role of law enforcement which had traditionally formed the operational and tactical response lead with regard to acts of domestic terrorism; and indeed where acts were undertaken abroad, the FBI's statutory authority meant that they also took the lead here. The FBI's role as lead investigative counter-terrorism agency for the United States originates from the signing of National Security Decision Directive No. 30 by United States President Ronald Reagan on 10 April 1982.[124] Their role, both domestically and internationally, is further solidified in the United States Code which states that through the Attorney General the FBI will have 'primary investigative responsibility for all Federal crimes of terrorism'.[125] The 9/11 terrorist attacks, as discussed below, spurred a reorientation of law enforcement. Where the function of law enforcement had been to investigate crimes in an after-the-fact manner, Mueller (Director of the FBI, 4 September 2001 to the present) and other commentators believed that law enforcement needed to adopt more of a preventative, intelligence-led approach.[126] This idea was supported in favour of the establishment of a domestic intelligence agency similar to that of the United Kingdom's Security Service.[127]

The United States' counter-terrorism strategy following 9/11 made note of the contribution of law enforcement: 'Not only do we employ military power, we use diplomatic, financial, intelligence, and law enforcement activities to protect the Homeland and extend our defences, disrupt terrorist operations, and deprive our enemies of what they need to operate and survive.'[128] The emphasis on law enforcement being used to protect the *homeland* was an indicator that counter-terrorism activity abroad would continue, in the post-9/11 era, to be led by the Armed Forces.[129]

The discussions regarding the role of the FBI in the period following 9/11 were significant, but also indicative of a level of uncertainty regarding the FBI's role in countering the transnational threat of terrorism. McMillan has argued that a law enforcement approach to countering the threat of transnational terrorism was insufficient and that the inability of law enforcement to deal with this had been evidenced by the failure to prevent the events of 9/11.[130] McMillan's argument centres on the belief that by and large law enforcement's role was reactive – occurring after events had taken place.[131] Pratt and Brook point out that law enforcement in the United Kingdom has a preventative function that allowed the police to intervene and, through the Crown Prosecution Service, to prosecute actions that were of a preparatory nature.[132] The same certainly applied to the United States context. However, in the United States it was seen that in terms of prevention, law enforcement was unable to act independently of other agencies, specifically intelligence and as such, due to the need to liaise with other agencies, was treated as a secondary consideration.[133]

Furthermore, the benefit of having an effective, retributive entity was not always realised. Indeed, one day after 9/11 Larsen attended a meeting at the White House. In attendance was the President, George W. Bush, and the Director of the FBI, Mueller, told the President that they were going to find the people who had committed the 9/11 attacks. President George W. Bush's response was: 'They're all dead. They flew airplanes into buildings and into the ground.'[134] While that was true, the investigative elements of the FBI and the prosecutorial role of the Department of Justice could have brought justice to financers or supporters of transnational terrorism.[135] The role of the FBI prior to 9/11 was 'devoted to after-the-fact investigations of major terrorist attacks in order to develop criminal cases' – a purpose or function that was considered to have been a contributing factor to the failure of the wider Intelligence Community to identify the 9/11 threat.[136]

If a distinction is to be made, therefore, between intelligence-led and law enforcement-led approaches and, further, if this is to be based on their statutory duties, then the following observation can be made. An intelligence-led approach, in the United States, to countering the threat of terrorism aimed primarily to find out about specific events in advance and notify those agencies capable of undertaking actions to ensure the security of the population. In contrast, while prevention, in the United States context, is ideal where law enforcement is concerned, the fact of the matter is that few law enforcement agencies had the means, mechanisms or finances to take on a preventative and inherently intelligence-led approach.[137] As such, law enforcement was primarily responsive to events.

What the United States needed was a domestic intelligence agency similar to the United Kingdom's Security Service – a topic discussed extensively during the 9/11 Commission.[138] Mueller argued forcefully against the idea of establishing a new domestic intelligence service. He believed that it would take a significant amount of time to set up a new intelligence agency and get it operating efficiently. What Mueller suggested, and was later adopted, was the rapid expansion of the intelligence function within the FBI – 'an agency within an agency'.[139]

Three years after the 9/11 attacks, Mueller noted the following in relation to the development of an intelligence-gathering function within the FBI: 'To the question of whether the FBI now has a fully-matured intelligence apparatus in place, the answer is that we have laid the structural foundation, and are developing the intelligence personnel and the capacities at a steady pace.'[140] By 2009, Larsen, who had originally accepted Mueller's argument for an agency within an agency, considered the FBI's attempt to adopt an additional role of intelligence collector to have failed.[141]

The United States, therefore, lacked a single intelligence-gathering agency and instead depended on law enforcement agencies that were answerable to the governors of each of the fifty states. This provided a lack of coherence in what was needed – a unified counter-terrorism approach. The decision by the FBI to try to adopt an intelligence capability, in addition to their law enforcement obligations, was understandable – especially as their authority was not restricted by state boundaries. The inability of the FBI to create a viable intelligence capability was a significant problem for the United States as a whole. This is despite the predominant view that they did not face a *home-grown* threat on a par with that experienced throughout Europe. It remained a significant problem, as the *9/11 Commission Report* noted in 2004, that it was not only a lack of intelligence sharing but also of intelligence gathering which led to the perpetrators managing to carry out acts of terrorism on 9/11.[142]

In addition to the FBI, discussed above, another federal organisation that has not yet been discussed, but that plays a crucial counter-terrorism role, is the National Counterterrorism Center.[143] The National Counterterrorism Center is made up of personnel from a number of different agencies of the Intelligence Community. A large part of United States intelligence sharing was organised horizontally and not vertically down to law enforcement organisations. Horizontal intelligence sharing, as in the purview of the National Counterterrorism Center, was considered a success.[144]

It was originally envisaged that the Department of Homeland Security, through the Office of Intelligence and Analysis, would assume this role, and indeed it continued to attempt to get into this area following the creation of the National Counterterrorism Center, which saw intelligence analysis as one of its specialist areas.[145] Recognising that the absence of a permanent state, local and tribal enforcement representation at the National Counterterrorism Center was detrimental to countering the threat domestically, the ITACG was established. The basis of the ITACG's legal authority came from the 2007 publication regarding the implementation of the *9/11 Commission Report* recommendations, which stated its purposes as being the establishment of a:

> Detail comprised of State, [L]ocal, and [T]ribal homeland security and law enforcement officers and intelligence analysts detailed to work in the National Counterterrorism Center with Federal intelligence analysts for the purpose of integrating, analysing, and assisting in the dissemination of federally-coordinated information within the scope of the information

sharing environment, including homeland security information, terrorism information, and weapons of mass destruction information, through appropriate channels identified by the ITACG Advisory Council.[146]

The idea for the ITACG was based on the United Kingdom's Police International Counter Terrorism Unit (also known as PICTU). This Unit, in conjunction with the United Kingdom's Joint Terrorism Analysis Centre, successfully established a 'process by which highly classified intelligence information is converted to a law enforcement sensitive-type format that could be widely disseminated to Officers to support both threat assessment and prevention planning'.[147] A proposal for a Vertical Intelligence Terrorism Analysis Link (VITAL) in the United States, as the ITACG Detail,[148] was adopted and situated within the National Counterterrorism Center.[149] One key problem in implementing the ITACG idea is similar to that discussed earlier regarding training in new technologies.

Secondments to the National Counterterrorism Center were often brief – six to twelve months in length – as the National Counterterrorism Center and, by extension the ITACG, was established with the broader notion of improving relationships between different agencies. Such short stints proved to be problematic. This, however, was noticed and ideas that were being tabled in 2009 centred on two areas. The first area was the provision of an online forum where officials could remain in touch. The second was in the development of a staggered rotation scheme, so that an overlap existed making the transition and indeed development of new relationships more seamless.[150] The long-term success of the ITACG is unknown but it is believed to be working well.[151]

One of the largest complaints levelled at the Office of Intelligence and Analysis was centred on the format of the information disseminated downwards. The mere fact that the ITACG was staffed by state and local law enforcement representatives, operating in conjunction with the Intelligence Community, increased its chances of successful approval from law enforcement officers.[152] This may be considered beneficial to the state insofar as it aided the wider dissemination of data to state and local law enforcement officials, and therefore increased the likelihood that terrorist attacks would be identified and thwarted early on.

The improved information sharing within the United States was not restricted to the dissemination of data from intelligence agencies. The creation, by law enforcement agencies, of Fusion Centers was also beneficial. In the aftermath of 9/11 one of the biggest concerns regarding law enforcement was over the ability to access and share intelligence and other information among agencies. In order to address this, in 2004 the State of Maryland established the first Coordination and Analysis Center, more commonly known as a Fusion Center.[153] A Fusion Center may be defined as a 'collaborative effort of two or more agencies that provide resources, expertise and information to the Centre with the goal of maximizing their ability to detect, prevent, investigate, and respond to criminal and terrorist activity'.[154]

By the time Kaplan wrote about them in February 2007, forty-two Fusion Centers were operating across the United States.[155] Kaplan stated that Fusion

Centers were 'designed to pool and analyse information from federal, [S]tate, and local sources in an effort to get vital information to the police officers who every day patrol on the home front of the "War on terror"'.[156] Although variations existed between different states' Fusion Centers, their basic task was to pool information and intelligence in one location so that analysts could look for suspect patterns and act in a way to either prevent crime, or terrorism, or facilitate investigations.

Members of Fusion Centers included state law enforcement, public health, social services, public safety and public works organisations. It is important to note that this initiative was not, at the state level and below, targeted exclusively at terrorist-related crimes. Indeed, as Gruber indicates, the primary intention of these Centers was simply to pool information in order to prevent crime or assist in investigations.[157]

Federal input into the state initiative of Fusion Centers really gained standing in February 2007 with the joint Department of Homeland Security–Department of Justice publication of nationally applicable guidelines.[158] These guidelines, along with the secondment of representatives from the Department of Homeland Security, the FBI, the Drug Enforcement Administration and the Bureau of Alcohol, Tobacco, Firearms and Explosives to Fusion Centers, brought an added bonus of inter-state coordination and sharing that was not previously present.[159] For example, the Department of Homeland Security developed what is known as the Homeland Security Data Network. This allowed the secure movement of intelligence, classified as Secret, to Fusion Centers.[160] Furthermore, access to the Network facilitated access to the National Counterterrorism Center's portal, which held the most current terrorist-related intelligence.[161]

The greatest benefit of Fusion Centers was that they allowed police, as Kaplan put it, to move from being 'first responders into first preventers'.[162] Moreover, by placing federal representatives with local officers, the sharing of information was increased, a key concern for the 9/11 Commission. The impact of Fusion Centers cannot be overstated. Fusion Centers allowed the sharing of intelligence between various agencies in a manner that had not been undertaken before. They helped in the identification of patterns of ordinary crime as well as terrorist-related activity. The development of Fusion Centers significantly improved the United States' ability to counter the threat and pursue the perpetrators of acts of terrorist violence.

When considering the contribution of United States law enforcement in countering transnational terrorism a number of key issues should be noted, such as the fact that there were estimated to be in excess of 18,000 law enforcement agencies in operation.[163] Furthermore, especially when compared to law enforcement in the United Kingdom, these agencies were structured in a much more autonomous manner. This applied as much to the federal law enforcement agencies as it did to state, local and tribal agencies. The problems that come with decentralisation, such as a lack of coordination, control and knowledge of what other colleagues are doing, provided the impetus for some of the changes, or transformations, that occurred during this period. A key issue was less to do with capability (as was the case with the United Kingdom, especially with regard to niche capabilities provided by the Armed Forces) and more with capacity.[164]

What was lacking – and this was recognised by federal authorities – was a technological capacity to process and share information in a timely fashion. A high capacity would mean that, for example, a State Trooper having pulled over a suspect would be able to run a search of their identity and receive results that took data from interlinked databases. Similarly, any data they filed would be available for others to see and indeed cross-reference in an effort to identify trends.[165] To be clear, the issue was not, when considering the totality of the United States' database system, a lack of information.[166] The concern was over the *interconnectability* of the various databases that hold this data. Beardsworth gave an example of an incident in 2005 which illustrates the benefits of improvements in this area. United States Customs and Border Patrol officers were alerted to the fact that they had twenty individuals with similar backgrounds of concern, who were converging on Miami in three separate aircraft. The horizontal intelligence sharing that ensued ensured that they were able to divert two of the three aircraft to different airports.[167]

Summary

It is interesting to note that the United Kingdom and United States seemingly had different dilemmas to contend with post-9/11. For the United Kingdom the focus was primarily around what Peter Clarke described as a 'deficit of trust'.[168] This deficit, according to Clarke, occurred due to concerns among the population about the manner in which policing resources were being used. Perceptions of the deliberate targeting of Muslims were supported by the manner in which counter-terrorism projects were funded. Furthermore, the apparent disproportionate use of stop-and-search powers of ethnic minorities, within the United Kingdom, served to further magnify these perceptions. In contrast, the United States' dilemmas were more institutional, with a focus on establishing the ways and means in which intelligence should be shared, the role of the FBI and the manner in which acts of terrorism should be conceptualised (as ordinary crimes or acts of war).

Why do these differences exist? One answer to this question may be due to the divergent structures of policing agencies in both states. In the United Kingdom, perhaps similar to the United States, a number of different police forces existed but there was no overarching, national, federal policing agency similar to the FBI. This suggests that communication between the United Kingdom's police forces had always needed to be well entrenched. In the United States, inter-state crimes became the purview of the FBI, while in the United Kingdom they were worked on jointly by the police forces concerned. Another reason may be that the United Kingdom had, due to Northern Ireland, been dealing with terrorism for a prolonged period. The United States, quite simply, had not. Furthermore, the United States characterised the threat it faced differently from the United Kingdom. In contrast to the United

Kingdom, the view from the United States, perhaps mistakenly, saw terrorism as an external threat (i.e. an absence of *home-grown* terrorists) and so focused attention on improving communication between those agencies responsible for dealing with immigration and those concerned with law enforcement. The United Kingdom's recognition of a *home-grown* threat indicates a perception that it was in their best interests to develop counter-radicalisation programmes to tackle this threat.

Notes

1 Inspector Jonathan Brook, South Yorkshire Police Constabulary, interview conducted by the author, held in Sheffield, UK, 19 August 2009.
2 More information may be found at Cabinet Office. United Kingdom government (19 January 2009), 'Public Service Agreements', Cabinet Office, www.cabinetoffice. gov.uk/about_the_cabinet_office/publicserviceagreements.aspx.
3 Metropolitan Police Service (n.d.), 'Statement of Our Common Purpose and Values', Metropolitan Police, www.met.police.uk/history/purpose.htm.
4 United Kingdom government (October 2007), 'PSA Delivery Agreement 26: Reduce the Risk to the United Kingdom and its Interests Overseas from International Terrorism', Her Majesty's Treasury, www.hm-treasury.gov.uk/d/pbr_csr07_psa26.pdf.
5 John Jackson, Royal Military Academy Sandhurst, interview conducted by the author, held at Royal Military Academy Sandhurst, 30 July 2008; Brook, op. cit.; Superintendent Andy Pratt, Lancashire Police Constabulary, interview conducted by the author, held in Preston, United Kingdom, 22 November 2009.
6 Brook, op. cit.
7 Pratt, op. cit.
8 Sir Richard Dearlove (former Chief of United Kingdom Security Service), Conference held at Royal United Services Institute, 23 October 2009.
9 Foreign Secretary David Milliband made note of the third-party rule in his response to the Court of Appeal's decision to publish excerpts of intelligence shared with the United Kingdom regarding the interrogation of terrorism suspect Binyam Mohamed. The then Foreign Secretary raised his concerns that publishing intelligence gathered by other intelligence agencies would hamper United Kingdom security. UK government (10 February 2010), 'Binyam Mohamed Case', Foreign and Commonwealth Office, www.fco.gov.uk/en/news/latest-news/?view=News&id=21722320, accessed 12 February 2010.
10 Pratt, op. cit.
11 United Kingdom government (25 July 2007), 'Pre-charge Detention Fact Sheet', Home Office, http://security.homeoffice.gov.uk/news-publications/publication-search/counter-terrorism-bill-2007/pre-charge-facts2835.pdf?view=Binary.
12 James Kirkup (8 July 2008), 'Eliza Manningham-Buller, Former MI5 Chief, Savages 42-day Plan', *Telegraph*, www.telegraph.co.uk/news/newstopics/politics/2269755/ Eliza-Manningham-Buller-former-MI5-chief-savages-42-day-plan.html.
13 Pratt, op. cit.
14 United Kingdom government (July 2006), op. cit.
15 Baroness Frances D'Souza, Joint Committee on Terrorism, interview conducted by the author, held in London, 13 October 2009; Pratt, op. cit.
16 Pratt, op. cit.
17 Kirkup, op. cit.
18 United Kingdom government (May 2008), op. cit., p. 39; Brook, op. cit.
19 United Kingdom government (May 2008), op. cit., p. 19.
20 Ibid.

21 For more information see Ministry of Justice, 'Protecting the Public – Multi-Agency Public Protection Arrangements', Ministry of Justice, www.noms.justice.gov.uk/ protecting-the-public/supervision/mappa/.

22 Superintendent Neil Haynes, 'MPS *Prevent* Delivery Strategy – Report 9', Metropolitan Police Authority, www.mpa.gov.uk/committees/mpa/2008/080724/08/; for results see Mark Hughes, 'Police Identify 200 Children as Potential Terrorists', *Independent*, www.independent.co.uk/news/uk/crime/police-identify-200-children-as-potential-terrorists-1656027.html.

23 United Kingdom government (May 2008), op. cit.

24 Ibid.; and see United Kingdom government, 'National Policing Plan 2005–08, Safer, Stronger, Communities', Home Office, http://police.homeoffice.gov.uk/publications/ national-policing-plan/national_policing_plan2835.pdf?view=Binary.

25 Brook, op. cit.

26 Angie Sarchet, 'Agenda Item 4: The Government's "Prevent" Strategy', Buckinghamshire County Council, www.buckscc.gov.uk/moderngov/Published/C00000127/ M00002795/AI00004223/$CCEF*Prevent*Briefing.docA.ps.pdf, p. 11.

27 Ibid.

28 Ibid.

29 Brook, op. cit.

30 Ibid.

31 United Kingdom government (May 2008), op. cit., p. 8.

32 The Security Service, Secret Intelligence Service (SIS) and General Communications Headquarters (GCHQ) are collectively known as the Security and Intelligence Agencies (or Agencies).

33 Kim Howells, 'Annual Report', *Intelligence and Security Committee Annual Report 2007–2008*, March 2009, pp. 8–9; see also Security Service, 'Funding', Security Service, www.mi5.gov.uk/output/funding.html (n.d.).

34 United Kingdom government (May 2008), 'The *Prevent* Strategy: A Guide for Local Partners in England', Department for Children, Schools and Families, p. 9.

35 Ibid., p. 6.

36 United Kingdom government (June 2011), op. cit., p. 7.

37 Ibid., p. 8.

38 Ibid., p. 97.

39 Brook, op. cit.; Pratt, op. cit.

40 Pratt, op. cit.

41 Ibid.

42 United Kingdom government (21 July 2000), 'Terrorism Act', Office of Public Sector Information, www.opsi.gov.uk/acts/acts2000/ukpga_20000011_en_5, p. 20.

43 Lord Alex Carlile, comments made during the CT EXPO held at London's Earls Court, 14 to 15 April 2010.

44 Steve Hewitt, The British War on Terror – Terrorism and Counter-Terrorism on the Home Front Since 9/11 (London: Continuum, 2008), p. 113.

45 Unknown Author, 'Muslim Police Stops "More Likely"', *BBC News*, http://news. bbc.co.uk/1/hi/uk/4309961.stm, 2 March 2005.

46 Pratt, op. cit.

47 Peter Clarke, 'Former Assistant Commissioner and Head of Counter Terrorism Command', Metropolitan Police Service, comments made during the CT EXPO held at London's Earls Court, 14 to 15 April 2010.

48 Andy Hayman, 'Former Assistant Commissioner in charge of Specialist Operations for the Metropolitan Police Service', comments made during the CT EXPO held at London's Earls Court, 14 to 15 April 2010.

49 A list of all those in England and Wales may be found at United Kingdom government (1996), 'Police Act – Schedule 1', legislislation.gov, www.legislation.gov.uk/ ukpga/1996/16/schedule/1.

50 Unknown Author (24 October 2007), 'UK Forces List', National Policing Improvement Agency, www.police.uk/forces.htm, accessed 20 February 2010.

51 The Scottish Drug Enforcement Agency has arrest powers but are restricted to Scotland and not the whole of the United Kingdom.

52 The MoD website stated: 'They operate at MOD establishments and units throughout the United Kingdom, wherever their services are required, and are the United Kingdom's only truly national police force.' Ministry of Defence, (n.d.) *About Ministry of Defence Police*, www.mod.uk/DefenceInternet/AboutDefence/WhatWeDo/SecurityandIntelligence/MDPGA/AboutMinistryofDefencePolice.htm.

53 Andy Hayman, 'Former Assistant Commissioner in charge of Specialist Operations for the Metropolitan Police Service', comments made during the CT EXPO held at London's Earls Court, 14 to 15 April 2010.

54 Unknown Author (24 October 2007), op. cit.

55 See Unknown Author (2 July 2007), 'Car Bombing Suspect "On the Run"', *BBC News*, http://news.bbc.co.uk/1/hi/6259924.stm, accessed 20 December 2009.

56 Jackson, op. cit.

57 Ibid.

58 Hoffman, 3 December 2009, op. cit.

59 Brook, op. cit.; Pratt, op. cit.

60 Pratt, op. cit.

61 The Armed Forces comprise the Royal Navy (including the Royal Marines), British Army and Royal Air Force.

62 Second Clerk to the House of Commons Defence Committee, interview conducted by the author, held in London, 6 August 2009.

63 Ministry of Defence (September 2007), 'Operations in the United Kingdom: The Defence Contribution to Resilience: Joint Doctrine Publication 02, 2nd Edition', Ministry of Defence, www.cabinetoffice.gov.uk/media/132712/defencecontributio1. pdf, accessed 15 January 2010, p.v.; and Second Clerk to the House of Commons Defence Committee, op. cit.

64 Ministry of Defence (September 2007), op. cit.

65 House of Commons Defence Committee (18 May 2009), 'The Defence Contribution to United Kingdom National Security and Resilience – Sixth Report of Session 2008–09', House of Commons, www.publications.parliament.uk/pa/cm200809/cmselect/cmdfence/121/121.pdf.

66 Ibid., p. 14.

67 Ibid.

68 Ibid.

69 Ibid., p. 47.

70 Ibid.

71 Jackson states that some of the expertise gained was through police recruitment of former military bomb disposal specialists who in turn trained up police bomb disposal. John Jackson, Royal Military Academy Sandhurst, interview conducted by the author, held at Royal Military Academy Sandhurst, 30 July 2008; Inspector Jonathan Brook, South Yorkshire Police Constabulary, interview conducted by the author, held in Sheffield, 19 August 2009; and Superintendent Andy Pratt, Lancashire Police Constabulary, interview conducted by the author, held in Preston, UK, 22 November 2009.

72 Metropolitan Police Service (n.d.), 'Specialist Operations', *Counter Terrorism Command*, www.met.police.uk/so/counter_terrorism.htm.

73 Second Clerk to the House of Commons Defence Committee, op. cit.; Patrick Mercer MP, Chair, Home Office, Sub-Committee on Counter-Terrorism, interview conducted by the author, held in London, 12 October 2009; Brook, op. cit.

74 Ministry of Defence (September 2007), op. cit.

75 Mercer, op. cit.

76 Brook, op. cit.; Pratt, op. cit.; House of Commons Defence Committee (18 May 2009), op. cit., p. 14.
77 Second Clerk to the House of Commons Defence Committee, op. cit.
78 House of Commons Defence Committee (18 May 2009), op. cit.
79 Military Liaison Officers are drawn usually from military establishments within a particular region.
80 Second Clerk to the House of Commons Defence Committee, op. cit.
81 Ministry of Defence (September 2007), op. cit., ch. 1, p. 3.
82 House of Commons Defence Committee (18 May 2009), op. cit., p. 6.
83 Ibid., p. 7.
84 Brian Jackson, Homeland Security Program, RAND Corporation, interview conducted by the author, held in Washington, DC, 10 February 2009.
85 Ibid.
86 In 2008 there were approximately 18,000 state and local (this does not include tribal) law enforcement agencies in the United States. These agencies employed approximately 1,133,000 officers on a full-time basis with approximately 765,000 having full powers of arrest.
87 Joseph McMillan, Institute for National Strategic Studies, National Defence University, interview conducted by the author, held in Washington, DC, 13 February 2009.
88 Hoffman, Georgetown University, interview conducted by the author, held in Oxford, UK, 3 December 2009.
89 Robert G. Ross, Department of Homeland Security, interview conducted by the author, held in Washington, DC, 9 February 2009.
90 Ibid.
91 Department of Homeland Security (September 2008), 'Overview: FY 2008 Commercial Equipment Direct Assistance Program (CEDAP)', Federal Emergency Management Agency, www.fema.gov/pdf/government/grant/cedap/fy08_cedap_overview.pdf, accessed 2 February 2010.
92 Ibid., p. 1; B. Jackson, 10 February 2009.
93 B. Jackson, 10 February 2009.
94 Department of Homeland Security (September 2008), op. cit., p. 2.
95 Randall J. Larsen, Retired; Director, Institute for Homeland Security, interview conducted by the author, held in Washington, D C, 10 September 2009.
96 Ibid.
97 Ibid.
98 Ross, op. cit.
99 Corey Gruber, Executive Director, National Preparedness Task-Force, Federal Emergency Management Agency, Department of Homeland Security, interview conducted by the author, held in Washington, DC, 11 February 2009.
100 Ibid.
101 Department of Homeland Security (September 2008), op. cit., p. 1.
102 B. Jackson, 10 February 2009.
103 Ibid.
104 Larsen, op. cit.
105 Anonymous Source G, interview conducted by the author.
106 Robert S. Mueller III (14 April 2004), 'Statement of Robert S. Mueller III – Director, Federal Bureau of Investigation', National Commission on Terrorist Attacks Upon the United States, http://govinfo.library.unt.edu/911/hearings/hearing10/mueller_statement.pdf.
107 Tribal law enforcement officials may be found on native American territory.
108 Senior House Committee on Homeland Security Staffer, op. cit.
109 Kean, op. cit., p. 408; Homeland Security Expert with Congressional and Executive Experience, op. cit.
110 Ibid.; Senior House Committee on Homeland Security Staffer, op. cit.

111 Kean, op. cit.

112 B. Jackson, 10 February 2009.

113 Hurricane Katrina hit the south coast of the USA on 29 August 2005. Preparedness of the Federal Emergency Management Agency in light of the emerging threat and the subsequent response came in for clear criticism in a report that was later published. See United States government (February 2006), 'The Federal Response to Hurricane Katrina Lessons Learned', White House, http://library.stmarytx.edu/acadlib/edocs/katrinawh.pdf, accessed 1 February 2010.

114 B. Jackson, 10 February 2009.

115 Inspector Jonathan Brook, South Yorkshire Police Constabulary, interview conducted by the author, held in Sheffield, 19 August 2009; and Superintendent Andy Pratt, Lancashire Police Constabulary, interview conducted by the author, held in Preston, UK, 22 November 2009; Director, Federal Bureau of Investigation, Robert S. Mueller III, stated in his evidence to the 9/11 Commission that the USA 'must remain accountable under the Constitution and the rule of law. We must respect civil liberties as we seek to protect the American people.' Robert S. Mueller III (14 April 2004), 'Statement of Robert S. Mueller III – Director, Federal Bureau of Investigation', p. 2.

116 Anonymous Source B, op. cit.; Ross, op. cit.

117 Anonymous Source B, op. cit.

118 McMillan, op. cit.

119 United States government (September 2006), op. cit., p. 1.

120 Ibid.

121 Ibid.

122 The Posse Comitatus Act, discussed in the following chapter, proscribes the role of the Armed Forces in a manner that essentially prevents their participation in domestic law enforcement activities except under specific circumstances.

123 McMillan, op. cit.

124 United States government (10 April 1982), 'National Security Decision – Directive Number 30 – Managing Terrorism Incidents', Federation of American Scientists, www.fas.org/irp/offdocs/nsdd/nsdd-030.htm.

125 Unknown Author (current as of 8 January 2008), 'Title 18 (Crimes and Criminal Procedure), Part I (Crimes), Chapter 113B (Terrorism), Section 2332b (Acts of Terrorism Transcending National Boundaries), Paragraph f', Cornell University Law School,www.law.cornell.edu/uscode/pdf/uscode18/lii_usc_TI_18_PA_I_CH_113B_SE_2332b.pdf, p. 2.

126 Mueller, op. cit., p. 6.

127 Larsen also tentatively supported this move at first. Gruber, op. cit.; Mueller, op. cit., p. 6.

128 United States government (September 2006), op. cit., p. 1.

129 Ibid., p. 14; Michael Jacobsen, Senior Fellow, Stein Program on Counterterrorism and Intelligence, interview conducted by the author, held in Washington, DC, 11 February 2009.

130 McMillan, op. cit.

131 Ibid.

132 Pratt, op. cit.; Brook, op. cit.

133 It should be noted, as pointed out by one interviewee, that some of the larger states in the United States have their own intelligence structure that in many ways rivals some of the national agencies. One of particular note is that seen in New York. Indeed, in many instances it was New York's inter-state intelligence agencies that passed information up to the national Intelligence Community. Senior House Committee on Homeland Security Staffer, interview conducted by the author, held in Washington, DC, February 2009.

134 Larsen, op. cit.

135 This was especially applicable, as United States law treats acts of terrorism against American citizens anywhere in the world in the same manner as those committed within the territorial boundaries of the state. Consequentially, under United States law they are able to hold a trial and enforce whichever penalties are deemed proportionate against people who have committed terrorist acts. United States government (10 April 1982), 'National Security Decision – Directive Number 30 – Managing Terrorism Incidents', Federation of American Scientists, www.fas.org/irp/offdocs/nsdd/nsdd-030.htm, accessed 1 October 2008; Unknown Author (current as of 8 January 2008), 'Title 18 (Crimes and Criminal Procedure), Part I (Crimes), Chapter 113B (Terrorism), Section 2332b (Acts of terrorism transcending national boundaries), Paragraph f', Cornell University Law School, www.law.cornell.edu/uscode/pdf/uscode18/lii_usc_TI_18_PA_I_CH_113B_SE_2332b.pdf, accessed 1 October 2009, p. 2.

136 Unknown Author (13 April 2004), 'Law Enforcement, Counterterrorism, and Intelligence Collection in the United States Prior to 9/11: Staff Statement No. 9', National Commission on Terrorist Attacks upon the United States, http://govinfo.library.unt.edu/911/staff_statements/staff_statement_9.pdf, p. 1.

137 United States government (n.d.), 'Seventeen Agencies and Organizations United Under One Goal', intelligence.gov, www.intelligence.gov/about-the-intelligence-community/, accessed 12 November 2010.

138 Senior House Committee on Homeland Security Staffer, op. cit.; Larsen, op. cit.

139 Larsen, op. cit.

140 Mueller, op. cit., p. 6.

141 Larsen, op. cit.

142 Kean, op. cit.

143 Prior to 2003 this was known as the Terrorist Threat Integration Center.

144 Jacobsen, op. cit.

145 Senior House Committee on Homeland Security Staffer, op. cit.

146 United States Senate (3 August 2007), 'Public Law 110–53: Implementing Recommendations of the 9/11 Commission Act of 2007', Senate Select Committee on Intelligence, http://intelligence.senate.gov/laws/pl11053.pdf.

147 United States House of Representatives (n.d.), 'Beyond Connecting the Dots: A VITAL Framework for Sharing Law Enforcement Intelligence Information', Committee on Homeland Security, http://homeland.house.gov/SiteDocuments/20060801150837–36075.pdf, accessed 22 February 2010, p. 2; Senior House Committee on Homeland Security Staffer, op. cit.

148 The 9/11 Commission Act of 2007 requires that the ITACG Detail comprise state, local and tribal law enforcement officers. Unknown Author (n.d.), 'Interagency Threat Assessment and Coordination Group', Information Sharing Environment, www.ise.gov/pages/partner-itacg.html, accessed 1 February 2010.

149 Senior House Committee on Homeland Security Staffer, op. cit.

150 Senior House Committee on Homeland Security Staffer, op. cit.; Gruber op. cit.

151 Jacobsen, op. cit.

152 For further information see United States government (n.d.), 'Intelligence Threat Assessment and Coordination Group – Intelligence Guide For First Responders', Information Sharing Environment, www.ise.gov/docs/ITACG_Guide.pdf, accessed 12 November 2010.

153 Maryland's establishment of the first Fusion Center was perhaps in response to the fact that on 9 September 2001 a Maryland State Trooper made a routine traffic stop for speeding of Ziad Jarrah. Jarrah was on a CIA watch list which was not available to the State Trooper at the time and two days later, on 11 September 2001, he was one of the four hijackers of United Airlines Flight 93 which crashed in Pennsylvania, assumed to be making its way to the White House.

154 United States Department of Justice (August 2006), 'Fusion Center Guidelines – Developing and Sharing Information and Intelligence in a New Era', Federation of American Scientists, www.fas.org/irp/agency/ise/guidelines.pdf, p. 2.

155 Eben Kaplan, (22 February 2007), 'Fusion Centers', Council on Foreign Relations, www.cfr.org/publication/12689/fusion_centers.html.

156 Ibid.

157 Gruber, op. cit.

158 United States Department of Justice (August 2006), 'Fusion Center Guidelines – Developing and Sharing Information and Intelligence in a New Era'.

159 Kaplan, op. cit.

160 Department of Homeland Security (16 September 2009), 'State and Local Fusion Centers', Department of Homeland Security, www.dhs.gov/files/programs/gc_1156877184684.shtm.

161 Ibid.

162 Kaplan, op. cit.

163 B. Jackson, op. cit. There are thousands of Federal, state, local and tribal law enforcement agencies/departments.

164 B. Jackson, op. cit.

165 Ibid.

166 Randy Beardsworth, former Assistant Secretary for Strategic Plans; former Director of Operations; former Under-Secretary for Border and Transportation Security Director; former Director for Defence Policy on the National Security Council, interview conducted by the author, held in Washington, DC, 10 September 2009.

167 Ibid.

168 Peter Clarke, 'Former Assistant Commissioner and Head of Counter Terrorism Command', Metropolitan Police Service, comments made during the CT EXPO held at London's Earls Court, 14 to 15 April 2010.

169 Ibid.

5   Military force

The use of military force formed the most visible part of the counter-terrorism approaches adopted by both the United Kingdom and the United States. In the post-9/11 period, the implementation of this strategic policy instrument served as both a deterrent and a recruiting sergeant for sympathisers of terrorist causes.

Military force and the United Kingdom: a qualitative assessment

Military force in the United Kingdom is implemented by the Armed Forces, which comprise the Royal Navy (including the Royal Marines), British Army and the Royal Air Force. The Armed Forces come under one unified government department: the Ministry of Defence. The Ministry of Defence is both a policy-making department and the most senior military headquarters in the United Kingdom, 'providing political control of all military operations'.[1] The contribution of the Armed Forces in the United Kingdom, when compared to law enforcement and intelligence, changed very little after 9/11. The reason for this is not clear-cut. Intuitively, it would make sense to suppose that the role of the United Kingdom's Armed Forces changed substantially, especially as, in terms of counter-terrorism and counter-insurgency, the Armed Forces increased their commitments significantly after 9/11.

The United Kingdom's Armed Forces, however, were already familiar with the broader threat and issues surrounding terrorism activity. Protracted terrorist activity in Northern Ireland, anti-colonial terrorism in Malaya (modern-day Malaysia and Singapore) and Kenya gave them a basic template that informed their decisions and approach to the post-9/11 threat. This approach, domestically, may be seen as very much hands-off and internationally as a tool of last resort. The Armed Forces were, as former British Major-General Tim Cross put it, very much in favour of acting in support of other, civilian agencies. The Armed Forces did not consider themselves to be a long-term solution to what they saw as a political problem.[2]

The United Kingdom's counter-terrorism strategy suggests that the primary purpose of military force in countering the threat of transnational terrorism is in deterring and pursuing violent extremists and offering specific tools that facilitate a reduction in the vulnerability of the state and the United Kingdom's population.[3] These include 'hostage recovery, maritime counter-terrorism, bomb disposal and the interception of renegade aircraft'.[4] Internationally, the role of military force is considered to be an option in situations where 'non-military tools cannot achieve' objectives.[5] The overarching aim of military force was, as articulated in CONTEST-2006, '[t]o deliver security for the people of the United Kingdom and the Overseas Territories by defending them, including against terrorism, and to act as a force for good by strengthening international peace and security'.[6]

In order to fully understand what is meant by a campaign plan, it is worth briefly summarising the recent history of the Armed Forces, focusing particularly on their relationship to one another. In order for the Armed Forces to engage effectively they operate in a unified manner. This approach became institutionalised with the establishment of the Ministry of Defence in 1964 which placed all the Armed Forces under one ministerial agency. With the end of the Cold War and downsizing of the Armed Forces, a new, additional body, known as the Permanent Joint Headquarters (PJHQ), was established in 1994. The role of the PJHQ has been central to the planning and execution of operations for the Armed Forces. It is, as Cross put it, 'the campaign [headquarters] of the Ministry of Defence'.[7] A campaign plan, from a purely Armed Forces perspective, articulates the objectives as laid down by government; it identifies the contribution that the Armed Forces are expected to provide, and the way in which it is to be fought and ultimately won.[8]

In the Global War on Terror, Cross argues, no such campaign plan has been developed.[9] This may be due to the ambiguity that underscores the objectives of the Global War on Terror, but even on a smaller scale in terms of reconstruction in Afghanistan and Iraq, no equivalent to an Armed Forces campaign plan existed in or between other United Kingdom government agencies.[10] This is a significant criticism made by Cross, who noted, in relation to the Iraq conflict (2003–2009), that the Department of Trade and Industry, the Foreign Office and the Treasury rarely operated in unison, even though they were working towards the same objectives.[11]

In a witness statement provided to the Iraq Inquiry (which was set up to investigate the United Kingdom's involvement in the conflict) chaired by Sir John Chilcot, Cross stated that the equivalent of PJHQ, 'possibly located in the Cabinet Office or expanding the current PJHQ', was needed in order to improve upon the level of coordination between the Armed Forces and other civilian agencies.[12] Indeed, the lack of a campaign plan to fight the Global War on Terror was exacerbated by the recognition by senior military personnel that the conflict could not be won through military means alone.[13]

The provision of a coordinated plan, as undertaken among the Armed Forces, allows for a more economical use of resources and, by extension, a reduction of the burden across government in countering the threat of terrorism. Without the level of coordination that Cross suggests is needed, progress is hindered in achieving the strategic aim of the United Kingdom's counter-terrorism strategy:

the reduction of the threat from terrorism.[14] Furthermore, the absence of a campaign plan means that no reasonable benchmarks for success are set.

The lack of a coordinated campaign plan had other repercussions. Counter-radicalisation initiatives were, it appears, absent from military thinking. In a House of Commons Defence Committee report it was stated by the Armed Forces Minister, Bob Ainsworth (29 June 2007 to 5 May 2009), that counter-radicalisation is an area in which the Ministry of Defence 'maybe needed to do more'.[15] He added that the extent of the Ministry of Defence's counter-radicalisation programme was an awareness of the use of language when engaging with local Muslim communities.[16] The primary purpose of the Armed Forces is to counter threats to the security and interests of the state. It is an instrument of last resort and as such does not necessarily focus on preventative measures. This is particularly important, as the use of the Armed Forces overseas to counter the threat of terrorism is most visible through, for example, deployments to Afghanistan and Iraq. The recognition of a home-grown threat to the United Kingdom does not, it is argued here, negate the clear and current danger posed by those overseas. The lack of centrality regarding counter-radicalisation in military thinking did not necessarily increase the number of sympathisers becoming practitioners; but it is argued that by not taking it into consideration, the Armed Forces were missing an opportunity to reduce the rhetoric potentially used by terrorist recruiters regarding the use of the military overseas.

The key issues on the subject of counter-terrorism, from the Armed Forces' perspective, relating to the United Kingdom's military deployment to Iraq, centred on the amount that the Armed Forces, with simultaneous deployments to Afghanistan and Iraq, were being asked to do. However, the deployment to Iraq also had an impact domestically that, arguably, affected the implementation of all three of the policy instruments: intelligence, law enforcement and military force. This impact concerns that of the increased radicalisation which the conflict may have caused.

Afghanistan was also used as a tool by terrorist recruiters in convincing sympathisers to become practitioners of violence, but Iraq was used to a greater extent because of the tenuous link made between Iraq and terrorism.[17] Pratt talks about protest marches being organised that centred on the topic of the Iraq conflict.[18] Indeed, in giving evidence to the Iraq Inquiry, Eliza Manningham-Buller, former Director-General of the Security Service (2002–2007), stated that:

> our involvement in Iraq radicalised, for want of a better word, a whole generation of young people, some British citizens – not a whole generation, a few among a generation – who were – saw our involvement in Iraq, on top of our involvement in Afghanistan, as being an attack on Islam.[19]

Military action, therefore, in Afghanistan, but more so in Iraq, was considered by some within the United Kingdom to be a motivating tool for recruiters of terrorist violence.[20]

The loss of life sustained by the Armed Forces as a result the military campaigns in Afghanistan and Iraq not only served as a motivating factor for those terrorists looking to demonstrate success in their tactics but may also have eroded support among the general population. The impact that loss of life, as a result of military campaigns, has on the capability of a policy instrument is difficult to fathom. The reason for this difficulty is that this book's focus is on providing an assessment in relation to the state. While the losses sustained by the Armed Forces, particularly in a small, professional and overstretched military such as the United Kingdom's, are regrettable, the number of losses has not been at such a rate as to, on their own, be considered so significant as to trigger an immediate exit. Indeed, material presented throughout the Iraq inquiry stated that morale among frontline Armed Forces personnel was constantly high.[21]

That said, loss of life does have an impact on the image, not just of the Armed Forces but of the state's commitment to the use of military force, particularly overseas. In a speech delivered at the Institute of Public Policy Research, former Armed Forces Minister Bill Rammell stated that in contemporary counter-insurgency warfare, such as that seen during the Iraq and Afghanistan conflicts, the public is much more questioning of why deaths have occurred.[22] Rammell stated that this questioning, although tough and fair, appeared to be causing a loss of perspective when it came to the strategic nature of warfare – especially as 'every loss of life is reported as if somebody or some institution on our side is fundamentally to blame'.[23] This culture of blame eroded the image of the United Kingdom Armed Forces and served as a further motivating tool for those wishing to recruit sympathisers as practitioners of terrorist violence, to the extent that deaths of representatives of the state, particularly military personnel, were glorified and encouraged.[24]

As stated above, the Armed Forces were concerned about how much they were being asked to do. Internationally, the use of military force to counter terrorism was most visible during the Afghanistan campaign that began shortly after 9/11. The controversial Iraq conflict, which began in 2003 and lasted, for the United Kingdom, until 2009, was not at the start about counter-terrorism but about a perceived or alleged threat regarding the possession, by Iraq of weapons of mass destruction. As time progressed, this intervention's focus became countering terrorist violence.

The governing authority in Afghanistan – the Taliban – had been identified by the United States as being the state primary sponsor (at least visibly) of al Qaeda. The Taliban's support came through the provision of territory for the development of terrorist training camps. The United States believed that the 9/11 hijackers received part of their training from here but more importantly that Osama bin Laden, leader and inspirational figurehead of the movement, was still based there. When the Taliban government refused to close training camps and extradite Osama bin Laden and associates, the United States led a campaign of retribution and regime change.[25] The United Kingdom provided a significant supporting contingent. This was a relatively un-contentious commitment given the significant public sympathy and support afforded the United States following the 9/11 attacks.[26]

Concerns did arise regarding the amount of equipment needed and indeed the sustainability of the campaign. The 1998 Strategic Defence Review indicated that United Kingdom Armed Forces would be structured in such a way as to be able to fulfil those requirements indicated in Box 5.1.

Box 5.1 Strategic defence review: defence planning assumptions[1]

[R]espond to a major international crisis which might require a military effort and combat operations of a similar scale and duration to the Gulf War when we deployed an armoured division [28,000 soldiers], twenty-six major warships and over eighty combat aircraft
Or
undertake a more extended overseas deployment on a lesser scale (as over the last few years in Bosnia) while retaining the ability to mount a second substantial deployment – which might involve a combat brigade and appropriate naval and air forces – if this were made necessary by a second crisis. We would not, however, expect both deployments to involve warfighting or to maintain them simultaneously for longer than six months.
[and]
[w]e must also retain the ability, at much longer notice, to rebuild a bigger force as part of NATO's [the North Atlantic Treaty Organisation's] collective defence should a major threat re-emerge in Europe.

Note
1 Ministry of Defence (July 1998), 'Strategic Defence Review – Modern Forces for the Modern World', Ministry of Defence, www.mod.uk/NR/rdonlyres/65F3D7AC-4340–4119–93A2–20825848E50E/0/sdr1998_complete.pdf, p. 32; see also Ministry of Defence (2007), 'Ministry of Defence Plan 2007', Ministry of Defence, www.mod.uk/NR/rdonlyres/A5810AB5–6CDB-4B97-A8CF-976D3B9676B4/0/defence_plan2007.pdf, pp. 13–14.

Following 9/11 the then Secretary of Defence, Geoff Hoon (11 October 1999 to 5 May 2005), ordered another Strategic Defence Review in order to clarify if force posture – what the Armed Forces were structured to do and what they were being expected to do – needed to be adjusted in light of the emerging terrorist threat.[27] While the findings of the report suggested that challenges to the interests and integrity of the United Kingdom may have changed, structure, it concluded, should remain in line with 1998 defence planning assumptions outlined in Box 5.1. Requirements could be met by current capacity.[28]

The Iraq conflict, which began in 2003 and ran simultaneously to that undertaken to Afghanistan, put the United Kingdom's Armed Forces in a position that exceeded the defence planning assumptions as outlined in the 1998 Strategic Defence Review. Areas such as reduced helicopter availability and a lack of suitably armed personnel vehicles became significant matters of debate during this period.[29] However, the largest problem was the amount the Armed Forces were being asked to do. In March 2003, a letter sent from the then

Foreign Secretary, Jack Straw (8 May 2001 to 6 May 2006) and the Secretary of State for Defence, Geoff Hoon, stated: 'It will be necessary to draw down our current commitment to nearer a third by no later than autumn in order to avoid long term damage to the Armed Forces. Keeping more forces in Iraq would be outside our current Defence Planning Assumptions.'[30] By the time General Sir Richard Dannatt became head of the British Army, in March 2005, the belief was that by autumn 2006 there would be about 1,000 troops based in Iraq. In reality, Dannatt states, '[w]hen it came to it in autumn 2006, we had 8,000 troops in Iraq, but were already by that stage committed into Afghanistan in a commitment that grew very quickly from 3,500 to 5,000 and has now risen to 10,000'.[31]

The sustained deployments to Afghanistan (2001 and ongoing) and Iraq (2003–2009)[32] did put a strain on the ability of the Armed Forces, both in terms of manpower and equipment, to meet requirements.[33] This began to manifest itself particularly as the initial deployment to Iraq transitioned into a prolonged and seemingly unexpected counter-insurgency and nation-building operation.[34] The latter perhaps represented the biggest counter-terrorism commitment of military force for the United Kingdom post-9/11. The role of military force domestically was, during this period, in support of the civilian authority.

As shown above, the overstretched nature of the Armed Forces had profound consequences regarding their ability to meet the defence planning assumptions set out in the 1998 Strategic Defence Review. The civil–military contract was a development of the British Army's military covenant that was codified in 2000 and related to the mutual obligations between the Armed Forces and the nation.[35] The Armed Forces are expected to perform their duty, while the state will in return provide adequate equipment, training and fair treatment to both those serving and their families.[36] As discussed above, the overstretched predicament, caused by the deployments to Afghanistan and Iraq, of the Armed Forces meant that the provision of adequate equipment was difficult for the United Kingdom government to provide.

In evidence to the Iraq Inquiry chaired by Sir John Chilcot, General Dannatt stated that the covenant 'progressively got out of balance' as the workload that the Armed Forces was expected to perform increased.[37] It is important to note that Dannatt also observes that the morale of frontline troops during this period was of an adequate standard.[38] The alleged breach of the civil–military contract also had an impact on the ability of the state to justify both to personnel in the Armed Forces and the wider public not only why troops were deployed in Afghanistan and Iraq, but why they should be supported.

The process through which other United Kingdom government agencies could call upon the Armed Forces for military assistance was continuously improving. This had a great benefit in countering the threat of terrorism, in that it increased understanding and awareness throughout government regarding what capabilities were available and how the Armed Forces could help other agencies. Military capabilities were split into three categories: augmentation through regular forces; augmentation through reserve forces; and niche capabilities.[39]

Augmentative capability refers to the provision of Armed Forces assistance in the form of logistical support or sheer manpower.[40] Such deployments are drawn from capabilities otherwise meant for 'standing or contingent operations overseas and [were] not planned for regular use on behalf of the civil authorities'.[41] An example of the provision of augmentative capabilities may be seen in the deployment of troops within the United Kingdom during flooding in late 2009 and the foot-and-mouth crisis of 2001.[42] The fulfilment of augmentation requests from the civil authority comes generally from government agencies other than law enforcement. The redevelopment of the structure that codified the processes, through which military aid could be requested, was spurred by the foot-and-mouth crisis of 2001.

The 2001 outbreak represented a turning point in the manner in which interactions were conducted between the Ministry of Defence and other government agencies. This proved particularly relevant to counter-terrorism.[43] During this crisis, the Department for Environment, Food and Rural Affairs was, due to the nature of the problem and their expertise, declared lead agency, responsible for the coordination of all agencies that would work towards its objectives of clearing the United Kingdom of foot-and-mouth disease. The post-crisis analysis noted that military assistance from the Ministry of Defence, in particular the British Army, had been requested six days after the outbreak, despite the clear augmentative contribution they could have made earlier in logistics and other areas such as carcass disposal.[44]

One reason suggested for the delay was the general lack of understanding of how government departments, such as the Department for Environment, Food and Rural Affairs that have irregular interactions with the Ministry of Defence, should go about requesting assistance and, furthermore, what capabilities could be provided.[45] As a direct consequence, the Ministry of Defence published a series of documents that described the circumstances, procedures, extent and funding arrangements associated with any requests for assistance.[46]

A key feature of these publications was the manner in which financial costs were to be recuperated. With the exception of events that involved imminent danger to human life, Treasury rules dictate that as the Ministry of Defence's primary purpose is defence from external threats, financial costs be recuperated from requesting agencies.[47] This principle was applicable to requests made on the basis of national security:

> [The MoD] will not waive costs on grounds of national security. Those aspects of national security for which the MOD has responsibility are funded within the Defence budget. A [...] request might be related to national security, but would by definition fall within the responsibilities, and therefore the budget, of the requesting Department or agency.[48]

This reflected the United Kingdom government's view that the Ministry of Defence is not for domestic *homeland* security – inasmuch as their focus is on countering threats to international security. As a result, the Ministry of Defence suggested that should a capability be needed on a frequent basis, the civilian authority, or lead agency, should consider developing and retaining it in-house.

The use of augmentative capabilities in the form of military force to counter the threat of terrorism of any type did not occur during this period. Indeed, both law enforcement and military force practitioners have argued that the provision of military force of this nature is unnecessary and is tantamount to imposing military rule.[49] Experiences of Northern Ireland highlighted, particularly for the British Army, the problems with using military force on their own population.[50] The Ministry of Defence in all circumstances, but particularly in this area, considers itself to be an instrument of last resort.[51] That said, the rules and procedures that came about due to a need for augmentative military force also helped shape those applicable for Standing Home Commitments and, despite the fear about what its use could signify, solidified what and how it could be used.

While the use of military force, strategically and internationally, may well have been simply a means of carrying out specific policy objectives set by the United Kingdom government, domestic deployments were more complicated. This was because the military, although retaining specialised tools, were not always considered to have the lead at either the operational, institutional or strategic levels. Experiences of Northern Irish terrorism in the 1960s reinforced opinions that protection of the *homeland* was a role for other civilian authorities, particularly those with a law enforcement remit.[52] Indeed, *homeland security* fell within the purview of the Home Secretary not the Secretary of State for Defence.[53]

It is important to understand the basic underpinnings upon which military force could be used domestically, as these reinforced a clear reluctance on behalf of the Armed Forces and the United Kingdom government to use this as an option in counter-terrorism and in many ways shaped the nature of relationships between the Armed Forces and other government agencies post-9/11.[54]

The use of military force within the territorial borders of the United Kingdom is known as Military Aid to the Civilian Authority (MACA). This, as is shown in Figure 5.1, is subdivided into three components: Military Aid to other Government Departments (MAGD); Military Aid to the Civilian Community (MACC); and Military Aid to the Civilian Power (MACP).

The use of MAGDs refers to the deployment of military forces 'on urgent work of national importance' and is codified in statutory law.[55] Notably, MAGDs do not empower the Armed Forces to requisition services, or facilities. The use of MAGDs is the provision, if necessary, of armed personnel in helping to maintain law, order and public safety. This is used in situations that are deemed beyond the capability of the civilian power, specifically the police.[56] The use of MACC is the provision of unarmed assistance and is divided into three categories. Category A is the provision of assistance in emergencies, especially major natural or manmade disasters; Category B is routine assistance on special projects or events; and Category C involves secondments of volunteers to other, appropriate agencies.[57]

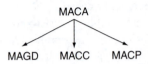

Figure 5.1 Divisions of military aid to the civilian authority.

When considering the use of military force and counter-terrorism in the United Kingdom, the emphasis that both the government and the Ministry of Defence placed on the primacy of civilian control and responsibility cannot be overstated.[58] Those resources that were made available to the civilian authority on a permanent basis fell under the military's Standing Home Commitments. Unlike augmentative capabilities, these Commitments were guaranteed to civilian authorities and as such were integrated into force structure planning and operation as well as in defence planning assumptions.[59] Standing Home Commitments were divided into four Military Tasks:[60]

- Military Task 2.1: Military Aid to the Civilian Authority;
- Military Task 2.2: Military Aid to the Civilian Authority in Northern Ireland;[61]
- Military Task 2.3: Maintenance of integrity of United Kingdom waters;
- Military Task 2.4: Maintenance of integrity of United Kingdom airspace.

Box 5.2 Extract of niche capabilities[62]

- A quick reaction capability to deter and defend against serious threats to the integrity of UK airspace, including air defence radar.
- A maritime capability to deter and defend against serious threats to the integrity of UK territorial waters.
- Counter-terrorist capabilities in support of the police on land or sea.
- Public order support in extremis to the Police Service of Northern Ireland.
- Fishery protection vessels in support of DEFRA.
- A maritime search and rescue capability in support of the Maritime and Coastguard Agency.
- An Explosive Ordnance Disposal 'render-safe' capability.
- Scientific support to police operations including a Technical Response Force with access to a wide range of relevant scientific expertise.
- Ministry of Defence Police support to the protection of key points in the critical national infrastructure.
- A regional command-and-control capability to provide an ability to coordinate larger scale defence contributions.
- Civil Contingency Reaction Forces, drawn from the reserve forces, which are potentially available if required to support the responsible authorities for dealing with civil contingencies.

Standing Home Commitments, or niche capabilities, therefore, are those that are retained by the Ministry of Defence in support of other agencies because they are 'not readily available in the civilian sector'.[63] Indeed, the conditions under which MACA is provided are that it is used as a last resort and that the civilian authority does not have the capability available to deploy it in sufficient time or quantity.[64] Domestically speaking, the largest contribution made by the Ministry of Defence in the area of countering terrorism comes in the provision of these niche capabilities, as shown in Box 5.2.

Military force and the United States: a qualitative assessment

Military force is undertaken by the Armed Forces of the United States which comprise the Army, Navy, Air Force, Marine Corps and Coast Guard.[65] Similar to the United Kingdom, the Armed Forces fall under one government department: the Department of Defense.[66] The Department of Defense continued its Cold War thinking of dividing the world into six regional Combatant Commands and Functional Commands. This division of resources formed the basic starting point from which United States strategy was developed.

The very structure of the United States Armed Forces is in many ways problematic in the Global War on Terror. This is because the overarching structure changed very little during the post-Cold War era. The function of the Department of Defense, after 9/11, was to 'maintain and employ Armed Forces' so that they may '[s]upport and defend the Constitution of the United States against all enemies foreign and domestic. [...] Ensure [...] the security of the United States, its possessions, and areas vital to its interest. [...] Uphold and advance the national policies and interests of the United States.'[67] The function of the Armed Forces, therefore, was considered to be a key component when developing foreign policy options at the national level and, as will be discussed below, was an inevitable policy instrument in the response to 9/11.

As discussed in earlier chapters, the United States' counter-terrorism strategy reinforced the belief that the role of the military, when it came to countering the threat of transnational terrorism, was to operate overseas. In order to meet the asymmetrical threat it was necessary to restructure the Armed Forces in a way that had not been undertaken since the end of the Second World War.[68] The centrality of military force in counter-terrorism strategy policymaking was also seen as an alternative to 'old orthodoxies that once confined [...] counterterrorism efforts primarily to the criminal justice domain' – a domain that was, as noted by McMillan, one that the George W. Bush administration seemingly wanted to shift away from and which operated in an after-the-fact manner.[69] Military force, according to McMillan, operated in an after-the-fact manner as the Armed Forces, primarily, responded to acts of aggression.[70] The difference between law enforcement and military force was that the latter appeared able to dispense swift responses, as opposed to legal mechanisms that generally take longer.[71]

The Army did, however, begin a restructuring programme, which is discussed further below, but this was not reflected throughout the wider Armed Forces.

Even though the United States military were capable of countering threats from state actors, the focus on military force to counter non-state threats seemingly undermined what was considered to be much-needed investment in more appropriate tools such as the Intelligence Community.[72] This in turn hindered the ability of the state to protect its population and interests.

In addition to diverting investment away from the Intelligence Community, this Cold War mind-set had an impact on other areas. It is important to note that the role of the Armed Forces during this period was considered to be that of a state policy instrument tasked with responding to aggression that originated from other states. The Armed Forces did have the capability of responding to non-state threats, but even here this was restricted to the projection of military power outside the domestic realm. Following 9/11, the declaration of a Global War on Terror, for which the stated aim was the defeat of terrorism, saw the military inevitably taking the lead in responding to the threat.[73] This view of the necessity and indeed inevitability of a military response was further compounded by the opinion, as noted in the previous chapter, that the United States faced a threat from international as opposed to domestic *home-grown* terrorists.[74] This thinking had consequences, including the striking lack of what Michael Jacobsen of the Washington-based Stein Program on Counter-Terrorism and Intelligence described as softer counter-terrorism measures, such as counter-radicalisation programmes.[75] Indeed, it was recognised by the Department of Defense that if the aim of the Global War on Terror was to defeat terrorism, then the Armed Forces alone could not do this due to the ideological dimension of the threat.[76]

A 2006 presentation made to the United States Armed Forces' senior leadership, the Joint Chiefs of Staff, entitled *The National Military Strategic Plan for the War on Terrorism*, looked at the role of the Armed Forces.[77] It concluded that the application of military force is not compatible with those techniques that would be expected within a strategy aiming to counter radicalisation.[78] However, the publication stated that although the Armed Forces may not have the lead, they can contribute in countering radicalisation by considering 'when, where, and how (or whether) to conduct operations'.[79] The primary tasking of military force was the seeking, apprehension, detention and, where applicable, killing of those suspected of terrorist-related activity.

Actions undertaken during this period by the United States Armed Forces, even if not directly related to counter-terrorism, such as the initial reasoning behind the Iraq campaign, did serve as a unifying, motivating factor for those that aimed to recruit others into terrorist groups. As a consequence a paradox of sorts appeared whereby military force was used as a means of suppressing an insurrection, while also motivating others to take up arms. This was recognised by the George W. Bush administration and is evidenced by former United States Secretary of Defense Rumsfeld's question to immediate staff, regarding whether United States actions were creating more terrorists than could be apprehended or killed.[80] Rumsfeld asked specifically: 'Are we capturing, killing or deterring and dissuading more terrorists every day than the madrassas [*sic*] and the radical clerics are recruiting, training and deploying against us?'

Although the question was asked and the likelihood of this being the case was acknowledged by senior administration officials, it did not lead to the establishment of initiatives that could be seen as beneficial. Indeed, the continued wide-scale use of military force, in Afghanistan and, as will be discussed further below, Iraq, did not reduce the threat of terrorism to the United States. Rather its use increased the likelihood of sympathisers becoming practitioners of terrorist violence.

The continued use of military force without increased counter-radicalisation programmes was further recognised by senior military figures such as General Stanley McChrystal (Commander of United States and the NATO Forces in Afghanistan) and Admiral James Stavridis (Supreme Allied Commander Europe) who noted that 'we cannot kill our way to victory' and that security in Afghanistan 'will not be delivered from the barrel of a gun'.[81] Thus the unifying and motivating impact that military force has upon sympathisers who become practitioners of terrorist-related violence reduced the effectiveness of this policy instrument.

The role of the military post-9/11 was always going to be central to the United States' response.[82] This was especially so, according to Larsen and another source, considering the disbelief by some in government that non-state actors could unilaterally be responsible for such a devastating attack.[83] Members of the George W. Bush administration saw the 9/11 attacks as a declaration of war with parallels to Pearl Harbor being drawn and inevitably necessitating a military response.[84]

This military response contrasted with the predominant European view that acts of terrorism were a concern for law enforcement.[85] The identification of the terrorists and their primary figurehead, Osama bin Laden, led the George W. Bush administration to demand that the Taliban regime that governed Afghanistan and provided safe haven for them should renounce terrorism, close their training camps and extradite Osama bin Laden or face military action. The failure of the Taliban regime to acquiesce to the demands led the United States, with its allies, to launch a military campaign against the country – not just against the al Qaeda network

The Afghanistan campaign affirmed the use of military force as the lead policy instrument in the Global War on Terror.[86] At inception, the George W. Bush administration did not appear interested in nation-building when it came to Afghanistan and may have been happy with ousting the Taliban regime and handing over control of the venture to the United Nations.[87] The administration believed that anti-Americanism, that had in part motivated the 9/11 suicide-hijackers, was not so much because of faults in United States foreign policy as because of misrepresentation of such policies by leaders of local, authoritarian regimes.[88]

Removing regimes like the Taliban would allow moderates to rise, and the country, both politically and economically, to flourish, necessitating minimal involvement by the United States or wider international community, particularly the armed forces.[89] As the United States' action took shape, an insurgency began forcing them to commit ever-greater resources to Afghanistan. McMillan states that the United States 'underestimated the difficulty of reinventing [Afghanistan's] systems of governance' and that while the justification of the conflict may have been widely acceptable within the international community, the consequences had a knock-on effect that not only undermined the United States' legitimacy, but distracted from the Global War on Terror itself.[90]

As the insurrection in Afghanistan progressed, the United States' Armed Forces found themselves in a position of overstretch with regard to what they were attempting to achieve in Afghanistan (the establishment of a safe, viable state) and indeed confused as to its strategic aim (the defeat of terrorism) and objectives.[91] Furthermore, it may be argued that later deployments, particularly to Iraq, further distracted from the overarching aim of the Global War on Terror.[92] This proved to be detrimental to the overall progress of the Global War on Terror by overstretching the resources of the United States' Armed Forces and detracting from the overarching aim and, by extension, decreasing the ability of the state's primary counter-terrorism policy instrument to reduce the threat of terrorism to the state.

The use of military force in the second Gulf conflict was authorised by the establishment of Operation Iraqi Freedom on 19 March 2003 with the first visible use of this policy instrument being the bombing of targets inside Baghdad a day later. On 9 April 2003, as United States-led coalition forces gained control of the capital, the toppling of a bronze statue of former Iraqi President Saddam Hussain signalled the decreasing grip of the Ba'ath regime in the country. On 1 May 2003 United States President George W. Bush, aboard the aircraft carrier USS *Abraham Lincoln*, standing before a banner that read 'Mission Accomplished', stated that 'Major combat operations in Iraq have ended'.[93] Following this, a period of low-intensity conflict, akin to an insurgency, emerged in Iraq.

The insurgency came from three fronts. First were elements of the Ba'ath regime loyal to Saddam Hussain; second were Shi'a groups; and third were external groups aiming to wage a war on behalf of al Qaeda.[94] These three groupings each used terrorist tactics.[95] Further evidence of a link between Saddam Hussein's regime and terrorism was put into the public domain by the capture and arrest of Abu Abbas, in Iraq, on 16 April 2003.[96] Abbas, a former leader of the Palestine Liberation Front, was suspected of masterminding the May 1986 hijacking of the *Achille Lauro* in which one passenger (a citizen of the United States) was killed.[97] Even with this taken into consideration it should be clear that the Iraq campaign was not at the start about counter-terrorism. It was, officially at least, about a state that had defied international demands, reneged on commitments to the international community, oppressed a people, had previously employed chemical weapons on its own people, and was suspected of reconstituting, or establishing a chemical, biological, radiological or nuclear programme to be used on its people or on regional, neighbouring states.[98] Moreover, Saddam Hussain was a sworn enemy of Osama bin Laden.

Terrorism arguably became a concern when expectations similar to those of Afghanistan, involving the quick establishment of a functioning state, failed to materialise. Instead, religious tensions that had been suppressed under the previous regime now provided the ignition for conflict – likely spurred and/or supported by external influences (i.e. Iran and al Qaeda). A sizeable insurrection that used terrorist violence emerged, necessitating military force to be used to counter terrorist activity both in Afghanistan and Iraq.

Considering counter-terrorism as a law enforcement issue appears to have made it easier for the United Kingdom to maintain a distinction between the military action in Iraq and other counter-terrorism activity. This distinction may have been eroded as the Iraq campaign developed from a liberation action towards counter-insurgency, but not as rapidly for the United Kingdom as it did for the United States This new conflict in Iraq, reinforced by the already established link between 9/11 and Afghanistan, made it difficult, when it came to Iraq, to divorce military action from counter-terrorism campaigns, and so may have proved to have been a distraction from the Global War on Terror.

By the time the 2007 Fiscal Year Budget was presented (February 2006), the George W. Bush administration, due perhaps to the similarities in terms of insurgencies, had defined their position so that both Iraq and Afghanistan were perceived as components of the Global War on Terror.[99] One view, therefore, was that Iraq, similar to Afghanistan, could be seen as a template for future military commitments. Iraq, a pariah of the international community, was to be brought back into the international fold, after over a decade of defying their wishes.[100] Afghanistan a state sponsor of terrorism, was now participating in international affairs. Indeed, McMillan states that former Secretary of Defense Donald Rumsfeld was more concerned with reshaping the military to carry out operations in support of this thinking, than he was with change within Iraq itself.[101]

A posse comitatus refers to the population from which a law enforcement official may draw assistance to aid in 'keeping the peace, in pursuing and arresting felons'.[102] The United States' Posse Comitatus Act describes the domestic role of the Armed Forces in a manner that prevents their participation in domestic law enforcement activities except under specific circumstances.[103] They may be used as a means of supplementing other areas such as the tasking of the Army Corps of Engineers in times of crisis.[104] According to Larson and Peters, other exceptions include: the use of the National Guard who are exempt due to their allegiance being to the state rather than to the nation; times of domestic civil unrest; search and surveillance undertaken by military personnel using aerial photographic equipment; the use of equipment and personnel in the war on drugs; and the Coast Guard in peacetime.[105] As an anonymous source indicates, it is perhaps the case that a scenario where military intervention is needed is difficult to imagine, due to the militarisation of law enforcement agencies.[106] Ross concurs, stating that domestically, much of what needed to be done during this period was non-military based.[107]

Counter-terrorism, especially in terms of the domestic realm, was not the exclusive purview of the Department of Defense; both the FBI and the National Counter-Terrorism Center had significant roles to play. This was not a view necessarily shared by the Department of Defense, which saw the broader concern of national security to be their specialist area of responsibility.[108] Especially when considered within the context of the establishment of the Department of Homeland Security, it appears clear that there was reluctance on the part of the Department of Defense to surrender elements, responsibility or authority relating to their counter-terrorism capability for deployments at home or abroad. This was due in large part to a belief that surrendering such capabilities would make the ability of the Armed Forces to deploy them, in future times of crisis, even harder.[109] That said, using military force domestically suggests that government cannot offer adequate protection in line with established rules and procedures and would have further hindered its ability to use law enforcement.[110]

In order to cater for the asymmetric threats of the twenty-first century, particularly that of transnational terrorism and as a means of easing the burden upon deployed units, in 2006 the United States Army initiated a process known as Army Modulation. Under this initiative the Army redesigned 'its current 10 active duty division force to a 42 or 43 [B]rigade [C]ombat [T]eam (BCT) force by [financial year] 2007.[111] This would make more troops available for deployment and provide greater interchangeability and flexibility within the Armed Forces.[112] The Army's Modularity process was undertaken within the context of the Global Posture Initiative announced by United States President George W. Bush in August 2004. The initiative called for a consolidation of the military, resulting in the stationing of fewer troops abroad and a reduction from 850 to 550 bases overseas.[113] Furthermore, it emphasised a need for a more flexible fighting force.

Counter-terrorism portfolios in the United States can be split between three primary agencies, as depicted in Figure 5.2. The FBI, which has responsibility for the investigation, pursuit, apprehension and, through its parent body the Department of Justice, prosecution of terrorist-related activities, is primarily, but not exclusively, a domestic agency. Indeed, United States law gives authority for the FBI to investigate terrorist-related cases that have occurred overseas.[114] The National Counter-Terrorism Center forms another part of the United States' counter-terrorism agencies, by creating an area in which members of the Intelli-

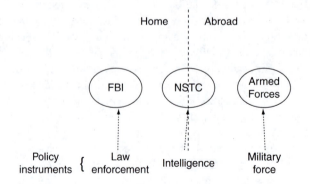

Figure 5.2 Counter-terrorism agencies of the United States.

gence Community could share information prior to sanitisation or redaction and distribution to appropriate law enforcement agencies at the state, local and tribal levels.[115] The third and final counter-terrorism agency is the United States Armed Forces which, through the Department of Defense, provides a counter-terrorism capability deliverable primarily in the overseas realm.[116]

Intelligence was used to gather information and, as Cohn (Deputy Assistant Secretary for Policy (Strategic Plans) within the Department of Homeland Security) states, law enforcement was for arrest and trial and, where applicable, the 'military [were] to go out and fix and kill'.[117] The clear division of roles between the domestic and international counter-terrorism agencies of the United States increases the ability of the state to do this. This is because resources can be developed and tailored to suit a particular environment. This, as discussed earlier, can only work efficiently if there are adequate lines of communication between the various agencies. This clear division of labour improved relationships and as such made the pursuit of terrorists more effective.

Summary

The use of military force for both of these states is, primarily, as a means of countering the threat of terrorist violence overseas. Even in the case of the United Kingdom, the use of military force, domestically, is restricted to times of extreme need and requires the retention of civilian control and responsibility. Arguably, particularly with regard to costs, the United States' use of military force has been more detrimental in their desire to achieve the overarching aim and objectives. It should be remembered that through the Army modulation redesign the United States, unlike the United Kingdom, has initiated a process to address the contemporary threat of transnational terrorism. A lack of movement on behalf of the United Kingdom's Armed Forces in this area can and should be considered as being an indicator that no structural changes were needed – due in no small part to previous counter-terrorism/counter-insurgency experiences.

The greatest differences in the use of military force between these two states come down to ability. Even though both states committed resources to Afghanistan and Iraq and indeed both were overstretched, the United States was undoubtedly able to put more *boots on the ground* and cope with the strain of the Armed Forces undertaking two simultaneous deployments. Furthermore, when it came to counter-insurgency and interacting with local people, the United Kingdom had far more experience than the United States due to previous experiences, particularly in Northern Ireland.

Notes

1 Ministry of Defence (n.d.), 'Defence Organisation', about defence, www.mod.uk/DefenceInternet/AboutDefence/Organisation/KeyFactsAboutDefence/DefenceOrganisation.htm.
2 Major-General Timothy Cross, Retired: British Army, interview conducted by the author, held in Aldershot, UK, 29 August 2009.

3 The strategy thus states that the primary focus of the Armed Forces is on the PREVENT and PURSUE strands of CONTEST-2006 with 'specialised elements' occurring in the PROTECT strand. United Kingdom government (July 2006), 'Countering International Terrorism', p. 28.

4 United Kingdom government (July 2006), op. cit., p. 28.

5 Ibid., p. 29.

6 Ministry of Defence (September 2007), 'Operations in the United Kingdom: The Defence Contribution to Resilience: Joint Doctrine Publication 02, 2nd Edition', Ministry of Defence, www.cabinetoffice.gov.uk/media/132712/defenceconrtibution1.pdf, ch. 1, p. 4.

7 Ibid.

8 Cross, 29 August 2009, op. cit.

9 Ibid.

10 Ibid.; and Major-General Timothy Cross, Retired (British Army) (7 December 2009), 'Witness Statement: Post-Invasion Iraq: The Planning and The Reality After The Invasion From Mid 2002 To The End Of August 2003', Evidence to the Iraq Inquiry – chaired by Sir John Chilcot, www.iraqinquiry.org.uk/media/39160/timcross-statement.pdf, pp. 26–27.

11 Cross, 29 August 2009, op. cit.

12 Cross, 7 December 2009, op. cit., p. 26.

13 Ibid.

14 United Kingdom government (March 2009), op. cit., p. 6.

15 House of Commons Defence Committee (18 May 2009), op. cit., p. 18.

16 Ibid.

17 Baroness Eliza Manningham-Buller (20 July 2010), 'Transcript: Baroness Manningham-Buller', Iraq Inquiry – chaired by Sir John Chilcot, www.iraqinquiry.org.uk/media/48331/20100720am-manningham-buller.pdf, p. 19.

18 Superintendent Andy Pratt, Lancashire Police Constabulary, interview conducted by the author, held in Preston, UK, 22 November 2009.

19 Manningham-Buller (20 July 2010), op. cit., p. 19.

20 It should be noted that claims relating to increased or decreased radicalisation made throughout this book are from the perspective of the state and not from sympathisers or practitioners of terrorist violence.

21 General Sir Richard Dannatt (28 July 2010), 'Transcript: General Sir Richard Dannatt GCB CBE MC DL', Iraq Inquiry – chaired by Sir John Chilcot, www.iraqinquiry.org.uk/media/48965/20100728am-dannatt.pdf.

22 Bill Rammell (13 January 2010), Speech, 'Generation Why?: Understanding the Armed Forces in Modern Society', http://webarchive.nationalarchives.gov.uk/+/www.mod.uk/DefenceInternet/AboutDefence/People/Speeches/MinAF/20100113GenerationWhyUnderstandingTheArmedForcesInModernSociety.htm.

23 Ibid.

24 Anonymous Source I, interview conducted by the author.

25 The campaign in Afghanistan was known as Operation Enduring Freedom – Afghanistan. Other campaigns in the Global War on Terror and under the banner of Operation Enduring Freedom were: Operation Enduring Freedom – Philippines; Operation Enduring Freedom – Horn of Africa; and Operation Enduring Freedom – Trans Sahara.

26 Paul Rogers, *Global Security and the War on Terror – Elite Power and the Illusion of Control* (Abingdon: Routledge, 2008), p. 157; Senior House Committee on Homeland Security Staffer, op. cit.; Anonymous Source B, op. cit.; Corey Gruber, Executive Director, National Preparedness Task-Force, Federal Emergency Management Agency, Department of Homeland Security, interview conducted by the author, held in Washington, DC, 11 February 2009; Michael Jacobsen, Senior Fellow, Stein Program on Counterterrorism and Intelligence, interview conducted by the author, held in Washington, DC, 11 February 2009; Hoffman, 12 February 2009, op. cit.

27 Ministry of Defence (July 2002), 'The Strategic Defence Review: A New Chapter', Ministry of Defence, www.mod.uk/NR/rdonlyres/79542E9C-1104–4AFA-9A4D-8520F35C5C93/0/sdr_a_new_chapter_cm5566_vol. 1.pdf.

28 Broader issues, such as strategic lift capability, were raised but it was recognised that these were not concerns for the contribution of military force to countering the threat of terrorism. Ministry of Defence (July 2002), 'The Strategic Defence Review: A New Chapter', pp. 28–29.

29 Dannatt (28 July 2010), op. cit., p. 110.

30 Jack Straw (Foreign Secretary) and Geoff Hoon (Defence Secretary) (19 March 2003), 'Declassified Extract from a Letter to the Prime Minister: Iraq United Kingdom Military Contribution to Post-conflict Iraq', Iraq Inquiry – chaired by Sir John Chilcot, www.iraqinquiry.org.uk/media/46615/uk-military-contribution-post-conflict-iraq.pdf.

31 Dannatt (28 July 2010), op. cit., p. 15.

32 Although a minimal force remained in place, offensive combat operations for the United Kingdom were completed in the summer of 2009.

33 In an exchange between Jenkins and Bob Ainsworth it was noted that the infantry departments were particularly overstretched. House of Commons Defence Committee (18 May 2009), 'The Defence Contribution to United Kingdom National Security and Resilience – Sixth Report of Session 2008–09', p. EV27; see also Second Clerk to the House of Commons Defence Committee, interview conducted by the author, held in London, 6 August 2009.

34 Ministry of Defence (July 1998), op. cit.

35 Helen McCartney, 'The Military Covenant and the Civil–Military Contract in Britain', *International Affairs*, 86 (2010), 2, p. 412.

36 British Army (n.d.), 'The Military Covenant', Army, www.army.mod.uk/join/terms/3111.aspx; Unknown Author (n.d.), 'Military Covenant', BBC: *Ethics Guide*, www.bbc.co.uk/ethics/war/overview/covenant.shtml.

37 Dannatt (28 July 2010), op. cit., p. 20.

38 Ibid., p. 20.

39 Ministry of Defence (September 2007), op. cit., ch. 2, pp. 9–10.

40 Second Clerk to the House of Commons Defence Committee, op. cit.

41 House of Commons Defence Committee (18 May 2009), op. cit., p. 8.

42 Iain Anderson (22 July 2002), 'Foot and Mouth Disease 2001: Lessons to be Learned Inquiry Report', Cabinet Office, http://archive.cabinetoffice.gov.uk/fmd/fmd_report/report.

43 Foot-and-mouth disease is a highly infectious disease that can spread rapidly among animals, particularly cattle, and also among humans. The disease spread in the United Kingdom in 2001 and the outbreak was described in a Cabinet Office Report as being 'one of the largest in history'. Iain Anderson (22 July 2002), 'Foot and Mouth Disease 2001: Lessons to be Learned Inquiry Report', p. 8; and United Kingdom government (1 November 2008), 'Disease Factsheet: Foot-and-Mouth Disease (FMD)', Department for Environment and Rural Affairs, www.defra.gov.uk/foodfarm/farmanimal/diseases/atoz/fmd/about/factsheet.htm, accessed 6 February 2010.

44 Iain Anderson (22 July 2002), op. cit.

45 Second Clerk to the House of Commons Defence Committee, op. cit.

46 For full list of linkages see Ministry of Defence (September 2007), Second Clerk to the House of Commons Defence Committee, op. cit., p. vii.

47 According to a Ministry of Defence publication, 'Treasury rules dictate that Government Departments charge for services that do not form part of their funded tasks', as these are an improper use of resources. Ministry of Defence (September 2007), 'Operations in the United Kingdom: The Defence Contribution to Resilience: Joint Doctrine Publication 02', p. 29.

48 Ministry of Defence (September 2007), op. cit., ch. 2, p. 30, fn. 81.

49 Inspector Jonathan Brook, South Yorkshire Police Constabulary, interview conducted by the author, held in Sheffield, 19 August 2009; Superintendent Andy Pratt, Lancashire Police Constabulary, interview conducted by the author, held in Preston, UK, 22 November 2009; Patrick Mercer MP, Chair, Home Office, Sub-Committee on Counter-Terrorism, interview conducted by the author, held in London, 12 October 2009; Brian Jackson, Homeland Security Program, RAND Corporation, interview conducted by the author, held in Washington, DC, 10 February 2009.
50 Jackson, op. cit.; Cross, 29 August 2009, op. cit.
51 House of Commons Defence Committee (18 May 2009), op. cit., p. 7.
52 Grant Wardlaw, *Political Terrorism – Theory, Tactics and Counter-measures*, 2nd edn (Cambridge: Cambridge University Press, 1989), pp. 87–99.
53 Cross, 29 August 2009, op. cit.; Jackson, 30 July 2008, op. cit.; Ministry of Defence (September 2007), op. cit., p. v.
54 In giving his evidence to the House of Commons Defence Committee, General Richards stated that the principle of recovering costs in non-life-threatening situations from other departments reflected the government's view that security of the homeland from internal threats is not the job of the military. House of Commons Defence Committee (18 May 2009), 'The Defence Contribution to United Kingdom National Security and Resilience – Sixth Report of Session 2008–09', p. 13.
55 Ministry of Defence (September 2007), op. cit., ch. 2, p. 11; ch. 3, pp. 1–6.
56 Ibid., ch. 4, pp. 1–6.
57 Ibid., ch. 5, pp. 1–9.
58 Doctrine dictates that military support provided in aid of the civil power is 'on the basis that responsibility and control over the situation is retained by the relevant civilian agency' (i). Indeed, responsibility for security of the homeland rests with the Home Secretary (ii). (i) Ministry of Defence (September 2007), 'Operations in the United Kingdom: The Defence Contribution to Resilience: Joint Doctrine Publication 02', ch. 1, p. 7. (ii) Ministry of Defence (September 2007), 'Operations in the United Kingdom: The Defence Contribution to Resilience', p. v.
59 Ministry of Defence (September 2007), op. cit., ch. 5, p. 8.
60 House of Commons Defence Committee (18 May 2009), op. cit., p. 7, pp. 9–10, p. 14; Ev, p. 19; Ev, pp. 22–24; Ev, p. 30; Ev, p. 36; Ev, pp. 39–44; Second Clerk to the House of Commons Defence Committee, op. cit.
61 Military Aid to the Civilian Authority in Northern Ireland was considered to necessitate a separate capability appraisal due to the level of frequent support needed in light of paramilitary terrorism activity.
62 Extract taken from House of Commons Defence Committee (18 May 2009), op. cit., p. 8.
63 House of Commons Defence Committee (18 May 2009), op. cit., p. 9; Second Clerk to the House of Commons Defence Committee, op. cit.
64 Ministry of Defence (September 2007), op. cit., ch. 1.
65 According to the United States Code, the Armed Forces consist of 'the Army, Navy, Air Force, Marine Corps, and Coast Guard'. See United States House of Representatives (1 February 2010), 'Title 10 (Armed Forces), Chapter 1 (Definitions), Section 101 (Definitions), Paragraph a, clause 4', United States Code: Office of the Law Revision Counsel U.S. House of Representatives, http://uscode.house.gov/, accessed 1 March 2010.
66 United States House of Representatives (1 February 2010), 'Title 10 (Armed Forces), Chapter 1 (Definitions), Section 101 (Definitions), Paragraph a, clause 4', p. 101.
67 Former Deputy Secretary of Defense Paul Wolfowitz (1 August 2002), 'Department of Defense Directive: Functions of the Department of Defense and Its Major Components', Department of Defense, www.dtic.mil/whs/directives/corres/pdf/510001p.pdf.
68 United States government (September 2006), op. cit.

69 Ibid.; McMillan, op. cit.
70 McMillan, op. cit.
71 Ibid.
72 Jacobsen, op. cit.
73 Rogers, op. cit., p. 157; Senior House Committee on Homeland Security Staffer, op. cit.; Anonymous Source B, op. cit.; Gruber, op. cit.; Jacobsen, op. cit.; Hoffman, 12 February 2009, op. cit.
74 Larsen, 10 September 2009, op. cit.
75 Jacobsen, op. cit.
76 Ibid.
77 United States government (13 March 2006), 'The National Military Strategic Plan for the War on Terrorism (NMSP-WOT) Special Operations/Low Intensity Conflict Conference', Joint Chiefs of Staff, www.dtic.mil/ndia/2006solic/renuart.pdf.
78 Ibid.
79 Ibid.
80 Defense Secretary Donald Rumsfeld (20 May 2005), 'Rumsfeld's War-on-Terror Memo – 16th October 2003', *USA Today*, www.usatoday.com/news/washington/executive/rumsfeld-memo.htm; McMillan, op. cit.
81 Admiral James Stavridis (17 November 2009), 'Remarks for NATO Parliamentary Assembly', Allied Command Operations, www.aco.nato.int/page277501841.aspx.
82 Cross, 29 August 2009, op. cit.
83 Larsen, op. cit.; Senior House Committee on Homeland Security Staffer, op. cit.
84 Randy Beardsworth, former Assistant Secretary for Strategic Plans; former Director of Operations; former Under-Secretary for Border and Transportation Security Director; former Director for Defence Policy on the National Security Council, interview conducted by the author, held in Washington, DC, 10 September 2009.
85 Ibid.
86 Hoffman, op. cit.
87 Anonymous comment made during the question-and-answer session of the Anthony Hyman Memorial Lecture presented by Astri Suhrke, Chair of the Michelsen Institute. Astri Suhrke (17 March 2010), 'The Case for a Light Footprint: The International Project in Afghanistan', Anthony Hyman Memorial Lecture: School of Oriental and African Studies, University of London, www.soas.ac.uk/cccac/events/anthonyhyman/file58420.pdf.
88 McMillan, op. cit.
89 Ibid.
90 McMillan, op. cit.; Hoffman, op. cit.
91 Larsen, op. cit.
92 Jacobsen, op. cit.
93 United States President George W. Bush (1 May 2003), 'Speech – President Declares End To Major Combat in Iraq', *CBS News*, www.cbsnews.com/stories/2003/05/01/iraq/main551946.shtml.
94 David Teather (10 February 2004), 'US Claims to Uncover War Plot', *Guardian*, www.guardian.co.uk/world/2004/feb/10/iraq.davidteather.
95 Ibid.
96 Ibid.
97 The *Achille Lauro* was an Italian cruise ship hijacked on 7 October 1985 by members of the Palestinian Liberation Front, a faction of the Palestinian Liberation Organisation (also known as the PLO). The hijackers demanded the release of Palestinian prisoners in Israeli gaols. During the hijacking the terrorists shot and killed a Jewish-United States passenger, and threw his body overboard.
98 Secretary of State Colin Powell (5 February 2003), 'A Policy of Evasion and Deception', *Washington Post*, www.washingtonpost.com/wp-srv/nation/transcripts/powell-text_020503.html.

99 On 8 April 2009, the Inspector General of DoD published a report which stated that Operation Enduring Freedom, undertaken in Afghanistan; Operation Iraqi Freedom, undertaken in Iraq; and Operation Noble Eagle, referring to domestic counterterrorism operations, were collectively referred to as being parts of the Global War on Terror. United States government (8 April 2009), 'DoD Components' Use of Global War on Terror Supplemental Funding Provided for Procurement and Research, Development, Test, and Evaluation', Department of Defense, www.dodig.mil/Audit/reports/fy09/09–073.pdf, p. 1; and United States government (n.d.), 'Budget of the United States Government: Fiscal Year 2007 – Department of Defense', United States Government Printing Office, www.gpoaccess.gov/USbudget/fy07/pdf/budget/defense.pdf, pp. 64–65.

100 Secretary of State Colin Powell (5 February 2003), op. cit.

101 McMillan, op. cit.

102 Eric Larson and John Peters, *Preparing the United States Army for Homeland Security: Concepts, Issues and Options* (California: RAND, 2001), p. 243.

103 The Posse Comitatus Act, found in the United States Code pertaining to Crimes and Criminal Procedure, states: 'Whoever, except in cases and under circumstances expressly authorized by the Constitution or Act of Congress, wilfully uses any part of the Army or the Air Force as a posse comitatus or otherwise to execute the laws shall be fined under this title or imprisoned not more than two years, or both.' United States House of Representatives (1 February 2010), 'Title 18 (Crimes and Criminal Procedure), Chapter 67 (Military and Navy), Section 1385 (Use of Army and Air Force as posse comitatus)', United States Code: Office of the Law Revision Counsel U.S. House of Representatives, http://uscode.house.gov/, accessed 1 March 2010; and Commander Gary Felicetti and Lieutenant John Luce, 'The Posse Comitatus Act: Setting the Record Straight on 124 Years of Mischief and Misunderstanding before Any More Damage is Done', *Military Review* 175 (n.d.), www.jagcnet.army.mil/JAGCNETINTERNET/HOMEPAGES/AC/MILITARYLAWREVIEW.NSF/20a66345129fe3d885256e5b00571830/47c2 b664085060fc85256e5b00576e6e/$FILE/Volume175Felicetti.pdf, accessed 2 November 2009, pp. 86–183.

104 Larson and Peters, op. cit., pp. 244–245; Gruber, op. cit.

105 Ibid.

106 Second Clerk to the House of Commons Defence Committee, op. cit.

107 Ross, 9 September 2009, op. cit.

108 Ibid.

109 John B. McGowan, former Director of Cargo and Port Security, Office of Homeland Security, Executive Office of the President, interview conducted by the author, held in Washington, DC, 11 September 2009.

110 Gruber, op. cit.

111 Andrew Feickert (5 May 2006), 'Report for Congress – United States Army's Modular Redesign: Issues for Congress', Department of State, http://fpc.state.gov/documents/organization/67816.pdf.

112 United States government (n.d.), 'Budget of the United States Government: Fiscal Year 2007 – Department of Defense', United States Government Printing Office, www.gpoaccess.gov/USbudget/fy07/pdf/budget/defense.pdf; see also United States government (16 March 2005), 'Testimony – Force Structure Preliminary Observations on Army Plans to Implement and Fund Modular Forces', Government Accountability Office, www.gao.gov/new.items/d05443t.pdf.

113 Ibid.

114 United States government (10 April 1982), 'National Security Decision – Directive Number 30 – Managing Terrorism Incidents', Federation of American Scientists, www.fas.org/irp/offdocs/nsdd/nsdd-030.htm; Unknown Author (current as of 8 January 2008), 'Title 18 (Crimes and Criminal Procedure), Part I (Crimes), Chapter

113B (Terrorism), Section 2332b (Acts of terrorism transcending national boundaries), Paragraph f', Cornell University Law School, www.law.cornell.edu/uscode/pdf/uscode18/lii_usc_TI_18_PA_I_CH_113B_SE_2332b.pdf, p. 2.

115 The combination of all those organisations that have a role in intelligence (collection, oversight, assessment, tasking) makes up an intelligence structure. In the United Kingdom this structure is referred to as the National Intelligence Machinery (NIM) and in the United States as the Intelligence Community.

116 Cohn, op. cit.

117 Ibid.

6 Conclusion

The purpose of this book is to facilitate discussion on the effectiveness of both the United Kingdom–United States counter-terrorism strategies in the years following the terrorist attacks of September 2001. In addition to other primary and secondary sources, this work has used previously unpublished interview material gleaned from practitioners and academics with a specialist expertise in terrorism and counter-terrorism. It has been argued here that purely quantitative metrics in assessing the effectiveness of counter-terrorism strategies is not enough and that qualitative appraisals, problematic though they may be, are crucial to understanding the full picture of counter-terrorism effectiveness during this period. This book began with a statement made by an individual in the United States who worked on an oversight committee of the Department of Homeland Security. When asked how effective the United States had been at countering the threat of transnational terrorism, the interviewee stated that as there had not been a major terrorist attack on United States soil since 9/11 the inference was that they could be seen as effective. While one can see how individuals on the frontline of counter-terrorism activity can buy into such logic, a broader consideration suggests the recognition that the failure of one does not necessarily denote the success of the other. Put another way, just because terrorists have failed to successfully target the United States domestically does not mean that this is due to the actions of the United States authorities. There are bound to be multiple factors such as expense and mistakes by the would-be-attackers enforced by their own making.

As of June 2013 there has not been a major terrorist attack on United States soil; nor since July 2005 has there been a domestic attack, resulting in comparable numbers of dead or injured, in the United Kingdom. This, however, cannot be the benchmark for judging whether or not these states have been effective at countering the threat of transnational terrorism since 9/11. It is fair to state that judging effectiveness is no easy feat, particularly when it is difficult to ascertain how much of the lack of success is due to state actions as opposed to terrorist limitations. Specifically, therefore, what this book is asking is not so much how effective the United Kingdom and the United States have been in countering the threat of transnational terrorism in the early 2000s but how effective they themselves believe they have been. This book is based not only on official statements, strategies and documents but also on interviews with some of those charged with the delivery of the strategies and implementing them at a more local level. Moreover, this book has focused on three critical policy instruments: intelligence, law enforcement and military force. It is these instruments that have been at the forefront of counter-terrorism activity not only since 9/11 but preceding it in both states.

When considering how to respond to the threat of terrorism via the implementation of these policy instruments, states face a number of dilemmas. Chief among these is that of the balance that must be struck between effectiveness and acceptability. Liberal democratic (broadly defined) states must consider whether they are willing to sacrifice some of those norms that make them democratic (e.g. freedom of speech, movement, tolerance, *habeas corpus*) in order to be more effective at countering the threat posed. For governments, the dilemma is a difficult one not least because the primary role of the state is to provide security for its citizenry. The question remains how much imposition is acceptable before the desire for ever more security plays into the terrorist recruiting sergeant's hands. This could be in the form of 'special measures' such as the transfer and detention of so-called 'non-combatants' to Guantánamo Bay or other 'Black sites', the stopping and searching of individuals based on appearance by law enforcement, or the curtailment of other civil liberties. A terrorist recruiter may well use such 'security' measures to enforce the belief that this really is a war against Islam as opposed to terrorism.[1] States, therefore, face a problem. How do we counter the threat of terrorism while adhering to our democratic traditions? How do we undermine the terrorist recruiters' pitch while responding to specific or broad threats of terrorism? How do we, the state, act effectively in countering the threat of transnational terrorist violence?

There is no easy way to judge effectiveness. An abstract quantitative methodology fails to consider the critically important aspects of terrorist activities that distinguish them from 'ordinary' criminality; mainly, that terrorist actions are intended to resonate beyond the immediate both in terms of time, proximity and numbers killed and physically injured. A qualitative approach that appreciates context, the idiosyncrasies of the threat posed to threatened/targeted states and the environment in which counter-terrorism responders must operate lends itself readily to an assessment of counter-terrorism effectiveness. This is not to say that a qualitative approach is foolproof. Indeed, subjectivity within a qualitative approach is a challenge that must be recognised. What this book has attempted to do is combine the analysis of strategies and previously unpublished interview material in an effort to ascertain how states themselves consider their counter-terrorism activities to have gone. This has been done by outlining the threat posed, the general response and ascertaining how the three main policy instruments used for responding to terrorist activity have fared.

A qualitative assessment of the effectives of counter-terrorism policy instruments requires an understanding of the threat to which they were responding and the context in which that threat existed. Terrorism, over the course of the twentieth century, went through a rapid evolution. At the start of the twentieth century, terrorist groups were primarily made up of anarchists who sought to overthrow the ruling elite by assassination but who also went to extraordinary lengths in order to avoid civilian casualties.[2] State-sponsored terrorism during the Second World War gave way to what is termed traditional terrorism – the use of violence in a random, indiscriminate manner which also sought political change.[3] Traditional and transnational terrorist organisations could be distinguished by the fact that the members of the former sought, primarily, to create fear and not mass casualties. In contrast, the latter sought both to cause fear and mass casualties. Indeed, the emergence of transnational terrorism through al Qaeda represented a significant shift in the evolution of terrorism. The al Qaeda network emerged as a result of United States military presence in Saudi Arabia during the 1980s and early 1990s. As the network grew, it challenged the perceived erosion of traditional Islamic practices in an increasingly globalised world as well as the continued presence and influence of the United States, not just in Saudi Arabia but throughout the Middle East. To the al Qaeda core, the United States and its supporters represented a clear and current danger to Islam. Although retaining political objectives akin to those espoused by traditional terrorist groups, it was clear that negotiation was not feasible – this was reinforced by the fusion of political objectives and religious rhetoric.[4]

Transnational terrorist organisations were also structured in a manner which made the use of traditional counter-terrorism approaches of detection and prevention almost redundant. Traditional terrorist organisations were hierarchically structured, meaning that by arresting the leaders of a particular group a state could significantly hinder their operations. The al Qaeda movement, the epitome of a transnational organisation, adopted a network of cells structure. The detection and, for example, the arrest of members of one cell did not impact upon the organisation as a whole, as another cell would simply fill their place. This cell structure became even more fragmented following the early intervention in Afghanistan. This intervention hindered the ability of the al Qaeda core to effectively retain command and control of its affiliates overseas. As such, Osama bin Laden became more of an inspirational figurehead. Affiliates overseas had already begun to work increasingly towards local grievances and not only those in the Middle East.

The transnational terrorist combination of political objectives, religious rhetoric, a network structure and a desire to acquire and use weapons of mass destruction represented a significant threat to the international community as a whole. The immediate response to 9/11 was to target al Qaeda's training camps in Afghanistan, oust the Taliban regime and declare a War on Terror. Over the following months and weeks both states developed new strategies to counter the threat of terrorist violence. New strategies were needed, as the events of 9/11 and 7/7 represented to both a significant change in the threat posed by terrorism broadly and transnational terrorism specifically.

For the United Kingdom, no stranger to terrorist violence, the counter-terrorism approach was primarily focused on tackling the home-grown threat. This is not to say that the United Kingdom was not heavily committed to engagements overseas but that in the early years overseas actions were considered to be more akin to counter-insurgency actions than counter-terrorism events. By January 2010 this view was shifting. Bill Rammel, the Armed Forces Minister, made a speech in which he advocated the commitment of the Armed Forces overseas due to the blurring between threats at home and abroad.[5] Furthermore, the Armed Forces offered niche and supplementary (otherwise known as augmentative) capabilities to other domestic agencies in the United Kingdom.

The United Kingdom's counter-terrorism approach is divided between four strands: PREVENT, PURSUE, PROTECT and PREPARE. The PREVENT strand is geared towards counter-radicalisation; the PURSUE strand identifies and prevents those that threaten to or already have committed acts of terrorist violence; the PROTECT strand provides broad instruments such as barriers to key areas, and scanners so as to stop attacks taking place; and the PREPARE strand highlights and improves the way in which a state will offer continuation of critical services following a successful terrorist attack. In many ways these strands overlap, and indeed the failure of some may well trigger the necessity for others such as the PREPARE strand. The lead institution was the Home Office, a branch of government that focuses on domestic policies. Similar to the United Kingdom, the United States' approach has also been based on previous counter-terrorism experience. The aim of the strategy under the George W. Bush administration has been to win the Global War on Terror. Under President Obama this was clarified with the word 'war' being interpreted to mean the process upon which the government would pursue terrorists and their supporters. The aim was thus a reduction in threat levels against the United States and its interests overseas.

In the immediate aftermath of 9/11 it was believed that the focus for the United States' counter-terrorism strategy should be on the prevention of individuals entering the state to conduct terrorist attacks. The rationale behind this stemmed not only from the knowledge that the 9/11 hijackers were non-United States citizens but also the belief that terrorist activity of this kind overseas (multiple, simultaneous) had rarely, if ever, involved United States citizens. As such, the United States' strategy focused first and foremost on the prosecution of the conflict in Afghanistan and later the suppression of terrorist activity in Iraq. The establishment of the Department of Homeland Security also saw the bringing together of a number of federal agencies that were responsible for border protection. The consideration of a domestic terrorist threat was not disregarded. The FBI, which had always had a counter-terrorism remit, had been criticised in the aftermath of 9/11 for not having the capability to gather, analyse and collate intelligence about emerging threats. As such, the FBI attempted to create an in-house intelligence-gathering facility which, according to Larsen, had failed by 2009.[6] This is somewhat unsurprising considering that the role of law enforcement is traditionally to investigate crimes that have already taken place or those which are plotted but either way to be driven by evidence rather than intelligence. This further added an argument to those suggesting that a separate, domestic intelligence-gathering capability akin to the United Kingdom's Security Service was needed.

In providing a qualitative assessment of a post-9/11 counter-terrorism strategy in both the United Kingdom and the United States the focus of this publication has been on the identification of threat, broad response and effectiveness of three policy instruments: intelligence, law enforcement and military force. These policy instruments have proven to be the primary tools through which states have responded to the threat of terrorist violence.

Intelligence, law enforcement and military force: a qualitative assessment

The United Kingdom's intelligence counter-terrorism contribution is led by the Security and Intelligence Agencies. The Agencies have the institutional lead in counter-terrorism domestically, making this an intelligence-led approach. One of the primary problems in having the Agencies, as opposed to the police, as the institutional lead in counter-terrorism is that the former does not have arrest powers and the competing aims of the police and the Agencies may cause problems when decisions pertaining to when to act need to be made. Counter-terrorism activity within the United Kingdom has benefited from increased funding in policies such as regionalisation of the Security Service – a clear recognition that terrorism activity not only occurs in the capital, London. The sharing of intelligence between the Agencies and the police post-9/11 has, on balance, been considered to be effective. The key issues, as is discussed below with law enforcement, lay in the police's desire to share some of that information that they considered to be unnecessarily restricted by the Agencies with other critical partners and decision-makers such as local authorities.

When comparing and contrasting the United Kingdom and United States approaches to the use of intelligence in counter-terrorism a key observation can be made. Issues concerning intelligence and the United States were less localised and more focused on structural areas; for example, the sharing of intelligence among agencies. The continuation of a Cold War mind-set facilitated a lack of desire among the agencies of the Intelligence Community to share intelligence with one another. The establishment of the Department of Homeland Security and the Office of Intelligence and Analysis was meant to address many of these concerns. This, however, did not occur due in part to the establishment of the Terrorist Threat Integration Center (later the National Counterterrorism Center) which took many of their powers away. Other concerns regarding the heavy investment in technology rather than in intelligence analysts may also be seen. Technology was considered to be a quick fix to counter-terrorism shortfalls. This was particularly so as the recruitment and investment in new analysts were not only costly but lengthy. Having a smaller number of analysts available increased the broad risk to the state insofar as emerging threats might go unnoticed. This was also noted in the *9/11 Commission Report*'s findings.[7] Another area of concern was the controversial practice of extra-ordinary rendition. Extra-ordinary rendition, the process of moving suspects of terrorist activity from one state to another in an extra-judicial manner, for the purpose of interrogation, or incarceration, highlighted the United States' inability, or lack of desire, to counter terrorism through conventional means and moreover offered recruiters a motivational tool to attract those who sympathised with terrorist causes.

The contribution of law enforcement for both the United Kingdom and the United States was particularly divergent within this policy instrument. For the United Kingdom, the primary issue centred around what Peter Clarke, former Assistant Commissioner and Head of Counter Terrorism Command with the Metropolitan Police Service, described as a 'deficit of trust'.[8] Clarke was, in his remarks, referring to a deficit of trust between the police and the public at large, particularly in the use of stop-and-search laws – disproportionately used on ethnic minorities – and criticisms over police-led community programmes, which suggested that the police were encouraging members of the public to spy on their neighbours. However, this deficit of trust may also be seen in the relations between law enforcement and those having the institutional lead for counter-terrorism, the Security and Intelligence Agencies. This is because although the Agencies regularly shared information with the police, they did not, as a matter of course, allow further dissemination by the police to other critical parties such as local authorities. This was particularly troublesome, as it often placed local authorities, which were responsible for authorising community counter-terrorism programmes, in the position of having to agree to something without being in full possession of the facts. That said, there was an improved relationship between the police and the Armed Forces.

The contribution of law enforcement to counter-terrorism in the United States context was dissimilar to that of the United Kingdom. One reason for this may be the structural differences between both states. For the United States, thousands of legal jurisdictions existed within the country, whereas the United Kingdom had forty-three separate, territorial, police forces. The characterisation of threat as originating from outside the United States meant that law enforcement agencies frequently did not get as much as they wanted, or expected, from federal agencies such as the Department of Homeland Security. Moreover, there was a lack of clarity over whether terrorism should be considered an ordinary crime or an act of war, and uncertainty over the role of the FBI. Where law enforcement did flourish was in the creation of agencies, such as the Interagency Threat Assessment and Coordination Group and Fusion Centres, as a means of improving communications between different jurisdictions.

Of the three policy instruments analysed in this book – intelligence, law enforcement and military force – military force presented the most similarities. For the United Kingdom, the primary issues centred on the overstretched position of the Armed Forces following deployments to Afghanistan and Iraq, the failure to engage more fully in counter-radicalisation programmes and the breaking of the civil–military contract. In contrast, the benefits were seen as the establishment of guidelines concerning the domestic role of the military and clarity over the use of the Armed Forces in the provision of specialist capabilities. Similarly, for the United States, overstretch in Afghanistan, the distraction from the Global War on Terror caused by the Iraq conflict and the distinct lack of focus regarding softer counter-terrorism techniques undermined effectiveness. A continued adherence to non-military participation in domestic counter-terrorism roles, except in exceptional circumstances, restructuring of the United States Army and a clear division of roles between the Armed Forces on the one hand and the intelligence and law enforcement agencies on the other are considered beneficial.

For both states, the use of military force is reserved for countering terrorism overseas. The use, both in terms of finance and rhetoric, of the Armed Forces in this role does, however, vary. The reason for this, as has been mentioned extensively throughout this book, is that the United States considers the threat of terrorism to be an overseas one. As such, the United States' primary instrument of counter-terrorism has been the deployment of military force overseas. In contrast, the United Kingdom considers there to be both an overseas and a domestic threat and thus sees overseas action as being just one part of its counter-terrorism strategy. From this, four broad policy recommendations may be made.

Policy recommendations

The analysis undertaken in this book has focused on the first decade post-9/11 – specifically 2001 to 2011. The policy recommendations below take into consideration not just the evidence presented within this publication from that period but also subsequent decisions and/or rationales that may have had an impact on their implementation. Furthermore, the policy recommendations below recognise the changed nature of the al Qaeda threat, specifically the death of key inspirational figureheads such as Osama bin Laden; the significantly reduced foothold in both Afghanistan and the border regions with Pakistan for the network; as well as the increased significance of stronger autonomous groups such as those found in Northern Africa – Algeria, Mali and Mauritania as well as Nigeria and Somalia. The proposals given below focus on improving the counter-terrorism response of both the United Kingdom and the United States, both domestically and internationally. As such it is important to note that in drawing generalisable conclusions it should be remembered that each threat of terrorist violence brings with it its own idiosyncrasies specific to the time, location and nature of the event(s).

Further investment in domestic counter-radicalisation programmes and a dialling down of ideological rhetoric

By far the most significant recommendation is that both states invest more in counter-radicalisation initiatives. The 2011 publication of a new PREVENT strategy under a newly elected Coalition government in the United Kingdom ushered in a division between community cohesion and counter-radicalisation. While a strong argument for this can be made (and this book does not purport to support or contest this decision), the fact of the matter is that a disproportionate amount of investment is not being channelled into counter-radicalisation projects. The United Kingdom government continues to see the development of new technologies and, more reasonably so, a strengthening of law enforcement and the Security and Intelligence Agencies as a key overarching necessity. A heavier investment, one that even matched the amount already committed to the aforementioned, would significantly impact upon efforts to address the root causes of radicalisation. The consequence of that would be to reduce the home-grown threat of terrorist violence as well as diminish perceptions of victimisation from segments of the domestic population.

Although still significantly behind with regard to counter-radicalisation initiatives, there has been an increased law enforcement focus on possible home-grown threats planned and/or undertaken by those who subscribe to the broad objectives of the al Qaeda movement within the borders of the United States. The reason for this focus has been an observed increased level of activity resulting in arrests of either citizens or long-term residents of the United States. Significant examples include the arrest of Rezwan Ferdaus (a citizen) on suspicion of planning to attack the Capitol Building and Pentagon using radio-controlled, explosive-laden aeroplanes – along with firearms involving six conspirators in September 2011; the November 2011 arrest of Jose Pimentel (a citizen) on suspicion of planning to bomb targets in New York and members of the Armed Forces returning from overseas duties; the January 2012 arrest of Sami Osmakac (a naturalised citizen) on suspicion of planning to use a weapon of mass destruction in Tampa, Florida; the arrest of Adel Daoud (a citizen) in September 2012 on suspicion of planting to bomb in a Chicago Bar; and the arrest of United States Army Major Nidal Hasan (citizen), who killed thirteen on a military base in Texas.

Another possible example of terrorist violence undertaken by long-term residents of the United States may be seen in the April 2013 bombing of the Boston Marathon. At the time of writing, brothers Tamerlan Tsarnev (aged 26) and Dzhokhar Tsarnev (aged 19) had been identified as the prime suspects of the attacks. Tamerlan had died in the pursuit shortly after the attacks and Dzhokhar had been indicted in what was the biggest single loss of life post-9/11 (domestically) for the United States. Over 250 were injured and three killed, when two simultaneous explosions occurred close to the finishing line of the race. In classic al Qaeda style, the explosions were designed to cause as much death and destruction as possible, with each device (a pressure cooker) packed with metal fragments (possibly nails). Both brothers had been in the United States for just under ten years, had become naturalised citizens and appeared to have fully integrated into their communities. It is too early to say exactly what motivated these suspects but Dzhokhar informed investigators from the High Value Detainee Interrogation group that the United States' participation in the conflicts of Iraq and Afghanistan had been their core grievance.

The above examples point to a need for the United States to begin to develop not just a law enforcement approach to home-grown threats but also a community-based approach that attempts to counter the threat of radicalisation. Lessons may be learned from the United Kingdom's experiences in this area, specifically the need to have broad community support and for it to be led by members of the community for which it is intended. This approach, if mishandled, can present its own difficulties, such as finances being diverted to questionable organisations. The potential benefits significantly outweigh the costs.

A dialling down in the rhetoric, as has been the case since the taking of office of United Kingdom Prime Minister David Cameron but particularly United States President Barack Obama, should be continued. Overly broad, combative or ideologically orientated statements that target many of those states for which international counter-terrorism initiatives may well depend is unhelpful. Moreover, this can further alienate domestic populations, leading to an increased propensity to the emergence of home-grown threats. Considering terrorism as an ordinary crime, as is highlighted below, would also be beneficial. That said, governments should beware of applying the term 'terrorism' too loosely and, to that end, should have a clear definition of what is and is not considered to be terrorist violence. Such a definition should be applied rigorously to all counter-terrorism agencies and not selectively adopted depending on the role or function of a particular department.

Additional investment in intelligence analysts and sustainable training regimes for new technologies

Even with the above, it is of course prudent to have analysts on hand in order to gather, analyse and suggest courses of action regarding intelligence data pertaining to those already radicalised and/or guilty of planning, or undertaking, terrorist violence. A key criticism of the 9/11 Commission was that the United States lacked the analysts, as well as the coordinating infrastructure, to join all the dots of information together and identify the threat. In the post-9/11 period there has, in the United Kingdom, been a steep increase in the number of intelligence analysts working for the Security and Intelligence Agencies, specifically the domestically focused Security Service. In the United States, although there has been an increase in the number of analysts, this appears to have been limited in favour of increased technology. A key argument behind this, as noted earlier in this publication, is the length of time it takes to recruit and train an analyst. Moreover, the specific cultural background of al Qaeda operatives, and the small pool from which the intelligence agencies of the United States is able to draw upon, adds an additional barrier to appropriate recruitment.

The issue of domestic intelligence gathering needs to be sufficiently addressed. At present, the United States does not have a wholly national domestic intelligence-gathering agency such as the United Kingdom's Security Service. Intelligence gathering and sharing is based on ad-hoc relationships between different law enforcement and intelligence-gathering agencies. The FBI had intended to set up an intelligence-gathering agency under its remit but has struggled to implement this to an adequate extent. This needs to not only be re-examined but perhaps further facilitated, as the alternative would involve setting up a new intelligence agency.

While the contribution of technology in certain areas, such as identifying money flows, highlighting internet activity or gathering communications data, is useful, there needs to be a more sustainable approach to the training and retaining of law enforcement officials on their use. As identified earlier, their remains, particularly in the United States, a problem of the training and retention of staff on counter-terrorism technologies. Indeed, this may also be extended to relationships within the counter-terrorism community. As law enforcement officials progress, career roles may, and indeed do, change. Furthermore, funding for further training is sometimes limited. A more sustainable method of retaining counter-terrorism skills needs to be developed. This may be through the Interagency Threat Assessment and Coordination Group.

Set a campaign plan and facilitate joined-up thinking

The perception of the threat posed to both the United Kingdom and the United States varies. For the United Kingdom the threat is seen to be from overseas and domestic quarters, while the United States, notwithstanding the above, considers the threat to be largely international in nature. The development of what former Major-General Tim Cross called a Campaign Plan is needed for both states.[9] Such a plan would identify the long-term objective and the steps to achieve it. This plan would not only consider the Armed Forces but would also take into consideration all branches of government that have a role in countering terrorism both overseas and domestically. The development of such a plan would lead, it is argued, to a clearly identifiable end-point in the Global War on Terror.

Under the recommendation of a Campaign Plan also comes the suggestion of more joined-up thinking, particularly, but not exclusively, in relation to intelligence sharing. Within the United Kingdom intelligence sharing between the Security and Intelligence Agencies and the police is considered to be very good. An issue was identified when members of the police want to pass some of that information on to other, critical stakeholders, such as local authorities which, up until 2011, had responsibility for counter-radicalisation projects. This adherence to what former Chief of the Secret Intelligence Service (1999–2004), Sir Richard Dearlove, called the third-party rule, meant that those responsible for authorising counter-radicalisation activities were sometimes not privy to the intelligence that made them necessary.[10] If a Campaign Plan is to be effective and indeed if coordination is to truly work, intelligence-sharing capabilities need to be significantly strengthened.

For the United States, the *standing-up* of the Department of Homeland Security and within this the Office of Intelligence and Analysis and separately the National Counterterrorism Center was supposed to increase the intelligence-sharing capabilities of the different agencies. While with the addition of small initiatives, such as the establishment of Fusion Centers, intelligence sharing did improve, there remain a number of institutional blocks, particularly among outwardly and inwardly focused agencies. As such, more power needs to be provided to the Department of Homeland Security to enforce intelligence sharing among agencies.

Terrorism should be seen as an ordinary crime

Broadly speaking, the overarching objective of a terrorist organisation's *modus operandi* is to demonstrate to the state that it cannot provide security and to the citizens that they cannot be secured. Furthermore, terrorists, particularly with regard to liberal democracies (broadly defined), aim to highlight the duality of treatment by the state upon those residing within their borders. The introduction of 'new', 'special' or 'emergency' legislation to tackle a threat, as long-lasting as terrorism, should be avoided in lieu of lengthy and considered deliberation. In essence, their needs to be an element of proportionality in the counter-terrorism approach adopted by both states. Death and injury from terrorist-related violence, even if broadly defined, equates to significantly lower than even the most conservative annual figures of either gun or car crime in either the United Kingdom or the United States. What makes terrorism unique to other crimes is the wider repercussions, the fear element that is induced and the visibility of the aftermath of terrorist atrocities. Yet the introduction of special laws and/or regulations in either state (including the United States Patriot Act and any suggestions of pre-trial detention in the United Kingdom) seems disproportionate to the threat posed. Of particular note in this area is the use of extraordinary rendition, targeted assassinations and harsh interrogation techniques also known as torture. Such programmes, it is accepted here, have led to intelligence that has saved lives, as Eliza Manning-Buller, former Director-General of the Security Service (2002–2007), stated in September 2011; but its use or perhaps its publicly acknowledged use has led to further rhetoric in the terrorist recruiters' arsenal.[11] If either state is to retain the moral high ground then both must adhere to the rule of law that each cherishes. There must be not only a perception of fairness but a process of it, along with a rigid adherence to *habeas corpus*.

While intelligence agencies and the Armed Forces play a critical role in countering the threat of terrorist violence, the need to gather evidence and prosecute cases according to both international and domestic legal norms highlights the importance of giving law enforcement agencies an even greater institutional lead. This is particularly so in the case of the United Kingdom, where, understandably, the Security and Intelligence Agencies do not have the power and associated responsibilities of arrest. One suggestion, which is endorsed here and made by a member of the law enforcement community in the United Kingdom and goes to the heart of the point being made, is that the extension of pre-trial detention for all crimes should be made and not just terrorist-related crimes. This is not so much about perception as about the complexities of modern-day crimes, particularly those involving high-end computer technology. This wider thinking, as opposed to considering terrorism as one item and all other crime as another, should be encouraged. Terrorism should therefore be seen as an ordinary crime and law enforcement should take the lead on it.

For the United States, the lead should continue to be through the FBI, though this needs to be reaffirmed. The United Kingdom needs to develop a single, unified police lead. At present this is nominally the Metropolitan Police in

London. This, however, is for the investigation of terrorist-related crimes. Problems, as highlighted earlier in this book, emerge when it comes to quick pursuits, particularly when firearms units need to cross into different constabularies. Permission in such scenarios must be sought in advance. This needs to be addressed.

Summary

A fundamental question remains regarding the analysis of intelligence, law enforcement and military force and that is which can be considered to have been the most effective in countering the threat of transnational terrorism. The threat posed by transnational terrorism is a result of evolutionary processes and not the emergence of a *new* type of terrorism. Transnational terrorists have taken advantage of the increased connectedness and speed associated with the globalisation of technologies – particularly communications. Transnational terrorist groups aim to undertake mass casualty attacks. The transnational nature of these groups means that they are not affiliated to the cause of any one state. Such groups form a network of small cells that are difficult for the security services of states to infiltrate. The threat posed by transnational terrorists was further heightened due to a desire, perhaps spurred by the religious rhetoric that underscored their political objectives, to seek and deploy chemical, nuclear, biological and/or radiological, weapons of mass destruction in order to achieve their aim and objectives. The primary reason for their non-use has been the problems inherent in the development of an effective delivery system and not, as was the case with traditional terrorist groups, moral restraints reinforced by a lack of desire by state sponsors.[12]

Transnational terrorists do not have one aim. Rather they have multiple, transnational and local aims and objectives. Transnational terrorist groups associated with the al Qaeda network are united through a shared dislike of (broadly defined) the West and its influence across the international community and a fanatical interpretation of Islam. The transnational terrorist combination of political objectives, religious rhetoric, a network structure and a desire to acquire and use weapons of mass destruction represents a significant threat to the international community as a whole. For both the United Kingdom and United States, victims of transnational terrorism, the attacks of 7/7 and 9/11 respectively triggered a systematic shift in the manner in which both states countered the threat of transnational terrorism. Despite knowledge and, particularly in the case of the United Kingdom, experience of countering prolonged terrorist campaigns, both states opted to re-examine their counter-terrorism strategies.

The strength in both states' counter-terrorism strategies has been their ability to implement broad, blunt instruments in order to counter the threat of transnational terrorism and to pursue those suspected of threatening to commit, or who have undertaken, terrorist violence, but at a significant cost to their ability to counter the root cause. Put another way, the counter-terrorism approaches implemented by both the United Kingdom and United States were short term and incapable of making significant progress towards achieving the overarching long-term aim of success in the Global War on Terror. The different ways in which both the United Kingdom and the United States conceptualised the threat of transnational terrorism had a significant impact on the way in which they countered it.

For the United Kingdom, the threat was both a domestic and an international one with a focus primarily on the former. In contrast, for the United States the threat was considered to be an international one necessitating a strengthening of military capability, but also the establishment of the Department of Homeland Security. The Department of Homeland Security, although concerned with counter-terrorism strategy domestically, was focused on areas such as migration of peoples and funds. Both states had significant issues when it came to sharing data among agencies concerned with counter-terrorism activity. For the United Kingdom this was, to a large extent, part and parcel of the new intelligence lead, whereas for the United States it was also due to an institutional aversion to sharing intelligence between inward- and outward-looking agencies. For the United States, investments in technology rather than intelligence analysts also proved to be questionable, while the United Kingdom invested in intelligence analysts and the process of regionalisation, which indicated their recognition of the domestic threat that had emerged. For both states, the use of military force proved to signify either the continuation of normal practice or significant change. The United States, for example, continued to observe posse comitatus, while the United Kingdom began to formalise guidelines concerning normal practice. The overstretching of the military in Afghanistan and the distraction caused by the Iraq conflict impacted upon military force deployments for each state.

This book makes reference to two debates that are found within traditional counter-terrorism literature. These are the acceptance versus effectiveness debate and the role of military force in counter-terrorism. This book suggests that neither the United Kingdom nor the United States found an acceptable balance between acceptability (adherence to civil liberties) and effectiveness (ability to seek those who threaten or have undertaken acts of terrorist violence) in their counter-terrorism strategies. Within the United Kingdom context significant shortcomings were centred on the failure of counter-terrorism agencies to share pertinent information and undertake counter-radicalisation programmes that do not appear to be disproportionately applied to one particular ethnic community. That said, the process of regionalising counter-terrorism assets throughout the state increased the perceived effectiveness of counter-terrorism agencies.

For the United States, continued confusion over roles of differing agencies including the FBI, the use of extra-ordinary rendition, reliance on technologies and the radicalisation effect of deployments of the United States Armed Forces undermined the effectiveness of the counter-terrorism policy instruments and strategy as a whole. Although perhaps not having a direct bearing on the effectiveness of United States counter-terrorism strategy, the establishment of civil liberty oversight of the Department of Homeland Security should be seen as beneficial, as was the establishment of coordinating agencies and the resulting improved communications. The United Kingdom, therefore, is perhaps furthest along in appreciating the importance of domestic counter-radicalisation in achieving the overarching aim of success in the Global War on Terror, by tackling the problem of sympathisers of terrorist causes from becoming practitioners. Neither state has sought to relax the procedures through which military force may be used domestically, and indeed the United Kingdom has formalised the guidelines for their use.

These strategies have their strengths in the identification and interdiction of those that intend to, or have already, committed acts of terrorist violence. Their weaknesses are in the establishment of counter-radicalisation programmes and, indeed, in the inability to tackle increased numbers of practitioners of terrorist violence that they were established to counter. The fact that intelligence agencies in both the United Kingdom and United States have struggled to infiltrate the cells that make up the al Qaeda network further highlights the importance of tackling the root causes. The overarching strategies, therefore, are not considered to be suitable for either reducing the threat of transnational terrorism or, as is the case with the United States, defeating terrorism, and in this sense, holistically speaking, may be seen as ineffective.

This qualitative assessment of United Kingdom and United States counter-terrorism strategies has not only highlighted problems in the sharing of data, recruitment of intelligence analysts, or benefits of regionalisation and formation of coordinating agencies, but has also picked up on the importance of counter-radicalisation programmes. For the United Kingdom, the counter-terrorism strategy was to reduce the threat of terrorist violence. As such, a limited counter-radicalisation programme would be understandable, as a reduction in such a threat could be achieved, although unwisely, through the use of broad instruments such as scanners and increased policing. For the United States, the aim at the start was to win the Global War on Terror, an aim that necessitates tackling terrorism at the root, which inevitably involves the use of effective counter-radicalisation programmes. The United Kingdom had, albeit numerous and disjointed, counter-radicalisation programmes in place. These were led by the police in collaboration with local authorities, schools and other critical partners. These were effective, insofar as information sharing between the police and communities improved. The United States had no significant counter-radicalisation programmes in place domestically and few internationally. For both states this failure to fully appreciate the role of counter-radicalisation in the implementation of their strategies, across all of those policy instruments discussed in this book, serves not only to ignore the root cause but to increase the probability that more sympathisers of terrorist causes will become practitioners of terrorist violence.

In providing a qualitative assessment of United Kingdom and United States counter-terrorism strategies, it should be noted that an effective counter-terrorism strategy would incorporate all three policy instruments, drawing on their strengths to provide a seamless response to the threat posed. The relationship between the agencies responsible for the delivery of each of these instruments in both states was and continues to be problematic, though this has been greatly improved. It is also important to add that each of the policy instruments not only had very different and localised aims but some, to be frank, were more difficult to achieve than others. For the Armed Forces, for example, tackling the threat in Afghanistan was easier than asking the intelligence services to infiltrate and gather intelligence on al Qaeda and its affiliates. Furthermore, the necessity for one policy instrument may well indicate the failure of another. The need to use law enforcement officials to investigate a suspected suicide terrorist following detonation is due to a failure of intelligence and other agencies to identify and apprehend that individual in advance. It is issues such as these that make it difficult to put forward a succinct argument as to which policy instrument has proven to be more effective than the others. That said, interviewees and policy instruments have indicated in both states that the counter-terrorism strategies are largely intelligence driven. As such, therefore, it would be fair to say that failure and/or success should first and foremost be attributed to those agencies responsible for the collection and analysis of intelligence.

Notes

1 Corey Gruber, Executive Director, National Preparedness Task-Force, Federal Emergency Management Agency, Department of Homeland Security, interview conducted by the author, held in Washington, DC, 11 February 2009.
2 Walter Laqueur, *Terrorism* (Boston, MA: Little Brown, 1978), p. 23.
3 David J. Whittaker, *The Terrorism Reader* (London: Routledge, 2001), pp. 24–28.
4 Paul Pillar, *Terrorism and United States Foreign Policy* (Washington, DC: The Brookings Institution, 2003).
5 Bill Rammell (13 January 2010), Speech, 'Generation Why?: Understanding the Armed Forces in Modern Society', http://webarchive.nationalarchives.gov.uk/+/www.mod.uk/DefenceInternet/AboutDefence/People/Speeches/MinAF/20100113Generatio nWhyUnderstandingTheArmedForcesInModernSociety.htm.
6 Randall J. Larsen, Retired; Director, Institute for Homeland Security, interview conducted by the author, held in Washington, DC, 10 September 2009.
7 Thomas H. Kean (Chair), *9/11 Commission Report* (London: W.W. Norton, 2004).
8 Peter Clarke (former Assistant Commissioner and Head of Counter Terrorism Command, Metropolitan Police Service), comments made during the CT EXPO held at London's Earls Court, 14 to 15 April 2010.
9 Cross, 29 August 2009, op. cit.
10 Sir Richard Dearlove (former Chief of United Kingdom Security Service), Conference held at Royal United Services Institute, 23 October 2009.
11 Edgar B. Tembo, 'Torture: Right Under Certain Circumstances?', in *Ballots and Bullets* (12 March 2012), http://nottspolitics.org/2012/03/12/torture-perhaps-right-under-certain-circumstances-torture-perhaps-it-is-right-under-some-circumstances/, accessed 28 April 2012.
12 David Claridge, 'Exploding the Myths of Superterrorism', *Terrorism and Political Violence*, 11 (1999), 4, pp. 133–138, pp. 133–147. Anonymous Source B, interview conducted by author, held in Washington, DC, February 2009.

Select bibliography

Books (including edited publications)

Alexander, Yonah. (ed.) (2006) *Counterterrorism Strategies – Successes and Failures of Six Nations*, Virginia: Potomac Books.

Alexander, Yonah. (2006) 'United States', in Alexander (ed.) *Counterterrorism Strategies – Successes and Failures of Six Nations*, Virginia: Potomac Books, pp. 9–43.

Andrew, Christopher. (2009) *The Defence of the Realm – The Authorized History of MI5*, London: Penguin Books.

Ball, Desmond. (2002) 'Desperately Seeking Bin Laden: The Intelligence Dimension of the War Against Terrorism', in Booth, Ken and Dunne, Tim (eds) *Worlds in Collision – Terror and the Future of Global Order*, Basingstoke: Palgrave Macmillan, pp. 60–73.

Blakesley, Christopher L. (2006) *Terror and Anti-Terrorism – A Normative and Practical Assessment*, New York: Transnational Publishers.

Bonner, David. (1993) 'The United Kingdom's Response to Terrorism', in Schmid, Alex P. and Crelinsten, Ronald D. (eds) *Western Responses to Terrorism*, London: Frank Cass, pp. 171–205.

Bremer III, L. Paul. (1993) 'The West's Counter-Terrorist Strategy', in Schmid, Alex P. and Crelinsten, Ronald D. (eds) *Western Responses to Terrorism*, London: Frank Cass, pp. 255–262.

Bull, Hedley. (2002) *The Anarchical Society – A Study of Order in World Politics*, 3rd edn, New York: Palgrave.

Burke, Jason. (2004) *The True Story of Radical Islam*, 2nd edn, London: Penguin Books.

Buzan, Barry. (1991) 'Is International Security Possible?', in Booth, Ken (ed.) *New Thinking About Strategy and International Security*, London: Harper Collins Academic, pp. 31–55.

Chandler, Michael and Gunaratna, Rohan. (2007) *Countering Terrorism – Can We Meet the Threat of Global Violence*, London: Resktion Books.

Chin, Warren. (2003) 'Operation "Enduring Freedom": A Victory for a Conventional Force Fighting an Unconventional War', in Mockaitis, Thomas R. and Rich, Paul B. (eds) *Grand Strategy in the War Against Terrorism*, London: Frank Cass, pp. 57–76.

Christie, Kenneth. (2008) *America's War on Terrorism – The Revival of the Nation-State versus Universal Human Rights*, Ceredigion, Wales: The Edwin Mellen Press.

Clark, Robert M. (2003) *Intelligence Analysis – A Target-Centric Approach*, 2nd edn, Washington, DC: CQ Press.

Clemens, Walter. (1998) *Dynamics of International Relations – Conflict and Mutual Gain in an Era of Global Interdependence*, Oxford: Rowman & Littlefield.

Clutterbuck, Richard. (1993) 'Negotiating with Terrorists', in Alex P. Schmid and Ronald D. Crelinsten (eds) *Western Responses to Terrorism*, London: Frank Cass, pp. 263–287.

Coogan, Tim Pat. (1993) *The I.R.A.*, 17th edn, London: Harper Collins.

Cooley, John K. (2002) *Unholy Wars – Afghanistan, America and International Terrorism*, 3rd edn, London: Pluto Press.

Crelinsten, R. (2009) *Counterterrorism*, Cambridge: Polity Press.

Curley, Edwin. (ed.) (1994) *Hobbes – Leviathan*, Indiana: Hackett Publishing Company.

Dalby, Simon. (1997) 'Contesting an Essential Concept: Reading the Dilemmas in Contemporary Discourse', in Krause, Keith and Williams, Michael C. (eds) *Critical Security Studies – Concepts and Cases*, Abingdon: Routledge, pp. 3–31.

Davis, Mike. (2008) *A Brief History of the Car Bomb*, 2nd edn, London: Verso.

Dewar, Colonel Michael. (1992) *War in the Streets – The Story of Urban Combat from Calais to Khafji*, Newton Abbot: David & Charles.

Donohue, Laura K. (2008) *The Cost of Counterterrorism – Power, Politics, and Liberty*, Cambridge: Cambridge University Press.

English, Richard. (2009) *Terrorism – How to Respond*, Oxford: Oxford University Press.

Farer, Tom. (2008) *Confronting Global Terrorism and American Neo-Conservatism – The Framework of a Liberal Grand Strategy*, Oxford: Oxford University Press.

Finlan, Alastair. (2003) 'Warfare by Other Means: Special Forces, Terrorism and Grand Strategy', in Mockaitis, Thomas R. and Rich, Paul B. (eds) *Grand Strategy in the War Against Terrorism*, London: Frank Cass, pp. 92–108.

Freedman, Lawrence. (ed.) (2003) *Superterrorism – Policy Responses*, Oxford: Blackwell.

Gardner, Hall. (2005) *American Global Strategy and the 'War on Terrorism'*, Aldershot: Ashgate.

Glanagan, Stephen J. and Schear, James A. (eds) (2008) *Strategic Challenges – America's Global Security Agenda*, Virginia: Potomac Books.

Gless, Anthony. (2008) 'In Search of a New Intelligence System: The British Experience', in Tsang, Steve. (ed.) *Intelligence and Human Rights in the Era of Global Terrorism*, Stanford, CA: Stanford University Press, pp. 145–157.

Gregory, Frank. (2007) 'An Assessment of the Contribution of Intelligence-led Counter-terrorism to UK Homeland Security after 9/11 Within "Contest" Strategy', in Wilkinson, Paul (ed.) *Homeland Security in the UK – Future Preparedness for Terrorist Attack since 9/11*, London: Routledge, pp. 181–202.

Grey, Stephen. (2006) *Ghost Plane – The Inside Story of the CIA's Secret Rendition Programme*, London: C. Hurst & Co.

Griffin, David Ray. (2004) *The New Pearl Harbour – Disturbing Questions about the Bush Administration and 9/11*, Gloucestershire: Arris Books.

Guelke, Adrian. (2006) *Terrorism and Global Disorder – Political Violence in the Contemporary World*, London: I.B. Tauris.

Gupta, Dipak K. (2008) *Understanding Terrorism and Political Violence – The life Cycle of Birth, Growth, Transformation, and Desire*, Abingdon: Routledge.

Handel, Michael L. (1993) *Masters of War: Sun Tzu, Clausewitz and Jomini*, London: Frank Cass.

Harmon, Christopher C. (2008) *Terrorism*, 2nd edn, London: Routledge.

Hastedt, Glenn. (1991) *Controlling Intelligence*, London: Frank Cass.

Hewitt, Steve. (2008) *The British War on Terror – Terrorism and Counter-Terrorism on the Home Front Since 9/11*, London: Continuum.

Heywood, Andrew. (2002) *Politics*, 2nd edn, Basingstoke: Palgrave.

Ignatieff, Michael. (2005) *The Lesser Evil – Political Ethics in an Age of Terror*, Edinburgh: Edinburgh University Press.

Johnson, Loch K. (2008) 'Intelligence Oversight in the United States', in Tsang, Steve (ed.) *Intelligence and Human Rights in the Era of Global Terrorism*, Stanford, CA: Stanford University Press, pp. 54–66.

Kepel, Giles and Milelli, Jean-Pierre. (eds) (2008) *Al Qaeda In Its Own Words*, Cambridge, MA: Harvard University Press.

Kitson, General Sir Frank. (1971) *Low Intensity Operations – Subversion, Insurgency, Peace-keeping*, London: Faber and Faber.

Larsen, Randall J. (2007) *Our Own Worst Enemy – Asking the Right Questions about Security to Protect You, Your Family, and America*, New York: Grand Central Publishing.

Larson, Eric and Peters, John. (2001) *Preparing the U.S. Army for Homeland Security: Concepts, Issues and Options*, California: RAND.

Laqueur, Walter. (1978) *Terrorism*, London: Sphere Books.

——. (1980) *Terrorism*, 3rd edn, Boston, MA: Little Brown.

——. (2001) *The New Terrorism: Fanaticism and the Arms of Mass Destruction*, London: Phoenix Press.

Levi, Michael. (2007) *On Nuclear Terrorism*, Cambridge, MA: Harvard University Press.

Littlewood, Jez and Simpson, John. (2007) 'The Chemical, Biological, Radiological and Nuclear Weapons Threat', in Wilkinson, Paul (ed.) *Homeland Security in the UK – Future Preparedness for Terrorist Attack since 9/11*, London: Routledge, pp. 57–80.

Lutz, James M. and Lutz, Brenda J. (2008) *Global Terrorism*, 2nd edn, Abingdon: Routledge.

Martin, Gus. (2004) *Understanding Terrorism – Challenges, Perspectives, and Issues*, 2nd edn, London: Sage.

McMillan, Joseph and Cavoli, Christopher. (2008) 'Countering Global Terrorism', in Flanagan, Stephen J. and Schear, James A. (eds) *Strategic Challenges – America's Global Security Agenda*, Virginia: Potomac Books, pp. 20–60.

Meisels, Tamar. (2008) *The Trouble with Terror – Liberty, Security, and the Response to Terrorism*, Cambridge: Cambridge University Press.

Meyer, Christopher. (2005) *DC Confidential – The Controversial Memoirs of Britain's Ambassador to the U.S. at the Time of 9/11 and the Iraq War*, London: Weidenfeld & Nicolson.

Mingst, Karen A. (2008) *Essentials of International Relations*, 4th edn, London: W.W. Norton & Company.

Mockaitis, Thomas R. (2003) 'Winning Hearts and Minds in the "War on Terrorism"', in Mockaitis, Thomas R. and Rich, Paul B. (eds) *Grand Strategy in the War Against Terrorism*, London: Frank Cass, pp. 21–38.

Mommsen, Wolfgang J. (1982) 'Non-legal Violence and Terrorism in Western Industrial Societies: An Historical Analysis', in Mommsen, Wolfgang J. and Hirschfeld, Gerhard (eds) *Social Protest, Violence and Terror in Nineteenth- and Twentieth-century Europe*, London: The Macmillan Press, pp. 384–403.

Morrison, John N.L. (2008) 'Political Subversion of Intelligence Services in the United Kingdom', in Tsang, Steve (ed.) *Intelligence and Human Rights in the Era of Global Terrorism*, Stanford, CA: Stanford University Press, pp. 41–53.

Primoratz, Igor. (ed.) (2004) *Terrorism – The Philosophical Issues*, Basingstoke: Palgrave Macmillan.

Rich, Paul B. (2003) 'Al Qaeda and the Radical Islamic Challenge to Western Strategy', in Mockaitis, Thomas R. and Rich, Paul B. (eds) *Grand Strategy in the War Against Terrorism*, London: Frank Cass, pp. 39–56.

Rogers, Paul. (2008) *Global Security and the War on Terror – Elite Power and the Illusion of Control*, Abingdon: Routledge.

Scheuerman, William E. (2009) *Morgenthau*, Cambridge: Polity Press.

Schmid, Alex P. (1993a) 'Terrorism and Democracy', in Schmid, Alex P. and Crelinsten, Ronald D. (eds) *Western Responses to Terrorism*, London: Frank Cass, pp. 14–25.

——. (1993b) 'The Response Problem as a Definition Problem', in Schmid, Alex P. and Crelinsten, Ronald D. (eds) *Western Responses to Terrorism*, London: Frank Cass, pp. 7–13.

Schmid, Alex P. and Crelinsten, Ronald D. (eds) (1993a) *Western Responses to Terrorism*, London: Frank Cass.

——. (1993b) 'Western Responses to Terrorism: A Twenty-Five Year Balance Sheet' in Schmid, Alex P. and Crelinsten, Ronald D. (eds.) (1993) *Western Responses to Terrorism*, London: Frank Cass, pp. 307–340.

Schmid, Alex P. and Jongman, Albert J. (1988) *Political Terrorism*, 2nd edn, Oxford: North-Holland Publishing Company.

Simons, Anna and Tucker, David. (date) 'United States Special Operations Forces and the War on Terrorism', in Mockaitis, Thomas R. and Rich, Paul B. (eds) *Grand Strategy in the War Against Terrorism*, London: Frank Cass, pp. 77–91.

Smith, G. Davidson. (1990) *Combating Terrorism*, London: Routledge.

Sookhdeo, Patrick. (2007) *Global Jihad – The Future in the Face of Militant Islam*, Virginia: Isaac Publishing.

Stern, Jessica. (1999) *The Ultimate Terrorists*, London: Harvard University Press.

Strachan, Hew. (1997) *The Politics of the British Army*, Oxford: Oxford University Press.

Taylor, Peter. (2000) *Loyalists*, 2nd edn, London: Bloomsbury Publishing.

Tsang, Steve. (2008) 'Stopping Global Terrorism and Protecting Rights', in Tsang, Steve. (ed.) *Intelligence and Human Rights in the Era of Global Terrorism*, Stanford,CA: Stanford University Press, pp. 1–14.

Turner, Admiral Stansfield. (1991) *Terrorism and Democracy*, Boston, MA: Houghton Mifflin.

Vasquez John A. (1998) *The Power of Power Politics – From Classical Realism to Neotraditionalism*, 2nd edn, Cambridge: Cambridge University Press.

Wardlaw, Grant. (1989) *Political Terrorism – Theory, Tactics and Counter-measures*, 2nd edn, Cambridge: Cambridge University Press.

White, Jonathan R. (2006) *Terrorism and Homeland Security*, 5th edn, USA: Thomas Wadsworth.

White, Terry. (1992) *Swords of Lightning: Special Forces and the Changing Face of Warfare*, London: Brassey's.

Whittaker, David J. (2001) *The Terrorism Reader*, London: Routledge.

——. (2004) *Terrorists and Terrorism in the Contemporary World*, London: Routledge.

Wieviorka, Michel. (1990) 'French Politics and Strategy on Terrorism', in Rubin, B. (ed.) *The Politics of Counter-Terrorism – The Ordeal of Democratic States*, USA: Foreign Policy Institute, pp. 61–90.

Wijk, de Rob. (2003) 'The Limits of Military Power', in Lennon, Alexander (ed.) *The Battle for Hearts and Minds – Using Soft Power to Undermine Terrorist Networks*, London: The MIT Press.

Wilkinson, Paul. (1974) *Political Terrorism*, Essex: The Macmillan Press.

——. (ed.) (2007a) *Homeland Security in the UK – Future Preparedness for Terrorist Attack since 9/11*, London: Routledge.

——. (2007b) 'The Threat from the Al-Qaeda Network', in Wilkinson, Paul (ed.) *Homeland Security in the UK – Future Preparedness for Terrorist Attack since 9/11*, London: Routledge, pp. 25–36.

Williams, Paul D. (2008) 'Security Studies', in Williams. Paul D. (ed.) *Security Studies An Introduction*, Abingdon: Routledge, pp. 1–12.

Wolf, John. (1991) *Antiterrorist Initiatives*, 2nd edn, London: Plenum Press.

Zerbe, Richard O. and Dively, Dwight D. (1994) *Benefit-cost Analysis in Theory and Practice*, New York: Harper Collins College Publishers.

Journal articles

Bamford, Bradley W.C. 'The United Kingdom's "War Against Terrorism"', *Terrorism and Political Violence*, 16 (winter 2004), 4, pp. 737–756.

Bar-Joseph, Uri and McDermott, M. 'Change the Analyst and not the System: A Different Approach to Intelligence Reform', *Foreign Policy Analysis*, 4 (April 2008), 2, pp. 127–145.

Byman, Daniel. 'Do Targeted Killings Work?', *Foreign Affairs*, 85 (March/April 2006), 2, pp. 95–111.

Claridge, David. 'Exploding the Myths of Superterrorism', *Terrorism and Political Violence*, 11 (1999), 4, pp. 133–147.

Enders, Walter and Sandler, Todd. 'Transnational Terrorism in the Post-Cold War Era', *International Studies Quarterly*, 43 (1999), pp. 145–167.

Field, Antony. 'Tracking Terrorist Networks: Problems of Intelligence Sharing Within the UK Intelligence Community', *Review of International Studies*, 35 (October 2009), 4, pp. 997–1009.

Foley, Frank. 'The Expansion of Intelligence Agency Mandates: British Counterterrorism in Comparative Perspective', *Review of International Studies*, 35 (October 2009), 4, pp. 983–995.

Freedman, Lawrence. 'International Security: Changing Targets', *Foreign Policy*, 110 (spring 1998), pp. 48–63.

Gearson, John. 'The Nature of Modern Terrorism', *The Political Quarterly* (2002), pp. 7–24.

Gibson, Stevyn D. 'Future Roles of the UK Intelligence System', *Review of International Studies*, 35 (October 2009), 4, pp. 917–928.

Gill, Peter. 'The Intelligence and Security Committee and the Challenge of Security Networks', *Review of International Studies*, 35 (October 2009), 4, pp. 929–941.

Gordon, Philip H. 'Can the War on Terror be Won – How to Fight the Right War', *Foreign Affairs*, 86 (November/December 2007), 6, pp. 53–66.

Heyman, Philip B. 'Dealing with Terrorism: An Overview', *International Security*, 26 (winter 2001–2002), 3, pp. 24–38.

Hoffman, Bruce. 'The Logic of Suicide Terrorism', *The Atlantic Monthly*, 291 (2003) 5, www.rand.org/pubs/reprints/2005/RAND_RP1187.pdf, accessed 12 August 2010, pp. 1–11.

Hoffman, Bruce and Hoffman, Donna K. 'The Rand – St Andrews Chronology of International Terrorist Incidents – 1995', *Terrorism and Political Violence*, 8 (1996), 3, pp. 89–127.

Holland, Jack. 'From September 11th, 2001 to 9–11: From Void to Crisis', *International Political Sociology*, 3 (September 2009), 3, pp. 275–292.

Jervis, Robert. 'Understanding the Bush Doctrine', *Political Science Quarterly*, 118 (2003), 3, pp. 365– 388.

Kennedy, Robert. 'Is One Person's Terrorist Another's Freedom Fighter? Western and Islamic Approaches to "Just War" Compared', *Terrorism and Political Violence*, 1 (1999), 1, pp. 1–21.

Kosnik, Mark. 'The Military Response to Terrorism', *Navy War College Review*, 53 (2000), 2, www.nwc.navy.mil/press/Review/2000/spring/art1-sp0.htm, accessed 23 July 2006.

Laqueur, Walter. 'Postmodern Terrorism', *Foreign Affairs*, 75 (September/October 1996), 3, pp. 24–36.

McCartney, Helen. 'The Military Covenant and the Civil–Military Contract in Britain', *International Affairs*, 86 (2010), 2, pp. 411–428.

Mendelsohn, Barak. 'Al-Qaeda's Palestinian Problem', *Survival*, 51 (August– September 2009), pp. 71– 86.

Morgan, Captain Matthew J. 'The Origins of the New Terrorism', *Parameters* (spring 2004), http://carlisle-www.army.mil/usawc/Parameters/04spring/morgan.htm, accessed 10 March 2006, pp. 29–43.

O'Brien, Kevin A. 'Managing National Security and Law Enforcement Intelligence in a Globalised World', *Review of International Studies*, 35 (October 2009), 4, pp. 903–915.

Piazza, James A. 'Incubators of Terror: Do Failed and Failing States Promote Trans-national Terrorism?', *International Studies Quarterly*, 52 (September 2008), 3, pp. 469–488.

——. 'Transnational Terror and Human Rights', *International Studies Quarterly*, 53 (March 2009), 1, pp. 125–148.

Pillar, Paul R. 'Intelligence, Policy and the War in Iraq', *Foreign Affairs*, 85 (March/April 2006), 2, pp. 15–28.

Raufer, Xavier. 'New World Disorder, New Terrorism: New Threats for Europe and the Western World', *Terrorism and Political Violence*, 11 (1999), 4, pp. 30–51.

Reinares, Fernando. 'The Madrid Bombings and Global Jihadism', *Survival*, 52 (April– May 2010), 2, pp. 83–104.

Romaniuk, Peter. 'Institutions as Swords and Shields: Multilateral Counter-terrorism since 9/11', *Review of International Studies*, 36 (July 2010), 3, pp. 591–513.

Shapiro, Jeremy and Suzan, Bénédicte. 'The French Experience of Counter-terrorism', *Survival*, 45 (2003), 1, pp. 67–98.

Silke, Andrew. 'Terrorism and the Blind Men's Elephant', *Terrorism and Political Violence*, 8 (1996), 3, pp. 13–28.

Simon, Steven. 'The New Terrorism: Securing the Nation Against a Messianic Foe', *The Brookings Institution*, 21 (winter 2003), 1, pp. 18–24.

Index